The Atonement of Christ

By Oliver B. Greene

The Gospel Hour, Inc., Oliver B. Greene, Director
Box 2024, Greenville, South Carolina 29602

First printing, March 1968 — 10,000 copies
Second printing, March 1969 — 15,000 copies
Third printing, February 1972 — 15,000 copies

$5.00

FOREWORD

"Every good gift and every perfect gift is from above, and cometh down from the Father of lights, with whom is no variableness, neither shadow of turning" (James 1:17).

It is with this truth in mind that this series of lessons on The Atonement is offered by The Gospel Hour ministry. It is impossible to over-emphasize the importance of the atonement, because it is upon that divine truth that the entire structure of God's plan and program rests.

All Old Testament prophecy points to the atonement, all Mosaic Law looked to the atonement for fulfillment, and all ceremonial and religious rites typified the atonement made by the Lamb of God at Calvary. Without it, not one sinner could ever have been saved. Without sufficient knowledge and understanding of its importance no Christian can grow to the maturity we should attain in Christ Jesus.

This study is offered with the hope and sincere prayer that it may cause unbelievers to get a vision of Christ crucified for the sin of the world, and that it may lead Christians into a deeper experience with the risen Christ and a more fruitful field in soul-winning.

—The Author

THE ATONEMENT OF CHRIST

CONTENTS

THE ATONEMENT
OF CHRIST

Chapter One

CHRIST'S ATONEMENT
A DIVINE NECESSITY ARISING FROM
THE TOTAL DEPRAVITY OF MAN

"Therefore being justified by faith, we have peace with God through our Lord Jesus Christ: by whom also we have access by faith into this grace wherein we stand, and rejoice in hope of the glory of God. And not only so, but we glory in tribulations also: knowing that tribulation worketh patience; and patience, experience; and experience, hope: And hope maketh not ashamed; because the love of God is shed abroad in our hearts by the Holy Ghost which is given unto us.

"For when we were yet without strength, in due time Christ died for the ungodly. For scarcely for a righteous man will one die: yet peradventure for a good man some would even dare to die. But God commendeth His love toward us, in that, while we were yet sinners, Christ died for us. Much more then, being now justified by His blood, we shall be saved from wrath through Him.

"For if, when we were enemies, we were reconciled to God by the death of His Son, much more, being reconciled, we shall be saved by His life. And not only so, but we also joy in God through our Lord Jesus Christ, *by whom we have now received THE*

ATONEMENT" (Rom. 5:1—11).

In order to put man in his right perspective—that is, to lay man low in the dust before a holy and righteous God—the doctrines declared by Jesus and His apostles were those of *human depravity,* and salvation from sin *by grace through faith in the Lord Jesus Christ,* minus anything man can do.

Jesus declared, "The Son of man is come to seek and to save that which was lost" (Luke 19:10).

He further declared, "They that be whole need not a physician, but they that are sick. . . for I am not come to call the righteous, but *sinners* to repentance" (Matt. 9:12,13).

Not only did Jesus come to seek and to save lost sinners, but no man under any other character could partake of salvation—and that is still true: *only those who realize and confess their lost estate* can partake of salvation. Man must recognize and confess that he is a sinner—unrighteous, spiritually sick, in need of the Great Physician, the Lord Jesus Christ. He must realize and confess this before Jesus can *or will* save him.

The Apostle Paul, called and ordained of God to reveal the grace of God to the Gentiles, declared the same message:

"And you hath He quickened, who were dead in trespasses and sins: Wherein in time past ye walked according to the course of this world, according to the prince of the power of the air, the spirit that now worketh in the children of disobedience: among whom also we all had our conversation in times past in the lusts of our flesh, fulfilling the desires of the flesh and of the mind; and were by nature the children of wrath, even as others.

"But God, who is rich in mercy, for His great love wherewith He loved us, even when we were dead in sins, hath quickened us together with Christ, (by grace

ye are saved;) and hath raised us up together, and
made us sit together in heavenly places in Christ Jesus:
That in the ages to come He might shew the exceeding riches of His grace in His kindness toward us
through Christ Jesus. *For by grace are ye saved
through faith; and that not of yourselves: it is the
gift of God: not of works, lest any man should boast"*
(Eph. 2:1—9).

Not only did Paul declare this message to the
Gentiles, but—*himself a Jew,* an educated Pharisee
belonging to "the straitest sect" of the Pharisees—he
declared, "Among whom *WE ALL* had our conversation in times past, fulfilling the desires of the flesh
and of the mind; and were by nature the children of
wrath (children of the devil), *even as others."* Thus
by his own testimony Paul, though a devout religionist,
declared that all Jews were in the same spiritual condition as the Gentile "dogs."

Writing to Titus Paul further confessed, "For *we
ourselves* also were sometimes foolish, disobedient,
deceived, serving divers lusts and pleasures, living in
malice and envy, hateful, and hating one another"
(Tit. 3:3). Paul declared in the New Testament what
the Prophet Isaiah declared: *"ALL we like sheep have
gone astray;* we have turned every one to his own
way; and the Lord hath laid on Him *the iniquity of
us ALL"* (Isa. 53:6).

However, in view of the doctrine of the universal
and total depravity of all men, Paul properly and joyfully proceeded to declare the rich mercy of God:

*"BUT GOD, who is rich in mercy . . . EVEN
WHEN WE WERE DEAD IN SINS, hath quickened
us together with Christ."* The humbling doctrine of
our great salvation—salvation undeserved because of
our sin but made possible because of the unmerited
favor of God through grace—so completely permeated
the mind and heart of the Apostle Paul that he could

not forbear declaring, *"By GRACE are ye saved!"*
But he did not leave it there.   Shortly he declared
more fully, "By grace are ye saved *through faith, AND
THAT NOT OF YOURSELVES!"*

Writing to Timothy, his son in the ministry, Paul
declared, "Who (God) hath saved us, and called us
with an holy calling, *not according to our works, but
according to HIS OWN PURPOSE AND GRACE*,
which was given us in Christ Jesus before the world
began" (II Tim. 1:9).

To Titus, Paul wrote: "Not by works of righteousness which we have done, but *according to HIS MER-
CY He saved us,* by the washing of regeneration, and
renewing of the Holy Ghost" (Tit. 3:5).

To the believers in Corinth Paul declared, "Ye see
your calling, brethren, how that not many wise men
after the flesh, not many mighty, not many noble, are
called: But God hath chosen the foolish things of
the world to confound the wise; and God hath chosen
the weak things of the world to confound the things
which are mighty; and base things of the world, and
things which are despised, hath God chosen, yea, and
things which are not, to bring to nought things that
are: that no flesh should glory in His presence.

*"But of HIM are ye in Christ Jesus, who of God
is made unto us wisdom, and righteousness, and sanctification, and redemption: That, according as it is
written, He that glorieth, let him glory IN THE
LORD"* (I Cor. 1:26—31).

The Natural Man

"But the natural man receiveth not the things of
the Spirit of God: for they are foolishness unto him:
neither can he know them, because they are spiritually
discerned" (I Cor. 2:14).

As we look into the composition of the human

mind, we see various passions and natural appetites; and if we closely inspect the operations of these passions and appetites, we immediately see in each a definite and marked aversion toward the true God and true Christianity.   By way of example, man loves to *think*.   It is utterly impossible for a rational man to live *without* thinking.   It is as natural for man to think as it is for the morning sun to rise in the east. But according to the Psalmist, *God* is not *in* the thoughts of the unregenerate man:

"The wicked, through the pride of his countenance, will not seek after God: God is not in all his thoughts" (Psalm 10:4).

Man is an active creature, *perpetually in motion;* but the natural man has no heart to act for a holy God.   He has no desire to act in a manner pleasing to a holy and righteous God.   Man also takes great pleasure in *conversation.*   He is never happier than when he is conversing with his fellowman.   But let someone begin to talk about *Jesus*—the shed blood of His cross and the saving grace of God—and men usually become very quiet.   In a matter of moments if the subject is not dropped, many will walk away. As John the Beloved declared, *"They went out from us, but they were not OF us; for if they had been of us, they would no doubt have continued WITH us: but they went out, that they might be made manifest that they were not all of us"* (I John 2:19).

Men delight in hearing and telling news—both good and bad.   In this day of newspapers, magazines, telephones, telegraph, radio, and television, millions of men spend millions of hours giving and receiving news; but if the good news of the glorious Gospel of God's saving grace is sounded out, many turn a deaf ear.   The good news of the Gospel is not welcomed by the masses of humanity.   Oh, yes—there is a small nucleus who welcome it and enjoy hearing it over and over again; but the majority of men have no heart, no love, and no desire for the good news of God's saving grace. They are like those of whom Jesus said:

"I speak to them in parables: because they seeing *see NOT;* and *hearing they HEAR not,* neither do they *understand.* And in them is fulfilled the prophecy of Esaias, which saith, By hearing ye shall hear, and shall not understand; and seeing ye shall see, and shall not perceive: For this people's heart is waxed gross, and their ears are dull of hearing, and their eyes they have closed; lest at any time they should see with their eyes and hear with their ears, and should understand with their heart, and should be converted, and I should heal them" (Matt. 13:13—15).

If you will study the seventeenth chapter of II Kings you will find a remarkable illustration of this in the conduct of the nations planted by the King of Assyria in the cities of Samaria. These people were consumed by wild beasts, and they considered the judgment that came upon them as an expression of anger from "the God of the land." They wanted to become *acquainted* with the God of the land, that they might worship and serve Him, so a priest of Israel was sent to teach them *"the manner* of the God of the land." But when the priest taught and instructed them concerning fear of Jehovah, the true God, the character and worship of Jehovah did not suit their taste and they continued to worship heathen gods; and (like the children of Israel, in verses 10 and 11) "they set them up images and groves in every high hill, and under every green tree: and there they burnt incense in all the high places."

In the same chapter we read, "every nation made gods of their own, and put them in the houses of the high places which the Samaritans had made, every nation in their cities wherein they dwelt. . . So they feared the Lord, and made unto themselves of the lowest of them priests of the high places, which sacrificed for them in the houses of the high places. *They feared the Lord, AND SERVED THEIR OWN GODS,* after the manner of the nations whom they carried away from thence" (vv. 29,32,33).

Bible Proof of Human Depravity

Time and space here will not allow me to give all the Scriptures that teach the total depravity of man, but I will point out just a few:

1. The Word of God declares that man is completely depraved to the point where even the *imagination of his heart* is evil—not just *part* of the time, but *continually:*

"And God saw that the wickedness of man was great in the earth, and that *every imagination of the thoughts of his heart was only evil continually"* (Gen. 6:5). The Hebrew word used here suggests not only the *imagination* of the unregenerate, but the purpose and desires as well.

Romans 3:11,12 declares: *"There is none that understandeth, there is none that seeketh after God. They are all gone out of the way, they are together become unprofitable; there is NONE that doeth good, no, NOT ONE!"*

Jesus Himself declared: *"From within, out of the heart of men, proceed evil thoughts,* adulteries, fornications, murders, thefts, covetousness, wickedness, deceit, lasciviousness, an evil eye, blasphemy, pride, foolishness: *all these evil things come from within, and defile the man"* (Mark 7:21–23).

The Prophet Jeremiah said, *"The heart is deceitful above all things, and desperately wicked: who can know it?"* (Jer. 17:9).

David, a man after God's own heart, cried out, "Behold, I was shapen in iniquity; and in sin did my mother conceive me!" (Psalm 51:5).

ALL men are born in sin and shapen in iniquity.
God commanded Adam, "Of the tree of the knowledge
of good and evil, thou shalt not eat of it: for in the
day that thou eatest thereof *thou shalt surely die*"
(Gen. 2:17). The day Adam deliberately and knowingly
broke God's commandment was the day *the entire
human race* was sold into sin:

"Wherefore, as by one man sin entered into the
world, and death by sin; and so death passed upon
all men, for that all have sinned" (Rom. 5:12).

Regardless of birth, environment, or opportunity;
regardless of how sincerely man may attempt to correct the evil of his heart, there is *only ONE way* man's
wicked heart can be changed, and that is through the
miracle of God's grace; but God's grace can be ours
only because of the atonement of the Lord Jesus Christ:
*"A new heart also will I GIVE you, and A NEW
SPIRIT will I put within you . . ."* (Ezek. 36:26).

II Corinthians 5:19 declares, *"God was in Christ,
reconciling the world unto Himself,* not imputing their
trespasses unto them; and hath committed unto us the
word of reconciliation."

God gave up flesh in the Garden of Eden. He
said to Adam, *"Dust thou art, and unto dust shalt
thou return"* (Gen. 3:19). But when God provided
coats of skins to cover the shameful nakedness of
Adam and Eve, He promised the Lamb of God who,
in the fulness of time, would come to take away sin
and provide grace, that poor lost sinners might be
redeemed and become children of God by faith in the
finished work and shed blood of the Lord Jesus Christ:

"I will put enmity between thee and the woman,
and between thy seed and her seed; it shall bruise
thy head, and thou shalt bruise His heel" (Gen. 3:15).

And *"WHEN THE FULNESS OF THE TIME
WAS COME, God sent forth His Son,* made of a

woman, made under the law, to redeem them that were under the law, that we might receive the adoption of sons" (Gal. 4:4,5).

2. Hebrews 11:6 gives further Bible proof that man is totally depraved, and clearly declares the utter impossibility of the unregenerate man doing *anything* to please God:

"Without faith it is IMPOSSIBLE to please Him: for he that cometh to God must believe that He is, and that He is a rewarder of them that diligently seek Him."

Without faith it is impossible to please God, and the only way to have faith in God is to *hear the WORD of God* (Rom. 10:17); *believe* the Word of God (John 5:24); and become *a child of God.* It is utterly impossible for an unregenerate person to exercise faith in God, *for he must know the SON in order to know the FATHER;* and if a man does not know the Lord Jesus Christ through faith in His shed blood and finished work, then *he does not know GOD, and he cannot have faith IN God.*

"Whosoever transgresseth, and abideth not in the doctrine of Christ, hath not God. He that abideth in the doctrine of Christ, he hath both the Father and the Son" (II John 9).

"To be carnally minded is death; but to be spiritually minded is life and peace. Because the carnal mind is enmity against God: for it is not subject to the law of God, neither indeed can be. *So then they that are in the flesh CANNOT please God"* (Rom. 8:6—8).

They who are "after the flesh"—in other words, unregenerate men—seek the things of the flesh and are therefore *carnal;* and to be carnal is to die, because *the unregenerate mind and heart are not subject to God.* The natural man cannot be subject to the law of God, for God's law is holy and righteous, and the unregenerate man *cannot* be subject to holiness and righteousness until the miracle of the new birth has been wrought in his heart!

God is not a hard Master. God is love. He is longsuffering, He is pleased with righteousness whenever and wherever He sees it; but there can *be* no righteousness in man until Christ—*who IS our righteousness* (I Cor. 1:30)—abides in the heart: *"Christ in you, the hope of glory"* (Col. 1:27).

"For (God) hath made (Jesus) to be sin for us, who knew no sin; *that we might be made the righteousness of God IN HIM"* (II Cor. 5:21).

Man can never merit the grace of God through anything he does, regardless of how good or how righteous he may try to become, or how good he may seem in his own eyes:

"We are all as an unclean thing, and all our righteousnesses are as filthy rags; and we all do fade as a leaf; and our iniquities, like the wind, have taken us away"* (Isa. 64:6).

3. The Scriptures which speak of the whole of goodness or true virtue as comprehended in love prove that man is totally depraved and incapable of loving until he possesses God, because *"God IS love"* (I John 4:8).

The law of God is holy: "Wherefore *the law* is holy, and *the commandment* holy, and just, and good" (Rom. 7:12).

On one occasion, a lawyer came to Jesus and asked Him a question—not because he wanted to love, worship, or follow Him, but *tempting* Him:

"Then one of them, which was a lawyer, asked Him a question, tempting Him, and saying, *Master, which is the great commandment in the law?*

"Jesus said unto him, *Thou shalt love the Lord*

thy God with all thy heart, and with all thy soul, and with all thy mind.   This is the first and great commandment.   And the second is like unto it, Thou shalt love thy neighbour as thyself.   On these two commandments hang all the law and the prophets" (Matt. 22:35—40).

To attain righteousness which would allow man to enter the Celestial City of God, man must love God supremely, and then he must love his neighbor as he loves himself.   Such love is utterly impossible apart from the miracle of God's grace, and the miracle of God's grace is utterly impossible apart from Christ's atonement.   Ungodly men are wanting in such love as God's law and God's holiness demand, because unregenerate men *have not the love of God in them* (John 5:42).

The law of God demands that *God be loved supremely*—and man cannot love his neighbor, his fellowman, as he ought until he *does* love God supremely. Where supreme love *to* God and love *in subordination* to God are disregarded—or where the latter of these is regarded on any other ground or account—such love has no true virtue, is hypocritical, and is of the nature of sin.   Paul declared to the Romans, *"Whatsoever is not of FAITH is sin"* (Rom. 14:23b).

4. The Word of God teaches that regeneration is divinely necessary to eternal life.   The only possible way for anyone to *possess* eternal life is *through* regeneration, and regeneration is impossible apart from the atonement—the blood of Jesus.

We find this clearly set forth in the conversation between Jesus and Nicodemus, the outstanding religious teacher in Israel:

"There was a man of the Pharisees, named Nicodemus, a ruler of the Jews: the same came to Jesus by night, and said unto Him, Rabbi, we know that

thou art a teacher come from God: for no man can do
these miracles that thou doest, except God be with
him.

"Jesus answered and said unto him, Verily, verily,
I say unto thee, *Except a man be born again, he cannot see the kingdom of God.*

"Nicodemus saith unto Him, How can a man be
born when he is old? Can he enter the second time
into his mother's womb, and be born?

"Jesus answered, Verily, verily, I say unto thee,
Except a man be born of water and of the Spirit, he
cannot enter into the kingdom of God. *THAT WHICH
IS BORN OF THE FLESH IS FLESH; and that
which is born of the Spirit is spirit.* Marvel not that
I said unto thee, *Ye MUST be born again*" (John
3:1–7).

Since Adam sinned, flesh *is, has been, and will be
FLESH.*   But even though God gave up flesh in the
Garden of Eden, man still attempts to *do* something,
give something, or *live* something in the flesh which
will please God; but this is utterly impossible! "That
which is born of the flesh is *flesh.*" God "borns"
the spirit, the inner man; and when God puts a new
heart and a new spirit within us we can live a life
of righteousness and purity—*but only by FAITH:*

". . . as it is written, *The JUST shall LIVE by
faith*" (Rom. 1:17).

"So then faith cometh by hearing, and hearing by
the Word of God" (Rom. 10:17).

God does not "repair" the flesh, He does not repair the human heart: "Therefore if any man be in
Christ, *he is a NEW creature:* old things are passed
away; behold, *ALL things are become NEW*" (II Cor.
5:17).

If there could be any degree of virtue in the unregenerate heart, anything pleasing to God, then regardless of how small or insignificant that virtue might

be *it could be cultivated, increased;* and in such a case *old* things need not pass away, *all things need not become NEW.* But man cannot gradually evolve or increase his virtue or righteousness by cultivating it. Such is utterly impossible apart from regeneration.

"Regeneration" is NOT "reformation" — nor is it "improving" one's way of life. Regeneration is not the improvement of principles born in man. God puts within man — *not* more "noble principles," but *a NEW HEART;* and it is from the heart that the issues of life proceed (Prov. 4:23).

There is *only ONE WAY* for man to be born again, thereby becoming a son of God and a citizen of heaven:

"Forasmuch as ye know that ye were not redeemed with corruptible things, as silver and gold, from your vain conversation received by tradition from your fathers; but with the precious blood of Christ, as of a lamb without blemish and without spot: who verily was foreordained before the foundation of the world, but was manifest in these last times for you. Who by Him do believe in God, that raised Him up from the dead, and gave Him glory; that your faith and hope might be in God. Seeing ye have purified your souls in obeying the truth through the Spirit unto unfeigned love of the brethren, see that ye love one another with a pure heart fervently: *Being BORN AGAIN, not of corruptible seed, but of incorruptible, BY THE WORD OF GOD, which liveth and abideth for ever"* (I Pet. 1:18—23).

5. The Scriptures promise the blessings of salvation and eternal life to all who are saved by grace — to all who possess righteousness and true holiness by faith in the finished work and shed blood of the Lamb of God.

It is not to those who are *full grown in the spirit-*

ual life that the Scriptures promise blessings, but to *any and all* who possess *any degree* of righteousness. Romans 8:28 declares, "We know that all things work together for good *to them that love God,* to them who are the called according to His purpose." It does not say, "to them that love God *with all of their heart, soul, mind, and strength,*" but simply to all *who "LOVE GOD."*

Any person who will be reasonable must agree that *some* believers love God more than *others* love Him. Some who are born again leave everything that is dear to them and go forth to hazard their own lives on the mission field—in the jungles, among the heathen, in the midst of disease and corruption. Nothing short of the love of God completely *permeating* the heart of man could lead him from the comforts of home to the disease-ridden and insect-infested jungles of the mission field!

So there are those who love to a greater degree than others. Jesus said of the woman who bathed His feet with her tears and wiped them with the hairs of her head, *"She loved much."* And to the woman He said, "Thy faith hath saved thee; go in peace" (Luke 7:47,50).

On the same occasion, to Simon the self-righteous Pharisee Jesus said, "Seest thou this woman? I entered into thine house, thou gavest me no water for my feet: but she hath washed my feet with tears, and wiped them with the hairs of her head. Thou gavest me no kiss: but this woman since the time I came in hath not ceased to kiss my feet. My head with oil thou didst not anoint: but this woman hath anointed my feet with ointment. Wherefore I say unto thee, Her sins, which are many, are forgiven; *for she loved MUCH:* but to whom little is forgiven, the same loveth little" (Luke 7:44—47).

But God's rule does not measure as man's rule

measures. His scales do not weigh as man's scales weigh. *He blesses believers abundantly regardless of the degree of righteousness or the degree of true virtue they possess.* Jesus declared:

"Whosoever shall give to drink unto one of these little ones *a cup of cold water only* in the name of a disciple, verily I say unto you, *he shall in no wise lose his reward*" (Matt. 10:42).

In Mark 9:41 we read, *"Whosoever shall give you a cup of water to drink in my name, because ye belong to Christ, verily I say unto you, he shall not lose his reward."*

A cup of cold water would cost very little in dollars and cents, and it would require very little effort to give it; yet Jesus assures us that if we give *just a cup of cold water* in His name and in the right spirit, we will receive a reward!

"And being made perfect, (Jesus) became the author of eternal salvation *unto ALL THEM THAT OBEY HIM* . . . Jesus the author and finisher of our faith; who for the joy that was set before Him endured the cross, despising the shame, and is set down at the right hand of the throne of God" (Heb. 5:9; 12:2). These Scriptures declare that God's unmerited, unearned, gracious promises are not made according to *this or that degree* of righteousness, but *to ANY degree of righteousness.* Why? Because *CHRIST is our righteousness,* and when we possess righteousness we possess Christ. It is for Christ's sake that God saves us (Eph. 4:32).

God saves and keeps us "that in the ages to come He might shew the exceeding riches of His grace in His kindness toward us through Christ Jesus" (Eph. 2:7).

It is not *the degree* of righteousness one possesses, but *the NATURE of righteousness.* Keep in mind that all of *our* righteousnesses are as filthy rags; but when we possess *the righteousness of God we possess God's SON, the Lord Jesus Christ.* Unregenerate man has not the slightest degree of righteousness or true virtue. He has *nothing* that pleases God. But when John the Baptist baptized Jesus in Jordan, God spoke from heaven and declared, "This is my beloved Son, *in whom I AM WELL PLEASED*" (Matt. 3:17).

When Moses and Elijah appeared with Jesus on the Mount of Transfiguration and Peter suggested that three tabernacles be built there—one for Jesus, one for Moses, and one for Elijah—God overshadowed the mountain and spoke from the shadows, proclaiming: "This is my beloved Son, *in whom I AM WELL PLEASED;* hear ye Him" (Matt. 17:5).

God found no pleasure in any sacrifice offered from Eden to Calvary:

"But in those sacrifices there is a remembrance again made of sins every year. For it is not possible that the blood of bulls and of goats should take away sins. Wherefore when He cometh into the world, He saith, Sacrifice and offering thou wouldest not, but a body hast thou prepared me: *In burnt-offerings and sacrifices for sin thou hast had no pleasure.*

"Then said I, Lo, I come (in the volume of the book it is written of me,) to do thy will, O God. Above when He said, *Sacrifice and offering and burnt-offerings and offering for sin thou wouldest not, neither hadst pleasure therein; which are offered by the law;*

"Then said He, Lo, I come to do thy will, O God. He taketh away the first, that He may establish the second. *By the which will we are sanctified through the offering of the body of Jesus Christ ONCE FOR ALL"* (Heb. 10:3—10).

This passage plainly declares that God found *no pleasure* in the blood of bulls and goats—Old Testament sacrifices; but in *the Lamb of God,* His only begotten Son, He was *pleased.* Therefore when we

possess Jesus, God is pleased with *us*—not because of
any merit of righteousness or holiness on our part,
but because Jesus abides within our hearts (Rom. 8:1;
Col. 1:27; 3:3).   Thus are we made acceptable unto
God, "to the praise of the glory of His grace, *wherein
He hath made us ACCEPTED IN THE BELOVED"*
(Eph. 1:6).

A Revelation from Heaven Was Necessary
As Ground for Saving Faith

"So then faith cometh by hearing, and hearing
by the Word of God" (Rom. 10:17).

Since man is guilty before God, lost and undone
without God; and since the ground for salvation is
believing on Jesus (John 3:16), it must follow that
apart from a divine revelation from heaven *there could
BE no saving faith,* therefore no salvation from sin.

Revelation was first given in types and shadows,
in promises and prophecies; therefore both *revelation*
and *faith* may exist in different degrees. For instance,
Abel had faith—it was *by faith* that he "offered unto
God a more excellent sacrifice than Cain" (Heb. 11:4).
The *Apostle Paul* had faith; and as to its nature and
object, both of these men had the *same* faith; but as
to the *degree* of faith, there was a vast difference because of the difference in the degree of *divine revelation* each of them possessed.   *Paul,* centuries after
Abel, had a *much greater* degree of revelation which,
like a shining light, *shone "more and more unto the
perfect day,"* and such was the path of the just (Prov.
4:18).

Since *revelation* and *faith* may exist in widely different degrees, we see the force of such passages as
Psalm 147:19,20:

"He sheweth His Word *unto Jacob,* His statutes
and His judgments *unto ISRAEL.* He hath not dealt
so with any nation: and as for His judgments, *they*

have not known them . . . ."

Now hear the words of the Apostle Paul to the Romans: "What advantage then hath the Jew? or what profit is there of circumcision? *Much every way: chiefly, BECAUSE THAT UNTO THEM were committed the oracles of God"* (Rom. 3:1,2).

Again, as Paul wrote to the believers in Ephesus we read: "Wherefore remember, that ye being in time past *Gentiles in the flesh,* who are called Uncircumcision by that which is called the Circumcision in the flesh made by hands; that at that time ye were without Christ, *being aliens from the commonwealth of Israel, and strangers from the covenants of promise,* having no hope, and without God in the world: *BUT NOW IN CHRIST JESUS ye who sometimes were far off are made nigh by the blood of Christ"* (Eph. 2:11–13).

There are those who question God's dealings with mankind, but hear the words of the Apostle Paul:

"What shall we say then? *Is there unrighteousness with God? GOD FORBID! . . . Nay but, O man, who art thou that repliest against God? Shall the thing formed say to Him that formed it, Why hast thou made me thus? Hath not the Potter power over the clay, of the same lump to make one vessel unto honour, and another unto dishonour?*

"What if God, willing to shew His wrath, and to make His power known, endured with much longsuffering the vessels of wrath fitted to destruction: and that He might make known the riches of His glory on the vessels of mercy, *which He had afore prepared unto glory, even us, whom He hath called, not of the Jews only, BUT ALSO OF THE GENTILES?"* (Rom. 9:14, 20–24).

As we study the Word of God and learn how He has dealt with the nations and peoples, we learn to make allowance for the *small degrees* of faith where light and revelation have been little known. Our Lord spoke of this in Matthew 11:20—24:

"Then began (Jesus) to upbraid *the cities wherein most of His mighty works were done,* because they repented not:

"Woe unto thee, *Chorazin!* Woe unto thee, *Bethsaida!* for if the mighty works, which were done in you, had been done in Tyre and Sidon, they would have repented long ago in sackcloth and ashes. But I say unto you, *It shall be more tolerable for Tyre and Sidon at the day of judgment, than for you.*

"And thou, *Capernaum,* which art exalted unto heaven, shalt be brought down to hell: for if the mighty works, which have been done in thee, had been done in Sodom, it would have remained until this day. But I say unto you, *That it shall be more tolerable for the land of Sodom in the day of judgment, than for thee.*"

Here, Jesus clearly stated that if the ancient cities of Tyre and Sidon had had *the light and revelation* which had been given to Chorazin and Bethsaida, and if *Sodom* had had the light and revelation given to *Capernaum,* those wicked places would have *repented* in sackcloth and ashes! *THEREFORE the judgment and damnation* upon the former people will be more tolerable than the damnation and judgment heaped upon Chorazin, Bethsaida, and Capernaum.

Unregenerated men become sons of God by calling upon the name of the Lord in faith; but even though the Word of God declares, *"Whosoever shall call upon the name of the Lord shall be SAVED,"* the Holy Spirit further enlightens us by asking, "How then shall they call on Him in whom they have not *believed?* and how shall they believe in Him of whom they have not *heard?* and how shall they hear *without a preacher?* and how shall they preach, except they be *sent?* As it is written, How beautiful are the feet of them that preach the Gospel of peace, and bring glad tidings of good things!" (Rom. 10:13—15).

The preaching of the Gospel as it is in this day and hour *is not the uniform method of divine proceeding* from the beginning of the human race. Previous to the time of Moses, there was no *written* revelation; people did not have the Word of God in a book or even on parchment; and until the Lord Jesus Christ came into the world to declare God (John 1:18), there was no ordinance for preaching the Word. There was no command, no program of ministers called and ordained of God to preach the Word as we know ministers today.   There were no *missionaries* until Jesus came.

Therefore, men under the Old Testament economy—even *good* men—stood on much lower ground than those under the New Testament economy. In Acts 10 we read of Cornelius, a Roman centurion who was stationed in Judaea.   He had learned enough about the God of Israel to live a just life, he was "a devout man, and one that feared God with all his house, which gave much alms to the people, and prayed to God alway" (Acts 10:1,2).   Even before he heard the good news of the atonement, the prayers and alms of this man were approved of God; but it was the Word spoken to him by Peter which brought salvation to his heart.

The angel of God appeared to Cornelius in a vision and said to him, *"Thy prayers and thine alms are come up for a memorial before God"* (Acts 10:4).   He then instructed Cornelius to "send men to Joppa, and call for Simon, whose surname is Peter; *who shall tell thee WORDS, whereby thou and all thy house shall be saved"* (Acts 11:13,14).

Cornelius had a *degree* of light, a degree of *revelation;* but in spite of the fact that he feared God and was "devout," *he needed to be SAVED by God's grace.* So God sent a messenger to tell him what to do. He sent for Peter, and when Peter came to the house of Cornelius he delivered a sermon that brought the entire household into the grace of God through saving faith. We find that sermon recorded in Acts 10:34—43:

Peter first declared that *God is no respecter of persons* (v. 34). He then declared that Jesus was "hanged on a tree," crucified for our sins according to the Scriptures (v. 39). The next point in his sermon was that God raised Jesus from the dead (v. 40); and then, *"To Him give all the prophets witness, that through His name WHOSOEVER BELIEVETH IN HIM SHALL RECEIVE REMISSION OF SINS"* (v. 43).

Cornelius was devout, he prayed, he gave much alms—but he had not believed unto salvation. Why? "How shall they *believe* in Him of whom they have not heard? and how shall they *hear* without a *preacher?*" So God sent Peter to the house of Cornelius to preach the Gospel, and in Acts 10:44 we read, *"While Peter yet spake these WORDS, the Holy Ghost fell on all them which heard the WORD!"*

Until Peter preached the message of salvation, Cornelius had a very limited knowledge of things spiritual; but he had followed and obeyed the light and knowledge that had been revealed to him. This does not suggest that there is another way of salvation, another way of acceptance with God aside from the way of salvation by grace through faith. No person can please God until he exercises faith in the finished work of Jesus. But Cornelius had faith in *all that he knew about God,* and when the final revelation was made to him through Peter's preaching, he fully embraced that revelation and *faith moved in* unto salvation by grace! Then Peter commanded that Cornelius "be baptized in the name of the Lord."

God's Testimony Concerning the Inhabitants
of the World Just Before the Flood

"And God saw that the wickedness of man was great in the earth, and that every imagination of the thoughts of his heart was only evil continually" (Gen. 6:5).

According to God's own infallible, unalterable Word, man's wickedness, in varying degrees, has been great upon the earth in all ages. Just before the flood men were evil—evil without mixture: *"EVERY IM-AGINATION of the thoughts of his heart"* was evil. He was evil without cessation—*"evil CONTINUAL-LY."* He was evil from the fountainhead of his actions: *"The imagination of the thoughts of his HEART."*

This is not a description of certain persons such as Cain or Judas. *It is a description of MAN.* And man left to himself is *incurably* evil, *entirely* evil and *apart from* righteousness; and anything he attempts to do righteously becomes "filthy rags" in the sight of God's holy eyes. *Without God,* man does not cease to be evil; and his heart is the fountainhead of every ungodly thing imaginable!

And God sees this. He sees things as they are. Man tries to veneer wickedness and call it by other names; but God sees it as it is, and this is the fundamental doctrine of the Gospel. Redemption rests upon it—and I declare that every false scheme of religion, every false doctrine which has been advanced by ungodly men, *originated* in the denial of the total depravity of man, and the necessity of the saving grace of God through the atonement of Jesus Christ!

Without the Shedding of Blood Is No Remission

"And almost all things are by the law purged with

blood; and without shedding of blood is no remission"
(Heb. 9:22).

When Adam and Eve sinned in the Garden of
Eden they immediately began to think and plan *in
their own minds* what they might do to correct their
terrible mistake! The devil had declared to Eve that
the reason God had forbidden them to eat of the fruit
of one tree was because He knew that if they *did*
eat of that certain fruit their eyes would be opened
and they would be "as gods, knowing good and evil"
(Gen. 3:5). Eve believed the devil's lie, she ate of the
fruit, she gave to Adam and *he* ate—and their eyes
were opened; they *did* know good and evil. They
immediately realized what a terrible thing had happened; but even so, they did not call on their Creator.
Instead, they planned a covering, and with the labor
of their own hands they manufactured aprons of fig
leaves to cover their nakedness (Gen. 3:7). They by-
passed God, they used their own ability to think,
reason, plan, and prepare their own covering, instead
of calling on God to deliver them and help them.

We do not know how long Adam and Eve wore
their fig-leaf aprons, but it could not have been for
very long, because "they heard the voice of the Lord
God walking in the garden in the cool of the day,"
and they ran to hide themselves among the trees of
the garden (Gen. 3:8).

Remember, "faith cometh by hearing," and atonement demands a revelation from God. Adam and Eve
heard His voice calling to them, asking, *"Where art
thou?"* Everything was lovely until then—but when
Adam heard the voice of God he immediately realized
the guilt of his own heart because of his disobedience
in eating the forbidden fruit! The only way unregenerate man today will know the fear of God and realize
his *need* of God is to hear *the voice* of God—and in
this Dispensation of Grace *we hear His voice through*

His Word.

Adam began to make excuse. He confessed to God that he had realized that he was naked, and this realization had caused him to be *afraid.* His fear had caused him to hide himself among the trees. Now *in reality,* Adam was not naked. I am sure the fig-leaf apron effectively covered his *body,* but it did not cover his naked spirit—and it is the spirit, the *inner man,* with which God deals. Therefore in Adam's heart he recognized the nakedness of his *spirit.*

God then asked the man what he had done, and Adam made excuse by declaring that *the woman* was the guilty party—and *she,* in turn, blamed the serpent. But God condemned *all* of their excuses and cursed the entire creation—*including* Adam and Eve; but for them He provided a covering:

"Unto Adam also and to his wife did the Lord God make coats of skins, and clothed them" (Gen. 3:21). These garments, divinely provided, are definitely a type of Christ, *"who of God is made unto us . . . righteousness"* (I Cor. 1:30). The "coats of skins" provided the first covering for the first sinners, to make them fit for the presence of a holy God!

These sacrifices teach man his true desert from God: *Man sinned,* knowing what God had commanded him not to do. Therefore God could have annihilated him; He could have destroyed both Adam and Eve, in justice, in holiness, and in all truth. But instead, He provided a covering, thereby teaching that there is *only one way* by which man can be delivered from the guilt of sin and made fit to appear before God; and *that ONE WAY* is through the covering God provided in the death of His only begotten Son.

Only GOD can provide a covering to hide the shame and spiritual nakedness of sinful man; and the covering He provides is the righteousness of our atoning Sacrifice—the Sacrifice God Himself provided in His only begotten Son, the Lord Jesus Christ.

I would also emphasize the fact that when Adam sinned and went away from God, he *hid* from his Creator. Therefore it was God who sought Adam, not Adam who sought God. It was God who saw the need for a sacrifice provided by an innocent substitute—the blood of innocent animals. (And I sincerely believe that the animals God slew in the Garden of Eden were *lambs*. There is no definite word in the Scripture to prove—or disprove—this, but it is my belief that the skins God provided to clothe Adam and Eve were the skins of little innocent lambs.)

After God provided an acceptable covering at the expense of the blood of innocent animals, He drove Adam and Eve from their garden home and sent them out to till the ground and provide their livelihood by the sweat of their brow. In the process of time, Cain and Abel were born, and eventually God demanded an offering from these first two sons of Adam.

In Genesis 4:3—5 we read, "In process of time it came to pass, that Cain brought of the fruit of the ground an offering unto the Lord. And Abel, he also brought of the firstlings of his flock and of the fat thereof. And the Lord had respect unto Abel and to his offering: but unto Cain and to his offering He had not respect . . . ."

In the offerings of these two sons of Adam we see the essential difference between an offering *acceptable* unto God (a spiritual offering of worship), and an offering of *formalism* which God *rejects*.

You will notice that there was nothing particularly *defective* about *either* of these offerings. The fruit Cain brought was not decayed or "wormy." I do not doubt that he brought *lovely* fruit, the best he had; and certainly *Abel's* offering was not defective, for he brought "of the firstlings of his flock." The chief difference in the offerings of these two brothers is pointed out in Hebrews 11:4:

"BY FAITH Abel offered unto God a more excellent sacrifice than Cain, by which he obtained WITNESS that he was righteous, God testifying of his gifts: and by it he being dead yet speaketh."

Cain's heart was not in his offering—he did exactly what a *self-righteous* man would do, proceeding on the principle that there was no real breach between himself and God. He had not committed any sin, therefore he did not need to *confess* sin. He needed no atonement, so why should he offer an innocent animal to be slain and consumed on an altar?

Such offerings are plentiful today in the world of "religion." Church members by the millions attend church on Sunday and participate in formal rituals and programs—but they have no heart for it. They do it because they feel it is their "duty," or because it is the "socially acceptable" thing to do. They do it *without faith*—and even *worship* which is not of faith becomes sin. Paul tells us in Romans 14:23 that *WHATSOEVER is not of faith is sin!*

Abel's offering was a blood-offering, an expiatory sacrifice; therefore *"the Lord had respect unto Abel and to his offering:* but unto Cain and to his offering He had not respect."

The Word does not say here that Abel's offering was consumed by fire from heaven, but I personally believe it was. Leviticus 9:23,24 records the fact that fire consuming the offering was a token of God's acceptance of the sacrifice:

"And Moses and Aaron went into the tabernacle of the congregation, and came out, and blessed the people: and the glory of the Lord appeared unto all the people. *And there came a fire out from before the Lord, and consumed upon the altar the burnt-offering and the fat: which WHEN ALL THE PEOPLE SAW, THEY SHOUTED, AND FELL ON THEIR FACES."*

We notice *"the Lord had respect unto ABEL,"* and then "to his *offering."* God accepted Abel first; then Abel's offering was accepted. If Abel had been justified on the ground of "good works," the order of acceptance would have been reversed: God would first have accepted the offering, and then He would have accepted Abel. Believing in the Messiah, Abel was accepted "for Christ's sake" (Eph. 4:32); and being so, his works were well pleasing in the sight of God. He brought his offering *by faith,* he *presented* it by faith, and God accepted both Abel and his offering. It was faith in the heart of the man that made his offering acceptable to God. Abel was accepted as a believer; Cain was *rejected* as an *unbeliever:* "He that believeth on (Jesus) is not condemned: but he that believeth not is condemned already, because he hath not believed in the name of the only begotten Son of God" (John 3:18).

Cain was angered by the Lord's rejection of his offering. The Scripture tells us that he "was very wroth, and his countenance fell." If the love of God had been in his heart, he would have fallen on his face before Jehovah and repented, as Joshua and his brethren did when Israel was defeated and driven back at Ai. Thirty-six of Joshua's men were slain because of the sin of Achan, and in Joshua 7:6—8 we read:

"Joshua rent his clothes, and fell to the earth upon his face before the ark of the Lord until the eventide, he and the elders of Israel, and put dust upon their heads. And Joshua said, Alas, O Lord God, wherefore hast thou at all brought this people over Jordan, to deliver us into the hand of the Amorites, to destroy us? Would to God we had been content, and dwelt on the other side Jordan! O Lord, what shall I say, when Israel turneth their backs before their enemies!"

Joshua had the love of God in his heart; he realized that something was drastically wrong, and he fell on his face and cried out to God; but it was quite different with *Cain!* His actions were those of a self-righteous, proud, unregenerated man—one who thinks highly of his ability, his offering, and whatever he does. Such a person thinks God should be pleased and honored that he would make an offering *at all.* Self-righteousness is an ugly, deadly sin. I do not doubt that Cain walked proudly into the presence of God and presented his gift of the fruit of the ground; but when God rejected Cain and his offering he went out from God's presence *filled with cruel passions* to which his fallen countenance was but the index. His *heart* was much uglier than his face, however, and finally the foul passions of his heart led him to murder his own brother (Gen. 4:8).

Philosophers—ancient and current—have taught many things in favor of morality. Many books have been written praising the achievement of mortal man. Many who, *from the human standpoint,* were great teachers and theologians, have cried long and loud on the subject of "the brotherhood of man"—all men free and equal, social equality on a universal scale. But the curious machine framed by philosophers, teachers, and theologians simply *does not work!*

Do not misunderstand me: I believe we should love our fellowman. I believe insofar as is humanly possible we should treat others exactly as we would like to be treated; but the only answer to the ills c⁵ mankind, the only answer to the needs of this world, is *the return of JESUS!* And *until* that time there will not be "peace on earth, good will toward men." Man has advanced intellectually to the highest point in history; but *in spite of all* of man's knowledge, understanding, and ability the earth is filled with violence, hatred, animosity, strife, poverty, misery, and woe such as has never before been known! You may search all of the writings of ancient philosophers and gather all of the opinions of current commentators; you may search all of the writings of great religious leaders, past and present—and *among them all* what principles have appeared in the world under the name of *philosophy OR religion* that can compare with John 3:16? *"For God so loved the world, that He gave His only begotten Son, that whosoever believeth in Him should not perish, but have everlasting life!"*

What philosopher or theologian has ever *loved* so deeply that he would give his only son on behalf of those who would nail his son to a cross and mock him as he died? What philosopher could love to the depth of *forgiving* the executioners of his beloved son? *Only GOD could love so much* because *God IS LOVE* (I John 4:8). We who love God love Him *"because He first loved US"* (I John 4:19), and not because of any principles set forth by philosophy or "religion." Had God not first loved us, *we could never have loved HIM:*

"Herein is love, not that we loved God, but that He loved us, and sent His Son to be the propitiation for our sins" (I John 4:10).

Why did God so love *me*, a poor, miserable, depraved son of Adam? Paul answers as the Holy Spirit spoke through him:

"Let all bitterness, and wrath, and anger, and clamour, and evil speaking, be put away from you, with all malice: and be ye kind one to another, tenderhearted, forgiving one another, *even as God FOR CHRIST'S SAKE hath forgiven YOU"* (Eph. 4:31,32).

Then in Ephesians 5:1,2 we read, "Be ye therefore followers of God, as dear children; and walk in love, *as Christ also hath loved us, and hath given Himself for us an offering and a sacrifice to God for a sweet-smelling savour."*

It is true that God first loved us and set forth

Jesus to be a propitiation for our sins. We are "a chosen generation, a royal priesthood, an holy nation, a peculiar people; that (we) should shew forth the praises of Him who hath called (us) out of darkness into His marvellous light" (I Pet. 2:9).

Because God so loved us and because Jesus died for us, words like these are sweet to our ears and we receive them joyfully in our hearts:

"Wherefore come out from among them, and be ye separate, saith the Lord, and touch not the unclean thing; and I will receive you, and will be a Father unto you, and ye shall be my sons and daughters, saith the Lord Almighty" (II Cor. 6:17,18).

What philosopher or liberal theologian could be the author of *these* words? "If there be therefore any consolation in Christ, if any comfort of love, if any fellowship of the Spirit, if any bowels and mercies, fulfil ye my joy, that ye be likeminded, having the same love, being of one accord, of one mind. Let nothing be done through strife or vainglory; but in lowliness of mind let each esteem other better than themselves. Look not every man on his own things, but every man also on the things of others.

"Let this mind be in you, which was also in Christ Jesus: Who, being in the form of God, thought it not robbery to be equal with God: but made Himself of no reputation, and took upon Him the form of a servant, and was made in the likeness of men: and being found in fashion as a man, He humbled Himself, and became obedient unto death, even the death of the cross" (Phil. 2:1—8).

Or *these?* "Dearly beloved, I beseech you as strangers and pilgrims, abstain from fleshly lusts, which war against the soul; having your conversation honest among the Gentiles: that, whereas they speak against you as evildoers, they may by your good works, which they shall behold, glorify God in the day of visitation" (I Pet. 2:11,12).

It is not principles set forth by philosophy, tradition, or man-made doctrines that constrain the believer to live morally, holy, and righteously in unselfishness toward his fellowman: *"For the LOVE OF CHRIST constraineth us;* because we thus judge, that if One died for all, then were all dead: and that He died for all, that they which live should not henceforth live unto themselves, but unto Him which died for them, and rose again" (II Cor. 5:14,15).

Through the atonement of our Lord Jesus Christ we have life and light: "When *Christ, who is our life,* shall appear, then shall ye also appear with Him in glory" (Col. 3:4).

"But ye, brethren, are not in darkness, that that day should overtake you as a thief. Ye are all *the children of LIGHT, and the children of the DAY:* we are not of the night, nor of darkness" (I Thess. 5:4,5).

Since we have life and light, we have the assurance that Jesus died for our sins and rose again for our justification "according to the Scriptures." Knowing this, we also have the assurance that all who sleep in Him will God bring with Him when He comes for His Church:

"For if we believe that Jesus died and rose again, even so them also which sleep in Jesus will God bring with Him. For this we say unto you by the Word of the Lord, that we which are alive and remain unto the coming of the Lord shall not prevent them which are asleep. For the Lord Himself shall descend from heaven with a shout, with the voice of the archangel, and with the trump of God: and the dead in Christ shall rise first: Then we which are alive and remain shall be caught up together with them in the clouds, to meet the Lord in the air: and so shall we ever be with the Lord. Wherefore comfort one another with these words" (I Thess. 4:14—18).

"But the day of the Lord will come as a thief in the night; in the which the heavens shall pass away with a great noise, and the elements shall melt with fervent heat, the earth also and the works that are therein shall be burned up. Seeing then that all these things shall be dissolved, what manner of persons ought ye to be in all holy conversation and godliness, looking for and hasting unto the coming of the day of God . . . ?" (II Pet. 3:10—12).

These *and only these* are the motives by which believers in every age have been induced and constrained to practice righteous living which automatically produces morality—a morality that can be ours only through the atonement made for us by the spotless Lamb of God. Atheists such as Ingersoll, Paine, Voltaire, and others have written many volumes against Christianity; but some of these men before their death were compelled to applaud the very faith they had condemned!

In this day and hour there are tens of thousands of religious leaders, ministers, and teachers who speak out against pure Christianity—the blood-bought redemption of Calvary's cross, the atonement made through the shed blood of the Lamb of God; but I ask, "What do *they* have to offer *instead of Christianity* that will produce the same righteousness and morality? What will they substitute that will be of equal efficacy?"

"The love of Christ" constrains believers. What does the liberal or modernist have to offer to constrain *their* followers? Self-love, the wisdom of man, the ability and accomplishments of man are certainly not the answer. All one need do is study the history of man and observe unregenerated men today, to learn that *apart from the atonement* man is strengthless, hopeless, without God, miserably condemned to an eternity of torment and damnation!

The total depravity of man *demands* the atonement

made by the Lord Jesus Christ!

Chapter Two

CHRIST'S ATONEMENT
IS THE HEART, SOUL, AND LIFEBLOOD
OF ALL PURE BIBLE DOCTRINE

"I will put enmity between thee and the woman, and between thy seed and her seed; it shall bruise thy head, and thou shalt bruise His heel" (Gen. 3:15).

"For I delivered unto you first of all that which I also received, *HOW THAT CHRIST DIED FOR OUR SINS ACCORDING TO THE SCRIPTURES*" (I Cor. 15:3).

"For He hath made Him to be sin for us, WHO KNEW NO SIN; that we might be made the righteousness of God IN HIM" (II Cor. 5:21).

"Who His own self *BARE OUR SINS in His own body on the tree,* that we, being dead to sins, should live unto righteousness: *BY WHOSE STRIPES YE WERE HEALED"* (I Pet. 2:24).

"And not only so, but we also joy in God *through OUR LORD JESUS CHRIST, BY WHOM WE HAVE NOW RECEIVED THE ATONEMENT"* (Rom. 5:11).

I do not hesitate to declare that the atonement of our Lord Jesus Christ is the greatest, grandest, most sublime and distinctive truth in the entire Bible. I further declare that His atonement is the greatest fact of Christianity—*the atonement IS Christianity.*

The atonement of the Lord Jesus Christ is the supplier of all human need, the answer to all human

questions, the minister to all human ills, the joy of
all human sorrows, the remover of all human guilt, and
the securer of all divine glory!   Yes, Christ's atonement is the heart, soul, and lifeblood of all pure Bible
doctrine.

The sum of the Gospel is: *"And this is life eternal, that they might know thee the only true God,
and Jesus Christ, whom thou hast sent"* (John 17:3).

Why did God send forth His only begotten Son?
Why was Jesus sent from the Father's bosom to a
world of sorrow, heartache, misery, and degradation?
Jesus answered that question in John 17:4 when He
said to the heavenly Father, *"I have glorified thee
on the earth: I HAVE FINISHED THE WORK
WHICH THOU GAVEST ME TO DO."*

Therefore the sum of the Gospel is to know the
Lord Jesus Christ in His finished work on the cross.
By knowing HIM we know GOD, and it is *only* by
knowing Him that we *can* know God in the provision
of His great love and saving grace.   He who knows
the Lord Jesus Christ knows God the Father; he who
does *not* know Jesus *does not know GOD.*

IN the Lord Jesus Christ—and Him crucified "according to the Scriptures"—all true Bible doctrines,
all of God's teachings, and all of man's experiences
culminate.   FROM the Lord Jesus Christ—and Him
crucified "according to the Scriptures"—all duties, all
works, and all ministries are to *emanate.*   No doctrine
is seen clearly and truly unless that doctrine leads
directly to the cross.   No work of *man* is God-pleasing,
no experience or attainment of man is genuine and
vital unless that work, experience, or attainment has
its source, root, and strength in the cross of the Lord
Jesus Christ.   No waiting for *the second coming* of
Jesus is spiritually healthy and purifying unless it is
called forth by the contemplation of the great God
and our Saviour Jesus Christ who gave Himself for us

that He might redeem us from all iniquity and purify
unto Himself a peculiar people. *Hallelujah* for the
simplicity of the Gospel! From this center—from the
cross of the Lord Jesus Christ—as from the heart of
man, are *"the issues of life"*:

"For the grace of God that bringeth salvation hath
appeared to all men, teaching us that, denying ungodliness and worldly lusts, we should live soberly,
righteously, and godly, in this present world; looking
for that blessed hope, and the glorious appearing of
the great God and our Saviour Jesus Christ; who gave
Himself for us, that He might redeem us from all
iniquity, and purify unto Himself a peculiar people,
zealous of good works" (Tit. 2:11—14).

The atonement of the Lord Jesus Christ is the
chief part of our salvation. It is the anchor of saving
faith, the refuge of our hope, and the rule of all pure
love. It is the true foundation of Christianity, the
richest treasure of the Christian faith. If the atonement were removed from the Word of God, the Bible
would be like a body without a spirit, like a tree
without a taproot; and the Gospel would be void of
the message of salvation.

In Luke 24:13—35 we read of Christ's appearing
to two of His disciples on the road to Emmaus, and
of how He showed them from the books of Moses,
Psalms, and the prophets that His death was essential
and the cross a divine imperative.

The Word of God contains the history of the *people*
of God. Other nations are introduced into the Bible
message only in an incidental manner and as they
have to do *with* the people of God who were chosen
and formed for Christ. God has appointed His Son
to be "heir of all things" (Heb. 1:2), and everything
the patriarchs and prophets did during the Old Testament economy was preparatory to the kingdom of the
Lord Jesus Christ. It was *in HIS field* that the Old

Testament prophets labored, and the apostles "entered into their labours" (John 4:38).

The Call of Abraham

"Now the Lord had said unto Abram, Get thee out of thy country, and from thy kindred, and from thy father's house, unto a land that I will shew thee: And I will make of thee a great nation, and I will bless thee, and make thy name great; and thou shalt be a blessing: And I will bless them that bless thee, and curse him that curseth thee: and in thee shall all families of the earth be blessed" (Gen. 12:1—3).

God's call to Abraham—and the unusual blessings He bestowed upon him—had reference to the kingdom of the Lord Jesus Christ, for it was through the seed of Abraham that *THE Seed* would come in the fulness of time, the Seed through whom all kindreds of the earth would be blessed.

When Melchisedec met Abraham returning from the slaughter of the kings (Gen. 14:18—20), why did he bless Abraham with such heart? Because Abraham had *the promise*—he was the seed through which Messiah would come.

Why was Esau's despising his birthright declared *profaneness?* (Gen. 25:34; Heb. 12:16). Simply because it referred to something sacred. God's promise to Abraham and his seed chiefly related to things a great many years in the future, but Esau desired something nearer at hand and therefore sold his birthright for a moment of pleasure and enjoyment.

Why is the reproach chosen by Moses in preference to the treasures and splendors of Egypt called "the reproach of Christ"? (Heb. 11:24—26) Because Israel was in possession of the promise that through that nation the Messiah would come, and Moses *believed* that promise. Therefore he cast his lot with the people of Israel, even though at that time they were slaves to Pharaoh. These were the "good" things to which he referred in persuading Hobab to go with them (Num. 10:29—33). Everything that was done for Israel —from their going down into Egypt to their settlement in Canaan and from thence to the coming of the Lord Jesus Christ—was in reference to the Messiah, Son of God, *the Lord Jesus Christ through whom we have the atonement.*

The *sacrifices* of the Old Testament under the Mosaic economy all *relate* to the doctrine of the atonement and point to the coming of Jesus. Consider the offering made by *Noah* immediately after the flood. The first objective of *a man of the WORLD* would have been a feast, a time of rejoicing, and probably the gathering of logs and whatever was at hand to build a house—but not so with Noah. He had neither a feast nor a day of rejoicing. *He built an altar;* and on that altar he offered burnt-offerings "of every clean beast, and of every clean fowl" (Gen. 8:20). The offering made by Noah that day was a substitutional sacrifice for the purpose of atonement.

The *process* of such a sacrifice was later given and is described in Leviticus 1:2—9:

"If any man of you bring an offering unto the Lord, ye shall bring your offering of the cattle, even of the herd, and of the flock. If his offering be a burnt-sacrifice of the herd, let him offer a male without blemish: he shall offer it of his own voluntary will at the door of the tabernacle of the congregation before the Lord. *And he shall put his hand upon the head of the burnt-offering; AND IT SHALL BE ACCEPTED FOR HIM TO MAKE ATONEMENT FOR HIM.*

"And he shall kill the bullock before the Lord: and the priests, Aaron's sons, shall bring the blood, and sprinkle the blood round about upon the altar

that is by the door of the tabernacle of the congregation.   And he shall flay the burnt-offering, and cut
it into his pieces.   And the sons of Aaron the priest
shall put fire upon the altar, and lay the wood in
order upon the fire: and the priests, Aaron's sons,
shall lay the parts, the head, and the fat, in order
upon the wood that is on the fire which is upon the
altar: but his inwards and his legs shall he wash in
water: and the priest shall burn all on the altar, to
be a burnt-sacrifice, an offering made by fire, of a
sweet savour unto the Lord."

The sinner confessed his sin upon the head of the
animal and the animal was then killed, thus being
treated as the transgressor; and as if the sin had actually *been transferred TO the animal,* the blood of
the substitute was shed and sprinkled "round about
upon the altar."   To show *Divine acceptance* of the
sacrifice on behalf of the one who offered it, fire de-
scended from heaven (or on some occasions was kindled
by the priest from the sacred fire kept for that purpose) and consumed the sacrifice.   In Leviticus 9:24
we read, *"And there came a fire out from before the
Lord, and consumed upon the altar the burnt-offering
and the fat: which when all the people saw, they
shouted, and fell on their faces."*

There can be no doubt that God *accepted* Noah's
offering, because Genesis 8:21 tells us that *"the Lord
smelled a sweet savour,"* and He bestowed upon Noah
and those who were with him a covenant promise
that the earth would never again be covered by water.
To guarantee that covenant, God put a rainbow in
the sky as a reminder to the peoples of earth that
"the waters shall no more become a flood to destroy
all flesh" (Gen. 9:13—15).

Noah's sacrifice bore a distinct and peculiar aspect
to the offering of the body of our Lord, and I believe
Paul had this in mind when he said, *". . . Christ also*

hath loved us, and hath given HIMSELF for us an offering and a sacrifice to God for a sweetsmelling savour" (Eph. 5:2).

The One Sacrifice Jesus Made Is Better
Than All the Sacrifices in the Old Testament

"For the law having a shadow of good things to come, and not the very image of the things, can never with those sacrifices which they offered year by year continually make the comers thereunto perfect. For then would they not have ceased to be offered? because that the worshippers once purged should have had no more conscience of sins. But in those sacrifices there is a remembrance again made of sins every year. For it is not possible that the blood of bulls and of goats should take away sins.

"Wherefore when He cometh into the world, He saith, Sacrifice and offering thou wouldest not, but a body hast thou prepared me: In burnt-offerings and sacrifices for sin thou hast had no pleasure. Then said I, Lo, I come (in the volume of the book it is written of me,) to do thy will, O God. Above when He said, Sacrifice and offering and burnt-offerings and offering for sin thou wouldest not, neither hadst pleasure therein; which are offered by the law;

"Then said He, Lo, I come to do thy will, O God. He taketh away the first, that He may establish the second. By the which will we are sanctified through the offering of the body of Jesus Christ once for all. And every priest standeth daily ministering and offering oftentimes the same sacrifices, which can never take away sins: but this Man, after He had offered one sacrifice for sins for ever, sat down on the right hand of God; from henceforth expecting till His enemies be made His footstool. For by one offering He hath perfected for ever them that are sanctified.

"Whereof the Holy Ghost also is a witness to us: for after that He had said before, This is the covenant that I will make with them after those days, saith the Lord, I will put my laws into their hearts, and in their minds will I write them; and their sins and iniquities will I remember no more. Now where remission of these is, there is no more offering for sin" (Heb. 10:1—18).

The Jewish institutions—feasts, holy days, offerings, temple, and tabernacle—were but *shadows* of good things to come, of which Christ was the *substance:*

The priests, the prophets, and the kings were typical of *our* great High Priest and King of kings—the Lord Jesus Christ.

The manna the children of Israel ate in the wilderness (Ex. 16:14,15) was a type of Jesus, the Bread of Life "which cometh down from heaven, and giveth life to the world" (John 6:31—35).

The rock in Horeb from whence water flowed when Moses *struck* it (Ex. 17:6) was typical of Jesus, the Water of Life. He declared, "Whosoever drinketh of the water that I shall give him shall never thirst; but the water that I shall give him shall be in him a well of water springing up into everlasting life" (John 4:14).

The cities of refuge in the Old Testament (Num. 35:9—14) represented Jesus as "the hope set before us" (Heb. 6:18).

The magnificent and glorious temple pointed to our Lord Jesus Christ, *the true temple.* In describing the New Jerusalem John said, "And I saw no temple therein: for the Lord God Almighty and the Lamb are the temple of it" (Rev. 21:22).

It is true that the moral law exhibited right things and the ceremonial law was a shadow of good things—*"but GRACE AND TRUTH came by JESUS CHRIST"* (John 1:17).

This Dispensation of Grace is to that of the Old Testament as the Jubilee was to the state of captivity (Lev. 25:8–12).   No doubt the Psalmist had such things in mind as he prayed, *"Open thou mine eyes, that I may behold wondrous things out of thy law"* (Psalm 119:18).

To Him Give All the Prophets Witness

It is most interesting to note that the spirit of inspiration in the prophets is called *the Spirit of Christ:*
"Of which salvation the prophets have inquired and searched diligently, who prophesied of the grace that should come unto you: searching what, or what manner of time *the Spirit of Christ which was in them* did signify, when it testified beforehand the sufferings of Christ, and the glory that should follow" (I Pet. 1:10,11).

There are *scores* of prophecies in the Old Testament Scriptures, and the Person and work of the Lord Jesus Christ is the principal theme of all of them:
"To Him give *ALL the prophets* witness, that through His name whosoever believeth in Him shall receive remission of sins" (Acts 10:43).
"And I fell at his feet to worship him.   And he said unto me, See thou do it not: I am thy fellow-servant, and of thy brethren that have the testimony of Jesus: worship God: for *the testimony of Jesus is THE SPIRIT OF PROPHECY"* (Rev. 19:10).
We find the first prophecy—the first mention of the coming of the Saviour—in Genesis 3:15:   "I will put enmity between thee and the woman, and between thy seed and her seed; it shall bruise thy head, and thou shalt bruise His heel."   From this first mention of *the Seed of the woman,* which Seed would eventually crush the serpent's head, to the day when Jesus appeared in flesh born of the Virgin, the language of

prophecy became more and more explicit and distinct
concerning His coming into the world to pay the sin-
debt and save the lost.

We do not know how much Adam and Eve understood of the prophecy spoken by the Lord God in the
promise of the Seed of the woman. We do not know
how much *Abel* understood about the blood sacrifice
he brought to the Lord, nor how much *Noah* understood about the ark and its significance. But when
God made the promise to *Abraham* and his seed, *Abraham understood* that the promise included the coming
of the Messiah, Saviour of sinners: "For what saith
the Scripture? *Abraham believed God, and it was
counted unto him for righteousness*" (Rom. 4:3).

From the first promise of the Saviour, given in
Genesis 3:15, God gave increased light step by step
through His prophets concerning the coming of the
Lamb of God, Saviour of sinners. And during His
public ministry Jesus Himself declared, "Your father
Abraham rejoiced to see my day: and he saw it, and
was glad" (John 8:56).

I would point out briefly here just *how* God revealed the coming of Messiah and how, as the time
of His coming drew nearer, additional light was given
which *pointed to* His coming:

To the Hebrews Paul said, "God, who *at sundry
times and in divers manners* spake in time past unto
the fathers by the prophets, hath in these last days
spoken unto us by His Son, whom He hath appointed
heir of all things, by whom also He made the worlds"
(Heb. 1:1,2).

(The Greek here reads—not "in divers *manners*,"
but "in divers *portions*.") This passage teaches *a
process* that reaches a definite climax, a process by
which God spoke *"in divers portions"*:

To Adam God revealed the manner of Christ's
coming—i. e., that He would be the seed of the *woman*,

not the seed of man (Gen. 3:15).

To *Abraham* He revealed that Christ would be from the nation Israel, of which Abraham was the head: "I will bless them that bless thee, and curse him that curseth thee: *and in thee shall all families of the earth be blessed*" (Gen. 12:3).

To *Jacob* God declared that the Messiah would belong to the tribe of Judah (the Jews): "The sceptre shall not depart from Judah, nor a lawgiver from between his feet, until Shiloh come; and unto Him shall the gathering of the people be" (Gen. 49:10).

To *David* He declared that Christ should *be of his family:* "The Lord hath sworn in truth unto David; He will not turn from it: Of the fruit of thy body will I set upon thy throne" (Psalm 132:11).

It was also to David that God revealed the manner of the *death* of Jesus: "For dogs have compassed me: the assembly of the wicked have inclosed me: *they pierced my hands and my feet*" (Psalm 22:16).

Again it was David to whom God revealed that Jesus would *rise from the dead:* "For thou wilt not leave my soul in hell; neither wilt thou suffer thine Holy One to see corruption. Thou wilt shew me the path of life: in thy presence is fulness of joy; at thy right hand there are pleasures for evermore" (Psalm 16:10,11).

To *Micah* God revealed that Christ would be born in the little, obscure village of Bethlehem: "But thou, Bethlehem Ephratah, though thou be little among the thousands of Judah, yet *out of thee shall He come forth unto me that is to be Ruler in Israel; whose goings forth have been from of old, from everlasting*" (Mic. 5:2).

To *Malachi* He revealed that Christ would be preceded by a forerunner who would announce the coming of Messiah: "Behold, *I will send my messenger, and he shall prepare the way before me:* and the

Lord, whom ye seek, shall suddenly come to His temple, even the Messenger of the covenant, whom ye delight in: behold, He shall come, saith the Lord of hosts" (Mal. 3:1).

To *Daniel* God revealed the time when Christ would be "cut off" in death—at the end of the sixty-ninth week of the seventy weeks of years: *"And after threescore and two weeks shall Messiah be cut off,* but not for Himself: and the people of the prince that shall come shall destroy the city and the sanctuary; and the end thereof shall be with a flood, and unto the end of the war desolations are determined" (Dan. 9:26).

To *Zechariah* God made known the fact that Christ would be betrayed and sold for thirty pieces of silver: "And the Lord said unto me, Cast it unto the potter: a goodly price that I was prised at of them. And *I took the thirty pieces of silver, and cast them to the potter in the house of the Lord"* (Zech. 11:13).

To *Isaiah* God revealed that Christ would die for the sins of the people, that He would be numbered with the transgressors, that He would intercede for those who put Him to death, and that He would be buried in a rich man's tomb:

"And *He made His grave with the wicked,* and with *the rich* in His death; because He had done no violence, neither was any deceit in His mouth. Yet it pleased the Lord to bruise Him; He hath put Him to grief: when thou shalt make His soul an offering for sin, He shall see His seed, He shall prolong His days, and the pleasure of the Lord shall prosper in His hand. He shall see of the travail of His soul, and shall be satisfied: by His knowledge shall my righteous servant justify many; for He shall bear their iniquities. Therefore will I divide Him a portion with the great, and He shall divide the spoil with the strong; because He hath poured out His soul unto death: and *He was numbered with the transgressors; and He bare the sin of many, and made intercession for the transgressors"* (Isa. 53:9—12).

The Psalms abound in prophecies concerning the coming of the Messiah. The plaintive part of Psalm 22 speaks of Him several times:

Verse 1 records His cry from the cross, *"My God, my God, why hast thou forsaken me?"*

The words recorded in verse 8 were used inadvertently by His enemies: *"He trusted on the Lord that He would deliver Him: let Him deliver Him, seeing He delighted in Him."*

The kind of death He endured is expressly pointed out in verse 16: *"They pierced my hands and my feet."*

The circumstances of the soldiers' casting lots for His garments is declared in verse 18: *"They part my garments among them, and cast lots upon my vesture."*

Isaiah prophesied concerning His miraculous *virgin birth:* "Therefore the Lord Himself shall give you a sign: Behold, a virgin shall conceive, and bear a Son, and shall call His name Immanuel" (Isa. 7:14).

Isaiah also prophesied of the humble, gentle *character* of Jesus: "A bruised reed shall He not break, and the smoking flax shall He not quench . . ." (Isa. 42:3).

Zechariah foretold the manner of Christ's public entry into the Holy City: "Rejoice greatly, O daughter of Zion; shout, O daughter of Jerusalem: behold, thy King cometh unto thee: He is just, and having salvation; *lowly, and riding upon an ass, and upon a colt the foal of an ass"* (Zech. 9:9).

There are many other "portions" of God's Word which make known His purpose concerning His only begotten Son; but Christ's coming was the culmination of the prophecies given here. The Word of God has said *all there IS to be said* concerning salvation, life, and godliness. "It is finished!" (John 19:30).

What is finished? What did Jesus accomplish? The Scriptures were fulfilled—every jot and tittle. The law was magnified. The justice of Almighty God was satisfied. The sin-debt was paid. Heaven was opened —Jesus declared, *"I am the DOOR"* (John 10:9). Hell was defeated—Jesus declared, "I have the keys of hell and of death" (Rev. 1:18). The "shadows" passed away because *reality* had come: *the Son of God appeared as prophesied* throughout the Old Testament.

The spirit of inspiration in the prophets is *correctly* called "the Spirit of Christ" because "it testified beforehand the sufferings of Christ, and the glory that should follow" (I Pet. 1:10,11).

The Jewish mercy seat during the Mosaic economy was a type of Christ; it was the medium of mercy and communion with God for all who worshipped God during the Old Testament economy:

"And thou shalt put the mercy seat above upon the ark; and in the ark thou shalt put the testimony that I shall give thee. And there I will meet with thee, and I will commune with thee from above the mercy seat, from between the two cherubims which are upon the ark of the testimony, of all things which I will give thee in commandment unto the children of Israel" (Ex. 25:21,22).

The Lord Jesus Christ is *in reality* what the mercy seat was *in figure;* but He is *not*—as the mercy seat was—*confined to a single nation or people.* Christ died for the sins of the whole world—Jew, Gentile, rich, poor, bond or free. He is "the Lamb of God, which taketh away the sin of the *world"* (John 1:29).

"For God so loved the world, that He gave His only begotten Son, that whosoever believeth in Him should not perish, but have everlasting life" (John 3:16).

"My little children, these things write I unto you,

that ye sin not. And if any man sin, we have an Advocate with the Father, Jesus Christ the righteous: And He is the propitiation for our sins, and not for our's only, but also *for the sins of the whole world"* (I John 2:1,2).

During the Old Testament economy, man *by faith* came to God with his sacrifices, *looking forward* to the coming of Messiah. In this Dispensation of Grace, we by faith *look back* to Calvary where Jesus paid the sin-debt in full. Christ is the only hope of man— through all ages and from all nations. *He is*—always has been and always will be—*the one Way.* There is no other door to heaven.

The Jewish sacrifices prefigured and pointed to the coming of the Messiah who was to become the sacrifice of atonement (the propitiation) for the sins of the world. Isaiah clearly prophesied that the iniquity of all mankind would be placed upon the Lamb of God and that His soul would be made *THE offering for sin:*

"ALL we like sheep have gone astray; we have turned every one to his own way; and the Lord hath laid on Him the iniquity of us ALL. . . Yet it pleased the Lord to bruise Him; He hath put Him to grief: when thou shalt make His soul an offering for sin, He shall see His seed, He shall prolong His days, and the pleasure of the Lord shall prosper in His hand. He shall see of the travail of His soul, and shall be satisfied: by His knowledge shall my righteous servant justify many; for He shall bear their iniquities. Therefore will I divide Him a portion with the great, and He shall divide the spoil with the strong; because He hath poured out His soul unto death: and He was numbered with the transgressors; and He bare the sin of many, and made intercession for the transgressors" (Isa. 53:6,10—12).

Since the Old Testament prophecies declared that the Messiah would be an *atoning sacrifice for sin,* the *apostles*, in declaring Jesus to be the *Messiah*, declared Him to BE the atoning sacrifice provided by God for sin. The Messiah prophesied by the Old Testament prophets was to be God manifest in flesh—God in a body like unto our body except for sin. Therefore when the apostles declared that Jesus was Messiah, they were announcing that He was God in flesh—and so He was!

Jesus Himself said, *"I and my Father are ONE"* (John 10:30). *Isaiah* declared that the Child to be born was to be called *"The Mighty GOD"* (Isa. 9:6). He further prophesied that the One who was to "feed His flock like a shepherd" and "gather the lambs in His arm, and carry them in His bosom" would be *none other than "THE LORD GOD"* (Isa. 40:10,11).

Since the prophecies in the Old Testament declared that Messiah would be God in flesh, the apostles *in declaring Jesus AS the Messiah* were proclaiming Him to be *the incarnate Son of God—man, yet God;* God in our nature (II Cor. 5:19). Jesus *said* He was the Son of God—and the Jews understood this. They knew He claimed equality with Jehovah, and it was because of this that they accused Him of blasphemy, declared that by their law He ought to be put to death, and finally *demanded* His death and had Him crucified. However, Jesus never claimed anything above and beyond what the prophets had said their Messiah would be.

When He healed a man on the Sabbath, the Jews "sought to slay Him, because He had done these things on the Sabbath day. But Jesus answered them, My Father worketh hitherto, and I work. Therefore the Jews sought the more to kill Him, because He not only had broken the Sabbath, but said also that God was His Father, making Himself equal with God" (John 5:16—18).

Then in John 19:7 the Jews said to Pilate, "We

have a law, and by our law He ought to die, because He made Himself the Son of God."

It was under these circumstances that the apostles, without explaining away the supposed blasphemy, declared that Jesus *was* the Son of God—thereby declaring Him to be *equal with God*—and called upon His murderers to repent and be baptized in His name for the remission of sins:

"Then Peter said unto them, Repent, and be baptized every one of you in the name of Jesus Christ for the remission of sins, and ye shall receive the gift of the Holy Ghost. . . Neither is there salvation in any other: for there is none other name under heaven given among men, whereby we must be saved" (Acts 2:38; 4:12).

The Old Testament is filled with prophecies concerning the coming of Messiah to save sinners. The New Testament relates *the fulfillment* of these prophecies. The *ordinances* of the Old Testament *prefigured* the coming of Messiah. The ordinances given to the Church in the *New* Testament *commemorate* His coming. However, both the Old and the New Testaments point to *the ONE Saviour*, the Lord Jesus Christ. Every divine truth of God's Word bears a distinct and definite *relation* to the Lord Jesus Christ; therefore the doctrine of the Gospel is *"THE TRUTH IS IN JESUS"* (Eph. 4:21). (The preposition "in" is not in the original language. The Greek reads, *"The truth IS Jesus."*) This is what the Lord said to Thomas in John 14:6:

"Jesus saith unto him, *I am the Way, THE TRUTH, and the Life:* no man cometh unto the Father, but by me."

Jesus also said, "Sanctify them through thy truth: *thy WORD is truth"* (John 17:17). In John 1:1 we read, *"In the beginning was the WORD, and the Word was with God, and the Word WAS God."* Therefore:

Jesus, God, and the Word are *inseparable.* The truth
is not "in" Jesus—*the truth IS Jesus* because *JESUS
is truth!*

Nothing Can Be Added

In Jesus "dwelleth all the fulness of the Godhead
bodily" (Col. 2:9). He came to take away sin (John
1:29). He came to lay His life down that *we* might
have life (John 10:17,18). He "bare our sins in His
own body on the tree" (I Pet. 2:24). And Jesus on
the cross satisfied the sin-debt once and forever through
His shed blood. He paid the sin-debt in full and declared, *"It is finished"* (John 19:30). Grace, mercy,
and peace are in Jesus (John 1:14; 14:27; Eph. 2:8;
Heb. 4:16). Resurrection to eternal life is through Jesus—and *only* through Him:

"If the Spirit of Him that raised up Jesus from
the dead dwell in you, He that raised up Christ from
the dead shall also quicken your mortal bodies by
His Spirit that dwelleth in you" (Rom. 8:11).

"When Christ, who is our life, shall appear, then
shall ye also appear with Him in glory" (Col. 3:4).

In the Lord Jesus Christ every precept finds its
most powerful motive. In Him every promise finds
its most perfect fulfillment. The Jews possessed—and
searched—the Scriptures, thinking that in them they
had eternal life; *but they would not come to Jesus,
THE WORD INCARNATE,* that they might have life
(John 5:39,40).

In Psalm 40:6—8 we read, "Sacrifice and offering
thou didst not desire; mine ears hast thou opened:
burnt-offering and sin-offering hast thou not required.
Then said I, Lo, I come: in the volume of the book
it is written of me, I delight to do thy will, O my
God: yea, thy law is within my heart."

No believer doubts that this passage speaks of the
Messiah, since the words here are clearly applied to

Jesus in the New Testament:

"In burnt-offerings and sacrifices for sin thou hast had no pleasure. Then said I, Lo, I come (in the volume of the book it is written of me,) to do thy will, O God. Above when He said, Sacrifice and offering and burnt-offerings and offering for sin thou wouldest not, neither hadst pleasure therein; which are offered by the law; then said He, Lo, I come to do thy will, O God. *He taketh away the first, that He may establish the second*" (Heb. 10:6—9).

It is impossible to explain these words on any other principle than that of specific and definite application to the Messiah. Who else could, with propriety, use the words spoken here? *David* certainly could not! Regardless of what one believes about the coming of Messiah—that is, whether He has already come (and we know *He has*), or is *yet TO come* (as the great majority of Jews believe)—it is *of His coming* that the prophets speak. Therefore the question is not whether the Scriptures prophesy of Messiah and characterize Him, but whether or not these prophecies and statements were *fulfilled in JESUS*. To accept the Bible as God's Word, to study and *rightly divide* the Word, comparing spiritual things with spiritual, is to know beyond any shadow of doubt that every jot and tittle of the prophecies pointing to the Messiah were *literally fulfilled* in the Lord Jesus Christ:

"Now we have received, not the spirit of the world, but the Spirit which is of God; *that we might know the things that are freely given to us of God*. Which things also we speak, not in the words which man's wisdom teacheth, but which the Holy Ghost teacheth; comparing spiritual things with spiritual" (I Cor. 2:12,13).

In the passage quoted from Psalm 40:6—8 we note three great peculiarities which distinguish the Messiah's coming:

1. *The sacrifices and ceremonies of the Mosaic Law
    would thence be superceded:* "Sacrifice and offer-
ing thou didst not desire... Then said I, Lo, *I come.*"

The Messiah would supercede the sacrifices and
ceremonies of the old economy. The prophets in the
Old Testament frequently spoke of those ordinances
in a depreciating strain. This they would not have
done if the sacrifices had been designed to continue
always:

I Samuel 15:22 declares, "Hath the Lord as great
delight in burnt-offerings and sacrifices, as in obeying
the voice of the Lord? *Behold, to OBEY is better
than sacrifice, and to HEARKEN than the fat of
rams!*"

In Psalm 50:8–15 we read, "I will not reprove thee
for thy sacrifices or thy burnt-offerings, to have been
continually before me. I will take no bullock out of
thy house, nor he goats out of thy folds. For every
beast of the forest is mine, and the cattle upon a
thousand hills. I know all the fowls of the mountains:
and the wild beasts of the field are mine. If I were
hungry, I would not tell thee: for the world is mine,
and the fulness thereof. Will I eat the flesh of bulls,
or drink the blood of goats? *Offer unto God thanks-
giving; and pay thy vows unto the most High: and
call upon me in the day of trouble: I will deliver thee,
and thou shalt glorify me.*"

Psalm 51:17 gives this great truth: *"The sacrifices
of God are A BROKEN SPIRIT: a broken and a con-
trite HEART, O God, thou wilt not despise!"*

In Isaiah 1:11,12 we read, "To what purpose is the
multitude of your sacrifices unto me? saith the Lord:
I am full of the burnt-offerings of rams, and the fat
of fed beasts; and I delight not in the blood of bullocks, or of lambs, or of he goats. When ye come
to appear before me, *who hath required this at your
hand,* to tread my courts?"

Jeremiah declared, "Thus saith the Lord of hosts, the God of Israel: Put your burnt-offerings unto your sacrifices, and eat flesh. For I spake not unto your fathers, nor commanded them in the day that I brought them out of the land of Egypt, concerning burnt-offerings or sacrifices: but this thing commanded I them, saying, *OBEY MY VOICE, and I will be your God, and ye shall be my people: and WALK YE IN ALL THE WAYS THAT I HAVE COMMANDED YOU, that it may be well unto you*" (Jer. 7:21—23).

Then in Jeremiah 31:31—34 we read, "Behold, the days come, saith the Lord, that *I will make A NEW COVENANT with the house of Israel,* and with the house of Judah: Not according to the covenant that I made with their fathers in the day that I took them by the hand to bring them out of the land of Egypt; which my covenant they brake, although I was an husband unto them, saith the Lord: *But this shall be the covenant that I will make with the house of Israel: After those days,* saith the Lord, *I WILL PUT MY LAW IN THEIR INWARD PARTS, AND WRITE IT IN THEIR HEARTS;* and will be their God, and they shall be my people. And they shall teach no more every man his neighbour, and every man his brother, saying, Know the Lord: for they shall all know me, from the least of them unto the greatest of them, saith the Lord: for I will forgive their iniquity, and I will remember their sin no more."

Paul speaks of this last passage in Hebrews 8:13: "*In that He saith, A NEW covenant, He hath made the first OLD. Now that which decayeth and waxeth old is ready to vanish away.*" And concerning Israel's sins and iniquities being *remembered no more* the Scripture declares, "Now where remission of these is, *there is no more offering for sin*" (Heb. 10:18).

The first reference to *sacrifice* in the Word of God is found in Genesis 3:21, where God clothed Adam and

Eve with "coats of skins." Innocent animals were
slain and their blood was shed that a covering might
be prepared for Adam and Eve.

The first *clear instance* of sacrifice is found in
Genesis 4:4 where Abel brought "of the firstlings of
his flock." In Hebrews 11:4 the Apostle Paul declared
that it was *"by faith"* that Abel brought his offering.
Therefore *his righteousness* was the result of his blood
sacrifice, not the result of his character.

Before God gave the law to Moses, the head of
the family was also the family priest. Then by the
law an *order of priests* was established and they alone
could offer sacrifices—but the sacrifices they offered
were but types and shadows. Although such sacrifices
expressed the guilt—and the need—of the offerer, *all
sacrifices in the Old Testament era pointed to the
Lord Jesus Christ and were FULFILLED IN HIM:*

Jesus said, "Think not that I am come to destroy
the law, or the prophets: *I am not come to destroy,
but to FULFIL"* (Matt. 5:17).

Therefore it is in perfect harmony with the tenor
of the Old Testament Scriptures that when Messiah
came into the world He should say, *"Sacrifice and
offering thou didst not desire; mine ears hast thou
opened: burnt-offering and sin-offering hast thou not
required. Then said I, Lo, I COME."* These words
clearly declare that Messiah came to accomplish *that
which could not BE accomplished* by or through sacrifices and offerings:

"For the law having a shadow of good things to
come, and not the very image of the things, can never
with those sacrifices which they offered year by year
continually make the comers thereunto perfect. For
then would they not have ceased to be offered? because that the worshippers once purged should have
had no more conscience of sins. *But in those sacrifices there is a remembrance again made of sins every*

year. For it is not POSSIBLE that the blood of bulls and of goats should take away sins" (Heb. 10:1—4).

Yes, it was impossible for the blood of bulls and goats to take away sins, it was impossible for the ceremonies under the Mosaic system to make the worshippers perfect— *"But THIS MAN, after He had offered ONE SACRIFICE for sins for ever, sat down on the right hand of God;* from henceforth expecting till His enemies be made His footstool. *For BY ONE OFFERING He hath perfected FOR EVER them that are sanctified"* (Heb. 10:12—14).

Jesus settled the sin-question *once and forever* through the sacrifice of His own blood. There is *nothing* man can do, live, or give to atone for sin because the sin-debt has been *paid in full.*

The question *now* is: *"What think ye of CHRIST? Whose Son is He?"* If we believe that Jesus is the Christ, the Son of God, *we are BORN of God.* When we believe on Jesus we have everlasting life (John 3:18,36; 5:24; Rom. 10:9,10).

Since Calvary, *sacrifice and oblation* have ceased. They ceased *virtually* when Jesus offered Himself on the old rugged cross; they ceased *in actuality* a few years *after* Calvary. The Jews who received Jesus as Messiah and Saviour ceased to offer sacrifices, and those who did *not* believe on Him were *compelled* to discontinue such practice for a season because of the destruction of their city and the temple.

2. The second peculiarity which distinguished the Messiah's coming was that *the great body of prophecy in the Old Testament Scriptures concerning His coming would be accomplished:* "Then said I, Lo, I come: *in the volume of the book it is written of me."*

In Luke 24:13—35 we find the account of the Lord Jesus, on the day of His resurrection, joining Himself to the company of two of His disciples who were on their way to Emmaus—"but their eyes were holden that they should not know Him." He asked them, "What manner of communications are these that ye have one to another, as ye walk, and are sad?" One of the disciples answered, "Art thou only a stranger in Jerusalem, and hast not known the things which are come to pass there in these days?" Jesus asked, "*What* things?" and they answered, "Concerning Jesus of Nazareth, which was a prophet mighty in deed and word before God and all the people."

They then went on to explain how the chief priests had had Jesus arrested and condemned to death, and had crucified Him. Then with a sad note they said, "But we trusted that it had been He which should have redeemed Israel: and beside all this, to day is the third day since these things were done."

They further related to Him that certain women had visited the sepulchre and had found the body of Jesus missing, and had "seen a vision of angels, which said that He was alive."

It was at this point that Jesus broke into their conversation: "Then He said unto them, *O FOOLS, and slow of heart to believe ALL THAT THE PROPHETS HAVE SPOKEN!* Ought not Christ to have suffered these things, and to enter into His glory? And beginning at Moses and ALL the prophets, *He expounded unto them in ALL THE SCRIPTURES the things concerning Himself.*"

"Beginning at *Moses*" (that is, the first five books in the Bible) "and *ALL the prophets*" (including both major and minor) "He expounded unto them *in ALL the Scriptures* the things concerning Himself." In other words, from Genesis 3:15 through the last verse in Malachi, Jesus preached to these disciples what the Scriptures declared concerning Himself, telling them that they were "fools, and *slow of heart to believe*" what the prophets had said.

The religious leaders in Israel when Jesus tabernacled among men knew that *the Seed of the woman* was to bruise the head of the serpent (Gen. 3:15). They also knew God had promised Abraham that *in his seed* all nations of the earth would be blessed (Gen. 12:3), therefore they knew Messiah would come through the seed of Abraham.

They knew that Jacob, when blessing the tribe of Judah, prophesied the coming of Shiloh, unto whom "the gathering of the people" should be (Gen. 49:10). They knew Moses spoke of "that Prophet" whom the Lord God would raise up from the midst of their own people, a Prophet like unto Moses, to whom His ancient people should listen (Deut. 18:15).

They knew that David and the prophets had prophetically described Messiah under a great variety of forms and names, such as "the Anointed of the Lord ...the King of kings...the Lord of David to whom Jehovah spoke...a Child born...a Son given, whose name would be called Wonderful, Counsellor, The mighty God, The everlasting Father, The Prince of Peace."

They knew He was prophesied to be "a rod out of the stem of Jesse" (Isa. 11:1); God's servant whom He upholds; His elect in whom His soul delighteth (Isa. 42:1); "Him whom man despiseth . . . Him whom the nation abhorreth" (Isa. 49:7). In Isaiah 53 — a passage read and loved by every Jewish religionist—it is plainly declared that Messiah would be "a Man of sorrows and acquainted with grief."

Thus it was that "in the volume of the Book" it was written of Him—the Messiah, only begotten Son of God, who came and offered Himself to the Jews; but they "denied the Holy One and the Just, and desired a murderer to be granted" unto them (Acts 3:14). They cried out, "We will not have this Man! Crucify Him! Let His blood be upon us and upon our children.''

In the Volume of the Book It Is Written

Inspired of Jehovah God and clearly marked out by the prophets, was *the time* when Messiah should come.

When Jacob was blessing the tribes, he said, ''The sceptre shall not depart from Judah, nor a lawgiver from between his feet, until Shiloh come; and unto Him shall the gathering of the people be'' (Gen. 49:10). What Jacob said was true, for although the ten tribes were scattered, *Judah* (the Jews) continued as a people and kept their government until the Lord Jesus came. However, soon after they rejected Jesus and crucified Him they were dispersed among the nations of the earth and scattered to the islands of the sea—and the vast majority of them are *still scattered.* It was in May, 1948, that Israel became a state for the first time in more than twenty-five centuries, and this is definitely a sign that the Lord's *second* coming is imminent.

In the prophecy of Haggai we learn that God put it in the hearts of the people to build a second temple, the Messiah would appear *during the time* this temple stood in Jerusalem, and His presence in this second temple would more than balance the inferiority of this temple as compared to Solomon's temple:

''For thus saith the Lord of hosts: Yet once, it is a little while, and I will shake the heavens, and the earth, and the sea, and the dry land; and I will shake all nations, and the desire of all nations shall come: and I will fill this house with glory, saith the Lord of hosts. The silver is mine, and the gold is mine, saith the Lord of hosts. The glory of this latter house shall be greater than of the former, saith the Lord of hosts: and in this place will I give peace, saith the Lord of hosts'' (Hag. 2:6—9).

All that was prophesied by Haggai was literally fulfilled in the Lord Jesus Christ; but soon after His crucifixion this second temple was completely destroyed and burned to ashes. Therefore it is clear that if Jesus were *not* the Messiah, it is impossible for the prophecy of Haggai to be fulfilled! *But Jesus WAS the promised Messiah.*

Gabriel spoke to Daniel of the time of the coming of Messiah, and Daniel prophesied:

"Know therefore and understand, that from the going forth of the commandment to restore and to build Jerusalem unto the Messiah the Prince shall be seven weeks, and threescore and two weeks: the street shall be built again, and the wall, even in troublous times. And after threescore and two weeks shall Messiah be cut off, but not for Himself: and the people of the prince that shall come shall destroy the city and the sanctuary; and the end thereof shall be with a flood, and unto the end of the war desolations are determined. And he shall confirm the covenant with many for one week: and in the midst of the week he shall cause the sacrifice and the oblation to cease, and for the overspreading of abominations he shall make it desolate, even until the consummation, and that determined shall be poured upon the desolate" (Dan. 9:25—27).

The prophecy of the seventy years was fulfilled in the Babylonian captivity; and this prophecy of *seventy weeks of years* was just as certainly fulfilled in the appearance and crucifixion of the Lord Jesus Christ. The effect of this and other clear prophecies upon the minds of the Jewish nation was that about that time there was a general excitement and expectation of the Messiah's appearance. Many Jews looked for the coming of "that Prophet" of whom Moses wrote.

God not only revealed to Daniel the time of *the coming* of Messiah, but also that He would be "cut off" and shortly thereafter the temple and the city would be destroyed. This occurred in 70 A. D. when Titus the Roman led his armies against the Holy City and so completely demolished it that not one stone was left standing upon another.

Also, "in the volume of the Book" the place where Messiah should be *born* is clearly pinpointed in Micah 5:2 and fulfilled in Matthew 2:4—6: "And when (Herod) had gathered all the chief priests and scribes of the people together, he demanded of them where Christ should be born. And they said unto him, *In Bethlehem of Judaea: FOR THUS IT IS WRITTEN BY THE PROPHET, And thou Bethlehem, in the land of Juda, art not the least among the princes of Juda: for out of thee shall come a Governor, that shall rule my people Israel.*"

It is further written "in the volume of the Book" concerning Messiah, "I the Lord have called thee in righteousness, and will hold thine hand, and will keep thee, and give thee for a covenant of the people, for a light of the Gentiles; to open the blind eyes, to bring out the prisoners from the prison, and them that sit in darkness out of the prison house" (Isa. 42:6,7).

Jesus referred to this prophecy in Matthew 4:16: "The people which sat in darkness saw great light; and to them which sat in the region and shadow of death light is sprung up."

"In the volume of the Book" is clearly declared *the family* through whom Messiah would come: "For unto us a Child is born, unto us a Son is given: and the government shall be upon His shoulder: and His name shall be called Wonderful, Counsellor, The mighty God, The everlasting Father, The Prince of Peace. Of the increase of His government and peace there shall be no end, *upon the throne of David,* and upon His kingdom, to order it, and to establish it with judgment and with justice from henceforth even for ever. The zeal of the Lord of hosts will perform this" (Isa. 9:6,7).

Gabriel referred to this prophecy when he announced to the Virgin Mary that she would be the mother of God's Son:

"And in the sixth month the angel Gabriel was sent from God unto a city of Galilee, named Nazareth, to a virgin espoused to a man whose name was Joseph, of the house of David; and the virgin's name was Mary. And the angel came in unto her, and said, Hail, thou that art highly favoured, the Lord is with thee: blessed art thou among women.

"And when she saw him, she was troubled at his saying, and cast in her mind what manner of salutation this should be. And the angel said unto her, Fear not, Mary: for thou hast found favour with God. And, behold, thou shalt conceive in thy womb, and bring forth a Son, and shalt call His name JESUS.

"He shall be great, and shall be called the Son of the Highest: *and the Lord God shall give unto Him the throne of His father David: and He shall reign over the house of Jacob for ever; and of His kingdom there shall be no end*" (Luke 1:26—33).

The kind of *miracles* Messiah would perform is also prophesied "in the volume of the Book." Seven hundred years before Mary conceived of the Holy Ghost and brought forth her firstborn Son, the Prophet Isaiah declared: "Then the eyes of the blind shall be opened, and the ears of the deaf shall be unstopped. Then shall the lame man leap as an hart, and the tongue of the dumb sing: for in the wilderness shall waters break out, and streams in the desert" (Isa. 35:5,6).

Such miracles as were prophesied by Isaiah were truly performed by the Lord Jesus Christ: "And it came to pass, when Jesus had made an end of commanding His twelve disciples, He departed thence to teach and to preach in their cities.

"Now when John had heard in the prison the works of Christ, he sent two of his disciples, and said unto Him, Art thou He that should come, or do we look for another? Jesus answered and said unto them, Go and shew John again those things which ye do hear and see:

"The blind receive their sight, and the lame walk, the lepers are cleansed, and the deaf hear, the dead are raised up, and the poor have the Gospel preached to them. And blessed is he, whosoever shall not be offended in me.

"And as they departed, Jesus began to say unto the multitudes concerning John, What went ye out into the wilderness to see? A reed shaken with the wind? But what went ye out for to see? A man clothed in soft raiment? Behold, they that wear soft clothing are in kings' houses. But what went ye out for to see? A prophet? Yea, I say unto you, and more than a prophet. *For this is he, of whom it is written, Behold, I send my messenger before thy face, which shall prepare thy way before thee.* Verily I say unto you, Among them that are born of women there hath not risen a greater than John the Baptist: notwithstanding he that is least in the kingdom of heaven is greater than he. And from the days of John the Baptist until now the kingdom of heaven suffereth violence, and the violent take it by force. *For all the prophets and the law prophesied until John. And if ye will receive it, this is Elias, which was for to come. HE THAT HATH EARS TO HEAR, LET HIM HEAR"* (Matt. 11:1—15).

The miracles of Jesus were works of mercy and benevolence, as well as demonstrations of divine power. He never performed one miracle to bring comfort to Himself, but to give healing and comfort to the needy. This is in accord with the prophecy in Psalm 72:12—14:

"He shall deliver the needy when he crieth, the

*poor also, and him that hath no helper. He shall
spare the poor and needy, and shall save the souls
of the needy. He shall redeem their soul from deceit
and violence: and precious shall their blood be in
His sight.*"

Many of the Jews traveled with Jesus through
much of His ministry, and they witnessed His miracles. His *enemies* witnessed His miracles—*but gave
Beelzebub the credit for them* (Matt. 12:24). He was
their Messiah, His miracles proved it; but in spite of
the fact that His works and His words fulfilled the
Old Testament prophecies with which the Jews were
familiar, they refused to accept Him as Messiah and
cried, "We will not have this Man! Crucify Him!"

One of the outstanding reasons for the Jews' rejection of Jesus was that they were expecting a powerful *military* leader who would deliver them from the
bondage of Rome and restore the former glory of Israel; but they were without excuse in this, because
"in the volume of the Book" it was clearly written
that Messiah, even though He would be King of kings,
would be humble and lowly. *Zechariah* even pointed
out the exact manner of His entry into the Holy City—
"lowly, and riding upon an ass" (Zech. 9:9).

In order for Zechariah's prophecy to be fulfilled
it was a divine imperative that Messiah should descend
from parents of humble and lowly circumstances, and
also that the rulers and leading dignitaries of the land
should not accompany Him when He rode into Jerusalem. (Mark 12:37 tells us that the "common people"
heard Him gladly.) It was *prophesied* that the common people would be those who would cry out, "Ho-
sanna to the Son of David! Blessed is He that cometh
in the name of the Lord!" (Please study John 12:
12—19.)

Even *the disciples* were disappointed and discour-
aged when Jesus was arrested and led away to be

tried in Pilate's hall—but they, too, were *without excuse,* for "in the volume of the Book" it was clearly written that Messiah would suffer and be put to death at the hands of ungodly men:

"As many were astonied at thee; His visage was so marred more than any man, and His form more than the sons of men" (Isa. 52:14).

I suppose no chapter in the Old Testament Scripture has been more loved by Israel than Isaiah chapter 53—and certainly there is no passage from Genesis through Malachi that more clearly labels the Messiah and more minutely describes His humble appearance, His cruel mockings, and the sufferings through which He passed. For that reason, we give the entire chapter here:

"Who hath believed our report? and to whom is the arm of the Lord revealed? For He shall grow up before Him as a tender plant, and as a root out of a dry ground: He hath no form nor comeliness; and when we shall see Him, there is no beauty that we should desire Him. He is despised and rejected of men; a Man of sorrows, and acquainted with grief: and we hid as it were our faces from Him; He was despised, and we esteemed Him not.

"Surely He hath borne our griefs, and carried our sorrows: yet we did esteem Him stricken, smitten of God, and afflicted. But He was wounded for our transgressions, He was bruised for our iniquities: the chastisement of our peace was upon Him; and with His stripes we are healed.

"ALL we like sheep have gone astray; we have turned every one to his own way; and the Lord hath laid on Him the iniquity of us ALL. He was oppressed, and He was afflicted, yet He opened not His mouth: He is brought as a lamb to the slaughter, and as a sheep before her shearers is dumb, so He openeth not His mouth.

"He was taken from prison and from judgment: and who shall declare His generation? for He was cut off out of the land of the living: for the transgression of my people was He stricken. And He made His grave with the wicked, and with the rich in His death; because He had done no violence, neither was any deceit in His mouth.

"Yet it pleased the Lord to bruise Him; He hath put Him to grief: when thou shalt make His soul an offering for sin, He shall see His seed, He shall prolong His days, and the pleasure of the Lord shall prosper in His hand. He shall see of the travail of His soul, and shall be satisfied: by His knowledge shall my righteous servant justify many; for He shall bear their iniquities.

"Therefore will I divide Him a portion with the great, and He shall divide the spoil with the strong; because He hath poured out His soul unto death: and He was numbered with the transgressors; and He bare the sin of many, and made intercession for the transgressors" (Isa. 53).

The enemies of Jesus *exactly and minutely fulfilled prophecy* in reproaching Him, demanding His death, and mocking Him as He hung on the cross. They used the very words spoken by the prophets and inflicted upon Jesus the exact cruelties the prophets had foretold. In Psalm 22 David prophesied, giving a graphic description of Christ's death by crucifixion:

His bones were out of joint (v. 14).

He was covered with perspiration because of His intense suffering (v. 14).

The action of His heart was affected (v. 14).

His strength was exhausted and He was extremely thirsty (v. 15).

His hands and His feet were pierced (v. 16).

He was partially nude; most of his clothing had been removed (v. 17).

His enemies quoted the words of prophecy as they mocked Him on the cross (v. 8).

If you will study Matthew 27:35—56 you will see that the prophecies recorded in Psalm 22 were fulfilled to the letter!

It is also written "in the volume of the Book" that death could not hold Him. It was prophesied that Messiah, after being "cut off" out of the land of the living and laid in the grave, would rise from the dead. *His resurrection* was a very definite part of the reward promised Jesus by the heavenly Father for His sufferings. *He did not enjoy the cross,* but "for *the joy* that was set before Him (He) *endured* the cross, despising the shame, and is set down at the right hand of the throne of God" (Heb. 12:2).

If Jesus had been just a man and had remained in the grave, how could He have "seen His seed" or "prolonged His days"? If His kingdom had been the kingdom of mortal man, how could that kingdom continue as long as the sun and the moon—never ceasing? How was He to see "of the travail of His soul" and be *satisfied* in seeing that travail *unless He SURVIVED it?* Yes, He rose again as prophesied—but even more than this, it was prophesied that He would rise early (shortly after death), because *He was not to see corruption:*

"Therefore my heart is glad, and my glory rejoiceth: my flesh also shall rest in hope. *For thou wilt not leave my soul in hell; neither wilt thou suffer thine Holy One to see corruption"* (Psalm 16:9,10).

Peter quoted this prophecy almost word for word in His sermon at Pentecost (Acts 2:25—27).

"In the volume of the Book" it is also foretold that the majority of the Messiah's own people, the Jews, would not believe Him, and that He would turn to the Gentiles:

"Then I said, I have laboured in vain, I have

spent my strength for nought, and in vain: yet surely
my judgment is with the Lord, and my work with
my God.   And now, saith the Lord that formed me
from the womb to be His servant, to bring Jacob again
to Him, Though Israel be not gathered, yet shall I
be glorious in the eyes of the Lord, and my God shall
be my strength.   And He said, It is a light thing that
thou shouldest be my servant to raise up the tribes
of Jacob, and to restore the preserved of Israel: I will
also give thee for a light to the Gentiles, that thou
mayest be my salvation unto the end of the earth"
(Isa. 49:4—6).

Speaking at the great council in Jerusalem, James
made this statement: "Men and brethren, hearken
unto me: Simeon hath declared how God at the first
did visit the Gentiles, to take out of them a people
for His name.   And to this agree the words of the
prophets . . ." (Acts 15:14,15).

The Scriptures prove beyond any shadow of doubt
that Jesus was Messiah.   The time and place of His
birth, His family, His character, His miracles, His
sufferings, His death, and His resurrection were all
fulfillments of prophecy.   He was truly the Messiah,
and He sits today at the right hand of God making
intercession for whosoever shall call upon His name.

3.   The third peculiarity which distinguished the Messiah's coming was the prophecy that *He would
perfectly fulfill the will of God:*   "I delight to do thy
will, O my God."

The Apostle Paul quoted this prophecy in Hebrews
10:5—7:

"Wherefore when He cometh into the world, He
saith, Sacrifice and offering thou wouldest not, but a
body hast thou prepared me: In burnt-offerings and
sacrifices for sin thou hast had no pleasure. Then said
I, Lo, I come (in the volume of the Book it is written

of me,) to do thy will, O God."

God's will sometimes denotes what He *approves,*
and sometimes it denotes what He *appoints.* What
God *approves* is the rule of our conduct; what He
appoints is *His own.* Both what He approved and
what He appointed were minutely and completely
fulfilled by His Son, the Lord Jesus Christ, the Messiah.

The life of Jesus perfectly conformed to each and
every divine precept. His every action was governed
by love. He challenged His enemies by asking, "Which
one of you convinceth me of sin?" They could not
find one sin in His life, and *false witnesses* were required to carry out the mock trial by which they demanded His death.

The Sanhedrin sent officers to *arrest* Jesus, and
when they returned *without* Him the Pharisees asked,
"Why have ye not brought Him?" The officers replied, "Never man spake like this Man!" (John 7:45,46).

In John 9:32, after Jesus opened the eyes of the
man born blind, we read, *"Since the world began* was
it not heard that any man opened the eyes of one
that was born blind!"

We could search the pages of history—both sacred
and secular—and we would find no record where *any
man* was born as Jesus was born, lived as He lived,
spoke as He spoke, wrought such miracles as He performed, died as He died, and whom the grave could
not hold! *"For such an High Priest became us, who
is holy, harmless, undefiled, separate from sinners, and
made higher than the heavens"* (Heb. 7:26).

Jesus came to declare the Father (John 1:18), but
He came to do more than fulfill the divine precepts:
He came "to seek and to save that which was lost"
(Luke 19:10). "For when we were yet without strength,
in due time Christ died for the ungodly" (Rom. 5:6).
Jesus fulfilled every jot and tittle of the law and the

prophets (Matt. 5:17), but His obedience to the law was subservient to the primary purpose of His coming—namely, "to save that which was lost." Otherwise, He could not have been *"the Lord of righteousness."*

As God's servant, Jesus came into the world, sent forth by God the Father, to save Israel—*and eventually Israel WILL BE SAVED.* (Study Romans chapter 11.)

He came to give light to the Gentiles and salvation to the ends of the earth (John 3:16). In accomplishing this, it was a divine necessity that Jesus endure the penalty as well as obey the precepts of God's holy law. His soul must be made "an offering for sin." He must be "cut off, *but not for Himself,"* that He might "make reconciliation for iniquity and bring in everlasting righteousness."

The death of Jesus on the cross is the *heart* of Christianity, for *without* His death on Calvary the sacrifices and prophecies of the Old Testament Scripture would be void and empty, and the great facts recorded in the New Testament giving *the fulfillment* of these prophecies would mean nothing.

The Apostle Paul declared to the Corinthian believers, "I determined not to know any thing among you, *save Jesus Christ, and Him CRUCIFIED"* (I Cor. 2:2). This is the hub of the wheel of Christianity, the center of God's plan and program foreordained before the world was, and all the spokes connected to the hub.

Paul did not mean, however, that he confined his preaching to a monotonous repetition of a favorite point, nor that he neglected other truths recorded in the Word of God. On the contrary, he declared, "I have not shunned to declare . . . all the counsel of God," and the doctrine of "Christ and Him crucified" *comprehends* all the counsel of God.

I close this chapter with the declaration that there

is not an important truth in all the Word of God but what is presupposed by, included in, or arising out of *the crucifixion of Jesus.* There is no part of practical Christianity but what hangs upon the doctrine of the cross of the Lamb of God, *"through which we have THE ATONEMENT."*

Chapter Three

JESUS MET THE DIVINE QUALIFICATIONS TO MAKE ATONEMENT FOR SIN

"Which of you convinceth me of sin? And if I say the truth, why do ye not believe me?" (John 8:46).

"I have glorified thee on the earth: I have finished the work which thou gavest me to do. And now, O Father, glorify thou me with thine own self with the glory which I had with thee before the world was" (John 17:4,5).

"Being justified freely by His grace through the redemption that is in Christ Jesus: whom God hath set forth to be a propitiation through faith in His blood, to declare His righteousness for the remission of sins that are past, through the forbearance of God; to declare, I say, at this time His righteousness: that He might be just, and the Justifier of him which believeth in Jesus. Where is boasting then? It is excluded. By what law? of works? Nay: but by the law of faith. Therefore we conclude that a man is justified by faith without the deeds of the law" (Rom. 3:24—28).

"For He hath made Him to be sin for us, who knew no sin; that we might be made the righteousness of God in Him" (II Cor. 5:21).

The Lord's question, "Which of you convinceth me of sin?" was not asked of friends or of people who loved Him dearly. It was asked of His bitterest enemies, those who were determined to destroy Him. No man *before or since* Jesus lived on earth has dared to ask such a question of his fellowmen because all rational human beings *know* that they have sinned, and neither friends nor enemies would have any difficulty in finding some degree of fault in every life.

But friends and enemies alike admitted that Jesus was a most unusual and extraordinary Person (John 9:32; 8:45,46; 11:47,48). He was "in all points tempted like as we are, yet WITHOUT SIN" (Heb. 4:15). As He tabernacled among men He never sinned in thought, word, or deed; and when He asked, "Which of you convinceth me of sin?" the mouths of His enemies were stopped. They could not answer because *He had DONE no sin!* Therefore He met every divine qualification necessary to atone for sin.

"I have glorified thee on the earth." Jesus glorified the heavenly Father in every minute detail of His life. He never walked one step, performed one miracle, or spoke one word that did not bring glory and honor to God.

"And now, O Father, glorify thou me with thine own self *with the glory which I had with thee BEFORE THE WORLD WAS."* The Man who spoke these words was either God's Christ, the only begotten *Son* of God, or the greatest impostor and counterfeit who ever set foot on God's dirt! Surely no mortal man would dare make such a statement. But Jesus was *not* an impostor: *He was very God in flesh.* He was "in the beginning" *with* the Father, He was *"in the bosom"* of the Father (John 1:1,2,18); but in the fulness of time He took a body made "in the likeness of sinful flesh" (Rom. 8:3), and in that body He conquered the world, the flesh, the devil, death, hell, and the grave, *and made atonement through His own shed blood!*

Jesus was *qualified* to make atonement for sin, and

He was set forth for that very purpose:

"Whom GOD hath set forth to be a propitiation through faith in His blood, to declare His (God's) *righteousness for the remission of sins THAT ARE PAST* (that includes *all* sins from Adam to Calvary), *through the forbearance of God; to declare, I say, at this time His righteousness: that He* (GOD) *might be JUST, and THE JUSTIFIER OF HIM WHICH BE-LIEVETH IN JESUS"* (Rom. 3:25,26).

Christ fulfilled every jot and tittle of the law (Matt. 5:17); therefore we are justified freely—*not by the deeds of the law, but by faith WITHOUT the deeds of the law, by the grace of God through the redemption that is in Christ Jesus.* What God Almighty demanded to make atonement for sin, only God Almighty *could*—and did—*provide* in the Person of His only begotten Son.

"Salvation Is of Jehovah"
(Jonah 2:9)

"Salvation belongeth unto the Lord . . ." (Psalm 3:8). Only Jehovah God could so love that He would sacrifice His only begotten Son in order that poor, helpless, hopeless, wicked sinners might be saved *from deserved damnation!*

Damnation is the sinner's just due because *"all have sinned"* and *"the WAGES of sin is DEATH"* (Rom. 3:23; 6:23). Therefore, "salvation *belongeth unto* Jehovah," and "salvation is *of* Jehovah." *Man* has nothing to do with the atonement, man cannot redeem himself. Salvation is ours by the grace of God, *"not of works, lest any man should boast"* (Eph. 2:8,9).

I repeat—what God demanded for an atonement, only God could provide. This is borne out in the following Scriptures:

"For God SO LOVED the world, that He gave

His only begotten Son, that whosoever believeth in Him should not perish, but have everlasting life" (John 3:16).

It was GOD who set forth His Son "to be *a propitiation" FOR sin* (Rom. 3:25).

It was GOD—yes, the eternal, holy God—who "commendeth His love toward us, in that, *while we were yet sinners,* Christ died for us" (Rom. 5:8).

It was GOD who made Jesus to be sin for *us.* I have always trembled when reading those words—but to fully appreciate this truth we must read the verse: *"For He* (God) *hath made Him* (Jesus) *to be sin for US, who knew no sin* (Jesus knew no sin); *that we might be made the righteousness of God in Him"* (II Cor. 5:21).

The cross of Jesus was foreordained before God created the universe, before there was a sinner to need salvation.   The Psalmist tells us that God has been "from everlasting to everlasting" (Psalm 90:1,2). God the Father, God the Son, and God the Holy Ghost agreed on an atonement and before the foundation of the world was laid, the blood of Jesus was foreordained to be shed:

"Forasmuch as ye know that ye were not redeemed with corruptible things, as silver and gold, from your vain conversation received by tradition from your fathers; but with the precious blood of Christ, as of a lamb without blemish and without spot: *who verily WAS FOREORDAINED BEFORE THE FOUNDATION OF THE WORLD, but was manifest in these last times for you.* Who by Him do believe in God, that raised Him up from the dead, and gave Him glory; that your faith and hope might be in God" (I Pet. 1:18—21).

Jesus was "the image of the invisible God" (Col. 1:15).

In Him dwelt "all the fulness of the Godhead

bodily" (Col. 2:9).

Those of us who have been born again are in the family of God because "He hath made us *accepted IN THE BELOVED*" (Eph. 1:6), and "the Beloved" is none other than the Lord Jesus Christ who died for our sins "according to the Scriptures" and is now our atonement.

Yes, God saves us—but *why?* Paul answers in his letter to the believers at Ephesus: "Be ye kind one to another, tenderhearted, forgiving one another, *even as God FOR CHRIST'S SAKE hath forgiven you*" (Eph. 4:32).

It is impossible to over-emphasize the fact that Jesus of Nazareth, God's only begotten Son, met all the qualifications necessary to make an atonement for our sins.

The Apostles Were Not Disappointed in Jesus

John the Baptist announced the coming of Jesus. He came out of the wilderness of Judaea preaching, "*Repent ye!* for the kingdom of heaven is at hand" (Matt. 3:2).

Jesus was baptized of John (Matt. 3:13–17), and shortly thereafter He called the twelve apostles to walk with Him. These men left their work, their homes, *their all* to follow the Lord. They saw His accomplishments, they saw in Him the fulfillment of what the prophets had prophesied, they loved Him deeply— and they were not disappointed in Him. Later, under inspiration of the Holy Ghost, John the Beloved wrote:

"*In the beginning was the Word, and the Word was with God, and the Word was God.* The same was in the beginning with God. All things were made by Him; and without Him was not any thing made that was made.

"In Him was life; and the life was the light of

men. And the light shineth in darkness; and the darkness comprehended it not. . . *And the Word was made
flesh, and dwelt among us, (and we beheld His glory,
the glory as of the only begotten of the Father,) full
of grace and truth. . . .*

"No man hath seen God at any time; *the only
begotten Son, which is in the bosom of the Father,
He hath declared Him. . .* The next day John seeth
Jesus coming unto him, and saith, *Behold the Lamb
of God, which taketh away the sin of the world. . .*
And looking upon Jesus as He walked, he saith, *Behold the Lamb of God!"* (John 1:1−5, 14, 18, 29, 36).

Approximately sixty years after John penned the
testimony of his Gospel he further testified:

"That which was *from the beginning,* which we
have *heard,* which we have *seen with our eyes,* which
we have *looked upon,* and our hands have *handled,*
of the Word of life; (for the life was manifested, *and
we have seen it, and bear witness, and shew unto
you that eternal life, which was with the Father,* and
was manifested unto us;) *that which we have seen
and heard* declare we unto you, that ye also may have
fellowship with us: and truly our fellowship is with
the Father, and with His Son Jesus Christ. And these
things write we unto you, that your joy may be full.

"This then is the message which we have heard
of Him, and declare unto you, that God is light, and
in Him is no darkness at all. If we say that we have
fellowship with Him, and walk in darkness, we lie,
and do not the truth: But if we walk in the light,
as He is in the light, we have fellowship one with
another, and the blood of Jesus Christ His Son cleanseth us from all sin" (I John 1:1−7).

The Apostle Peter testified, "Moreover I will en-
deavour that ye may be able after my decease to have
these things always in remembrance. *For we have
not followed cunningly devised fables, when we made*

known unto you the power and coming of our Lord
Jesus Christ, *BUT WERE EYEWITNESSES OF HIS
MAJESTY.* For He received from God the Father
honour and glory, when there came such a voice to
Him from the excellent glory, This is my beloved Son,
in whom I am well pleased. *And this voice which
came from heaven WE HEARD, when we were with
Him in the holy mount"* (II Pet. 1:15—18).

Thomas vowed that he would not believe *in the
resurrection* of Jesus unless he could see the nailprints
in His hands and thrust his hand into the Saviour's
wounded side. But when Jesus appeared to the disciples when Thomas was present with them and said
to him, "Reach hither thy finger, and behold my
hands; and reach hither thy hand, and thrust it into
my side," *Thomas*—in a mixture of shame and grief
but still in true love—*exclaimed, "My LORD and my
GOD!"* (John 20:24—28).

The *Epistle to the Hebrews* literally *breathes* with
love to Christ, and is intermingled with the same
kind of language used by John, Peter, Thomas, and
others of the disciples. I believe the Apostle Paul
penned the Epistle to the Hebrews. It was to him
that God revealed the mystery of the Church, the
mystery hidden from the ages but made known through
Paul.

There is no possible way to misunderstand the
language of Hebrews 1:1—3, penned under inspiration:
"*GOD*, who at sundry times and in divers manners
spake in time past unto the fathers by the prophets,
hath in these last days spoken unto us by His SON,
whom He hath appointed heir of all things, by whom
also He made the worlds; *who being the brightness of
His glory, and THE EXPRESS IMAGE OF HIS PER-
SON*, and upholding all things by the word of His
power, *when He had BY HIMSELF purged our sins,
SAT DOWN ON THE RIGHT HAND OF THE MAJ-*

ESTY ON HIGH."

In these tremendous verses God is recognized as the same God who spoke through the prophets and who, "in these last days" has spoken through His Son, the Lord Jesus Christ. The Son was *the brightness of God's glory,* the *"express image"* of *God's Person.* He purged our sins and having accomplished that for which God sent Him into the world, He sat down at the Father's right hand on the throne on high—*and there He sits today, the ONE MEDIATOR between God and men* (I Tim. 2:5).

Paul further declared that Jesus was "much better than the angels," and *by inheritance* has obtained "a more excellent name than they." God never said to any angel, "Thou art my Son, this day have I begotten thee." Neither did God say of any of the angels, "I will be to him a Father, and he shall be to me a son."

"But UNTO THE SON He saith, Thy throne, O God, is for ever and ever: a sceptre of righteousness is the sceptre of thy kingdom. Thou hast loved righteousness, and hated iniquity; therefore God, even thy God, hath anointed thee with the oil of gladness above thy fellows. And, Thou, Lord, in the beginning hast laid the foundation of the earth; and the heavens are the works of thine hands: They shall perish; *but thou remainest;* and they all shall wax old as doth a garment; and as a vesture shalt thou fold them up, and they shall be changed: *but thou art the same, and thy years shall not fail"* (Heb. 1:4—12 in part).

There is no excuse for musunderstanding here. Paul—writing under inspiration—declares that *Jesus is ETERNAL.* And then he asks a question: "To which of the *angels* said (God) at any time, *Sit on my right hand, until I make thine enemies thy footstool?"* God never made this statement to any angel, but He *did* make it to His Son. In Psalm 110:1 we read, "The

Lord said unto my Lord, *Sit thou at my right hand, until I make thine enemies thy footstool!"* (Paul also refers to this passage from Psalms in I Corinthians 15:25: "For He must reign, till He hath put all enemies under His feet.")

Then following the marvelous testimony given in Hebrews 1:4—14—parts of which we have just quoted—Paul thunders out:

"Therefore we ought to give the more earnest heed to the things which we have heard, lest at any time we should let them slip. For if the word spoken by angels was stedfast, and every transgression and disobedience received a just recompence of reward; *HOW SHALL WE ESCAPE, IF WE NEGLECT SO GREAT SALVATION; which at the first began to be spoken by the Lord, and was confirmed unto us BY THEM THAT HEARD HIM;* God also bearing them witness, both with signs and wonders, and with divers miracles, and gifts of the Holy Ghost, according to His own will?" (Heb. 2:1—4).

Paul could not mention the name of the Lord Jesus Christ without adding words of warm and tender praise. We find a good example of this in Romans 9:4,5, where Paul ennumerated the things that rendered his countrymen (the Jews) dear to his heart. He spoke of them as being his kinsmen *according to the flesh,* "who are Israelites; to whom pertaineth the adoption, and the glory, and the covenants, and the giving of the law, and the service of God, and the promises; whose are the fathers, *and of whom as concerning the flesh Christ came"*—and it seems that Paul might have stopped here. But having mentioned the name of the Lord Jesus Christ, he could not be content without adding, *". . . who is over all, GOD BLESSED FOR EVER. Amen!"*

We find the same principle in Colossians 1:15—19. Having declared that God had made it possible, through His dear Son, for us to have redemption, and having made it clear that redemption is *only* through the blood of Jesus, it seems this would have been enough to say. But the Apostle Paul went on to describe Jesus as *"the image of the invisible God,* the firstborn of every creature: for *by Him were all things created,* that are in heaven, and that are in earth, visible and invisible, whether they be thrones, or dominions, or principalities, or powers: *ALL THINGS WERE CREATED BY HIM, AND FOR HIM: AND HE IS BEFORE ALL THINGS, AND BY HIM ALL THINGS CONSIST.* And He is the head of the body, the Church: who is the beginning, the firstborn from the dead; *that in all things He might have the preeminence. For it pleased the Father that IN HIM SHOULD ALL FULNESS DWELL!"*

All who accept the Scripture as the Word of God believe that God the Father is a Divine Person—the Scriptures clearly teach this. But the Scriptures also teach that Jesus is *God's Son.* Therefore, whatever proves the divinity and personality of God *also proves the divinity of God's SON.* Thus we see the *plurality* of Divine Persons in the Godhead. God the Father is a Person, Jesus the Son is a Person, and the Bible clearly teaches that Jesus the Son was with the Father in the beginning. We need not use space here to give Scriptures to prove this accepted Bible fact.

Divine *perfections* are ascribed to Jesus, divine *worship* is paid to Him by both men and angels, and if Jesus Christ was *not* God in flesh and *equal with* the Father as He claimed to be, then I declare that Christianity must have tended to establish a religious system of idolatry that is far more dangerous (because it is *more plausible*) than the system it came to destroy!

Jesus was very God—yet He was very *man;* and the union of the divine and human natures in the

Person of the Lord Jesus Christ is a subject on which the holy men of old (through whom God gave the Scriptures) delighted to dwell — and so should *we*, because herein is *the heart and glory of the Gospel:* "unto us a child is born . . . and His name shall be called . . . *The mighty God*" (Isa. 9:6).

The Lord Jesus Christ was born in Bethlehem but *HIS "GOINGS FORTH have been from of old, from everlasting"* (Mic. 5:2). He was "made of the seed of David according to the flesh, and declared to be the Son of God with power" (Rom. 1:3,4).

God is an eternal Spirit (Psalm 90:1,2; John 4:24), and He cannot die. *Jesus is God* — He is the second Person of the Godhead. John 1:18 tells us, "No man hath seen God at any time; *the only begotten SON, which IS in the bosom of the Father*, He hath declared Him." Notice, this does not say, "the only begotten Son *which WAS* in the bosom of the Father," nor does it say, "the only begotten Son *which WILL BE* in the bosom of the Father." It says, "the only begotten Son *which IS* (present tense) in the bosom of the Father." Therefore, Christ in His original state could not die, and it was a divine imperative that He take flesh in order to die for the sins of the world:

"But we see Jesus, who was made a little lower than the angels FOR THE SUFFERING OF DEATH, crowned with glory and honour; that He by the grace of God SHOULD TASTE DEATH FOR EVERY MAN. . . . Forasmuch then as the children are partakers of flesh and blood, He also Himself likewise *TOOK PART OF THE SAME;* that through death He might destroy him that had the power of death, that is, the devil; and deliver them who through fear of death were all their lifetime subject to bondage. For verily *He took not on Him the nature of angels; but He took on Him the seed of Abraham"* (Heb. 2:9, 14—16).

Do not ask me to explain it — I cannot. The Scrip-

tures declare it and I accept it by faith. *Jesus was
GOD IN FLESH:*

"And all things are of God, who hath reconciled
us to Himself by Jesus Christ, and hath given to us
the ministry of reconciliation; *to wit, that GOD WAS
IN CHRIST, reconciling the world unto Himself,* not
imputing their trespasses unto them; and hath committed unto us the word of reconciliation" (II Cor.
5:18,19).

Jesus was the Son of God—yet He was "touched
with the feeling of our infirmities." He was "in all
points tempted like as we are, yet without sin. Let us
therefore come boldly unto the throne of grace, that
we may obtain mercy, and find grace to help in time
of need" (Heb. 4:14—16).

The Word of God puts great emphasis and stress
upon what Christ was, antecedent to His assumption
of human nature, and of the official character of our
Mediator and Saviour:

"In the beginning was the Word, and the Word
was *with* God, and the Word *was* God" (John 1:1).

The Scripture emphasizes the fact that our Mediator—He who made the atonement for us—was rich,
and for our sakes He became poor, *that we, through
His poverty, might be rich* (II Cor. 8:9). He was the
brightness of God's glory, the express image of His
Person; He was "in the form of God" and "thought
it not robbery (or usurpation) to be *equal* with God."
But He took a body, "made Himself of no reputation,
and took upon Him the form of a servant, and was
made in the likeness of men." He "humbled Himself"
and died *the death of the cross* (Phil. 2:5—8).

Christ is definitely and clearly *distinguished from*
the Father as the express image (or character) of God's
Person—and this while yet in His pre-incarnate state.
Father, Son, and Holy Ghost were in the beginning.
Then in the fulness of time *the Son*—second Person of

the Trinity—took a body like unto our body except that He was without sin, and in that body He paid the sin-debt and made atonement possible.

"WHEREFORE God also hath highly exalted Him, and given Him a name which is above every name: That at the name of Jesus every knee should bow, of things in heaven, and things in earth, and things under the earth; and that every tongue should confess that Jesus Christ is Lord, to the glory of God the Father" (Phil. 2:9—11).

The Word of God places great emphasis on the character of the Lord Jesus Christ as the Son of God. The main link in the Christian faith is, *"I believe that Jesus Christ is the Son of God."* Anyone who *refuses* to believe that Jesus Christ is the Son of God *is not a Christian* and has no part of Christianity in his heart or life! The question in this Day of Grace is *"What think ye of Christ? Whose SON is He?"* (Matt. 22:42). The way you answer that question will determine your eternal destiny. All who confess that Jesus is the Christ, the Son of God, are *born* of God (I John 5:1); all who *deny* that Jesus is the Son of God *make God a liar—because they believe not the record God has given of His Son* (I John 5:10).

I repeat: believing that Jesus is the Son of God is the main link in the chain of Christianity, and the whole chain of evangelical truth is connected to that link—*"for God so loved the world, that He gave His only begotten SON"* (John 3:16).

God the Father *gave* His only begotten Son; and the fact that though Christ *was* the Son He *obeyed* shows the condescension of His obedience to the heavenly Father.

The *efficacy* of His precious blood is shown in that "the blood of Jesus Christ *GOD'S SON* cleanseth us from all sin" (I John 1:7).

Hebrews 7:26 sets forth *the dignity* of Christ's

priesthood: "For such an high priest became us, who is *holy, harmless, undefiled, separate from sinners, and made higher than the heavens.*"

John 3:18 spells out the sin that has robbed heaven and populated hell, the sin that is an *insult* to Almighty God, the *greatest sin* man can commit: "He that believeth on Him is not condemned: *but he that BELIEVETH NOT is condemned already, BECAUSE HE HATH NOT BELIEVED in the name of the only begotten Son of God!*"

Mark adds: ". . . *he that BELIEVETH NOT shall be damned!*" (Mark 16:16).

The incarnation of the Lord Jesus Christ, His bodily resurrection from the dead, and His exaltation to the right hand of God the Father *declared* Him to be the Son of God—*but did not MAKE Him so.* Nor did *His offices* make Him the Son of God, for to all these His Sonship was antecedent. *Jehovah God,* He who was in the beginning, *sent* His only Son into the world, which fact implies that Christ was God's Son *antecedently* to His being sent into the world, just as Christ's sending out His *disciples* implies that they were His disciples *before He SENT them.*

The same may be said of Christ's being *"MADE of a woman,* made under the law" (Gal. 4:4). The term "made of a woman" no more expresses that which *rendered* Him the Son of God than His being *made flesh* expresses that which rendered Him *the WORD:*

"*In the beginning was the WORD . . . and the Word was made FLESH*" (John 1:1,14). By like token, *in the beginning was the SON—BEFORE He was born of Mary!*

". . . the Son of God was *manifested* that He might destroy the works of the devil" (I John 3:8); therefore He (the Son of God) must have *been* the Son of God antecedently to His being manifested in flesh.

The only begotten Son of God was not "in the bosom of the Father" in some prehistoric time, nor will He *be* "in the bosom of the Father" at some future date. The Scripture speaks in the present tense, declaring "the only begotten Son of God *which IS in the bosom of the Father*"—and at the time these words were spoken *Jesus was here in a body of flesh, tabernacling among men.* Yet even though He was walking among men, the holy, infallible Word of God declares that He was *also* in the bosom of the Father! This denotes the eternity and the immutability of His character. *There has never been a moment since "the beginning" when God has existed without His Son!*

In the Word of God we often read where Jesus declared that He performed miracles through the power of the Father, or through the power of the Holy Spirit. Concerning His resurrection we read that the Father raised Him, or that the Spirit raised Him. Many times He referred to the power of the Father or the power of the Holy Spirit, rather than to *His own* power or His own *divinity;* but the Word of God makes it very plain that the Father upheld His Servant, His only begotten Son in whom He was "well pleased."

In the Garden of Gethsemane (Luke 22:43), God the Father sent an angel to strengthen His Son in the horrible conflict when all hell was marshalled against Him, with the devil himself leading the attack in an attempt to destroy the Lord Jesus before He reached Calvary. Jesus was acting as the Father's Servant, and therefore the Father supported Him; but when the value, virtue, and efficacy of what Jesus did and what He suffered are touched upon, *these are NOT ascribed to the Father nor to the Holy Spirit, but always to the SON OF GOD* "who being the brightness of (God's) glory, and the express image of His Person, and *UPHOLDING ALL THINGS BY THE WORD OF HIS POWER, when He had by HIMSELF*

purged our sins, SAT DOWN ON THE RIGHT HAND
OF THE MAJESTY ON HIGH" (Heb. 1:3).

". . . *ye were not redeemed with CORRUPTIBLE
things, as silver and gold . . . BUT WITH THE PRE-
CIOUS BLOOD OF CHRIST, as of a lamb without
blemish and without spot"* (I Pet. 1:18,19).

". . . *the BLOOD OF JESUS CHRIST His Son
cleanseth us from ALL sin"* (I John 1:7).

". . . *Jesus Christ . . . in whom we have redemption through HIS BLOOD, the forgiveness of sins,
according to the riches of His grace"* (Eph. 1:5,7).

"*In whom* (Jesus) *we have redemption THROUGH
HIS BLOOD, even the forgiveness of sins"* (Col. 1:13,
14).

"For it pleased the Father that *IN HIM should
all fulness dwell; and, having made peace THROUGH
THE BLOOD OF HIS CROSS, by Him to reconcile
all things unto Himself;* by Him, I say, whether they
be things in earth, or things in heaven" (Col. 1:19,20).

Yes, *the blood of Jesus Christ God's Son* cleanses
from all sin, and *only* through the blood are we
cleansed. God the Father loved us, God the Son died
for us, and thank God for the Holy Spirit—but in
John 16:13—15 we read:

"Howbeit when He, *the Spirit of truth,* is come,
He will guide you into all truth: *for He shall NOT
speak of HIMSELF;* but whatsoever He shall hear,
that shall He speak: and He will shew you things
to come.   *HE SHALL GLORIFY ME: for He shall
receive OF MINE, and shall shew it unto you.   All
things that the Father hath ARE MINE: therefore
said I, that He shall take OF MINE, and shall shew
it unto you.*"

I thank God for the Holy Spirit! He convicted me
of sin, drew me to the place of prayer, and I was born
into the family of God through the miracle of the new
birth.   He indwells my heart, He seals me until that

glorious day of redemption. *But the Holy Spirit is NOT the grand and glorious object of ministerial exhibition in this day of God's saving grace.* The grand and glorious One whom we need to put on exhibition each and every time we step into the pulpit is the Son of God, the Lord Jesus Christ, crucified, buried, risen, seated at the right hand of God the Father making intercession for us.

When Philip was preaching in Samaria, "the people with one accord gave heed unto those things which Philip spake" (Acts 8:6), great revival broke out "and there was great joy in that city" (Acts 8:8). But Philip did not go down into Samaria to preach *the Holy Spirit* unto the Samaritans. According to the Word of God, "Philip went down into Samaria, *and preached CHRIST unto them*" (Acts 8:5). Great blessings followed his preaching, great miracles were wrought, and great joy came to the city *because Philip magnified THE LORD JESUS CHRIST.*

Then in verse 26 of the same chapter, God called Philip away from the revival in Samaria and sent him south toward Gaza. As he traveled, he saw an Ethiopian eunuch who was returning home from Jerusalem. As the eunuch rode along in his chariot he was reading from the Prophet Isaiah. The Holy Spirit directed Philip to go near and join himself to the chariot.

As Philip approached the eunuch he asked, "Understandest thou what thou readest?" The man replied, "How can I, except some man should guide me?" Philip then began to read aloud from the well known fifty-third chapter of Isaiah, and when he had finished reading he *"began at the same Scripture, and preached unto him JESUS."* The eunuch believed, he was saved, and as "they came unto a certain water" Philip baptized him and "he went on his way rejoicing" (Acts 9:26—39).

Believers are *led* by the Spirit, and ministers should

never enter the pulpit without the assurance that the
Spirit is leading; but if we make the ministry of the
Spirit the theme of our preaching and the grand object
of our ministry, then we shall be doing that which
the Spirit Himself does not do, thereby counteracting
the operations of the Holy Spirit. Remember—He
came on the Day of Pentecost, *NOT to magnify HIM-
SELF, but to magnify THE LORD JESUS CHRIST!*

Do not misunderstand me. The Holy Spirit is a
Person; He is not an "energy" or an "influence." He
is the third Person of the Holy Trinity. I believe in
one God manifested in three Persons—Father, Son,
and Holy Spirit.

The First Sermon After Pentecost

Peter preached the first sermon after Pentecost.
We find the record in the second chapter of Acts. His
message was addressed to the Jews upon principles
of the truth of which they, *in conscience,* were convinced. He said, "Ye men of Israel, hear these words:
Jesus of Nazareth, a Man approved of God among you
by miracles and wonders and signs, which God did
by Him in the midst of you, as ye yourselves also
know: Him, being delivered by the determinate counsel and foreknowledge of God, ye have taken, and by
wicked hands have crucified and slain" (Acts 2:22,23).

It was upon these principles that Peter based other
truths of which they were *not* convinced—i. e., the
bodily resurrection of Jesus from the dead (Acts 2:24—
32), the exaltation of Christ at the right hand of God
the Father (Acts 2:33), His being made both Lord and
Christ (Acts 2:36), and remission of sins through His
name (Acts 2:38).

In his *second* sermon, Peter declared Jesus to be
the Son of God, the Holy One, the Just One, the
Prince of life:

"The God of Abraham, and of Isaac, and of Jacob,

the God of our fathers, hath glorified *His Son Jesus;*
whom ye delivered up, and denied Him in the presence of Pilate, when he was determined to let Him
go.   But ye denied *the Holy One and the Just,* and
desired a murderer to be granted unto you; and killed
the Prince of life, whom God hath raised from the
dead; whereof we are witnesses" (Acts 3:13—15).

In his *first* sermon Peter appealed to what the
Jews themselves knew of Christ. In his second sermon
he declared what *he* knew concerning Christ. He, with
his fellow apostles, had looked upon Him, handled
Him, beheld His glory—yes, even the glory as of the
only begotten of the Father, full of grace and truth.

The Doctrine of the Atonement
and the Divinity of Christ Are Inseparable

The atonement and the doctrine of the divinity of
Christ rise or fall together.   The importance of the
atonement is acknowledged by all Bible-believing Christians; but there are some who *claim* to be Christians
who suppose that the doctrine of the atonement is
not necessarily connected with the divinity of the Lord
Jesus Christ.   They say that *the Person* of Christ suffered.   They further declare that since *Divinity could
not suffer,* it was just the *Man* Jesus who suffered,
and not His divine nature—to which it might be answered that though the *Person* of Christ suffered, yet
that He suffered *in ALL that pertained to His Person*
is quite another thing.   For instance, a virtuous person might suffer death in the electric chair or in the
gas chamber, which would be suffering death in his
person although he might not suffer in his honor or
in his character, and therefore would not suffer *in
ALL that pertained to him.*   It is possible for the body
to be destroyed and yet the character be unmarred.
Many believers in the past have suffered martyrdom—

they have been burned at the stake, fed to lions, sawn asunder—thus the *body* was destroyed but the *soul* was happy and immediately went to be with Jesus. The body suffered but the soul made its exit into Paradise, *not* suffering.

To object that Christ did not suffer in His Person because He was God and *not ALL that pertained to Him COULD suffer* is reasoning very inconclusively. It is quite sufficient if Christ suffered in that part of His Person which was *susceptible* to suffering. You can rest assured that Jesus suffered all the agony, misery, woe, disappointment, and pain of an eternal separation from God in the lake of fire. *He took the sinner's place;* therefore He suffered all that *sinners* were supposed to suffer because of their sin. He made *atonement,* and in so doing it was a divine necessity that He suffer the penalty that sin brought upon man.

There are those who teach that since only *humanity* is capable of suffering, only humanity is necessary to make atonement. However, this teaching proceeds upon the supposition that the *value* of the atonement arises only *from SUFFERING,* and not from *the CHARACTER OR DIGNITY of the One who suffered;* but the Word of God places the atonement in the latter, not in the former: *"The BLOOD of Jesus Christ, GOD'S SON,* cleanseth us from all sin" (I John 1:7). Jesus Himself purged our sins (Heb. 1:3).

When Paul was speaking to the Ephesian elders, he said, under inspiration of the Holy Spirit, "Take heed therefore unto yourselves, and to all the flock, over the which the Holy Ghost hath made you overseers, *to feed the Church of God, which He hath purchased WITH HIS OWN BLOOD"* (Acts 20:28). I do not profess to understand the depth of the spiritual aspect of that statement, but I *can* understand the *language.*

In Matthew 16:18 Jesus said to Peter, "Upon this

rock I will build my Church; and the gates of hell shall not prevail against it."

In I Corinthians 3:11 we learn that Jesus is the foundation of the Church. In Ephesians 5:21—33 we learn that He is head of the Church and Saviour of the body. In verse 30 of that chapter we learn that each and every believer is a *member* of His body: "For we are members of His body, of His flesh, and of His bones." Jesus purchased the Church when He died on the cross, and the blood shed on Calvary was *God's* blood. It is true that the Holy Ghost overshadowed Mary, she conceived and brought forth God's Son. Mary gave Jesus His *flesh*—but God gave Him His blood:

The angel said to Mary, "The Holy Ghost shall come upon thee, and the power of the Highest shall overshadow thee: therefore also *that holy thing which shall be born of thee shall be called THE SON OF GOD"* (Luke 1:35).

Fifteen centuries before the birth of Christ, God revealed to Moses that the life of the flesh is in the blood (Lev. 17:11). God gave Jesus His flesh through the Virgin Mary, but the flesh without the inner man is dead (James 2:26). The blood of Jesus was the blood of God. The atonement was made by the Lord Jesus Christ—not simply through His suffering, although He suffered as no *mortal* ever has; but the character and dignity of Jesus made possible the atonement. If He had been just a "good man," just a "righteous man," He could not have made atonement for sin; but He was the God-Man—He was God, yet He was man. He possessed a body like unto man's body, but *in that body He possessed THE NATURE OF GOD and the BLOOD of God*—yea, He was *very God* (II Cor. 5:19; John 10:30). Therefore the value of Christ's atonement does not rest simply upon His suffering. It rests primarily upon His character and dignity. He suffered, yes—but His suffering alone could not have provided atonement. The Word of God places the value of His atonement *on the fact that He WAS the Son of God.*

Mark tells us that when Jesus cried with a loud voice and gave up the ghost, "the centurion, which stood over against Him, saw that He so cried out, and gave up the ghost," said, *"Truly THIS MAN WAS THE SON OF GOD!"* (Mark 15:37—39).

What did Jesus cry out in His dying hour that caused the centurion to confess that he had just witnessed the death of the Son of God? What convinced him? It was not the terrible suffering through which Jesus had passed, but the fact that after hanging on the cross for hours, bleeding, without food or water, this Man could still cry out with a loud voice (the Greek indicates "a strong, vigorous voice"). The centurion heard His strong cry and saw Him literally give His life back into the hands of God; and it was that which he heard and saw that convinced him that he had just witnessed the death of the Son of God.

There are those who teach that sin is an infinite evil and therefore deserves eternal punishment—but they say that *an infinite ATONEMENT* is not a divine necessity because the question is not *what SIN DESERVES*, but *what GOD REQUIRES* in order to exalt the dignity of God's character and divine government *while DISPLAYING THE EXCEEDING RICHES OF HIS GRACE IN FORGIVING SINS and justifying the ungodly through faith* (Rom. 3:24,26).

But this objection implies that it would be consistent with the divine perfection of God's government to admit *not only what sin DESERVES and what is EQUIVALENT to the actual ETERNAL PUNISHMENT that MUST be meted out to the sinner* (because the wages of sin is death and God cannot acquit the wicked—Rom. 6:23; Nah. 1:3), *but by the same token*

DIVINITY would be admitting knowing that which is NOT EQUIVALENT TO THE ACTUAL ETERNAL PUNISHMENT DESERVED BY THE SINNER.

God knew the only sacrifice that would (or could) satisfy the wages of sin and make possible the salvation of the sinner. He also knew that sin must be met, dealt with, and overcome in every minute detail— *and THAT by a WORTHY SUBSTITUTE,* one who would be able to satisfy God's holiness, God's righteousness, and God's holy law. God also knew that *a substitute which would fall short* in one jot or tittle would come short of His demands to meet sin's wages. Therefore such a sacrifice could not and would not take the sinner's place because *such a substitute would not be CAPABLE of suffering the ACTUAL PUNISHMENT* (soul, spirit, and body) *deserved by the sinner.*

THEREFORE—if LESS than an INFINITE A-TONEMENT were consistent with God's character and divine government, there is not one legitimate reason why God might not have dispensed with a divine satisfaction for sin and pardoned sinners WITHOUT an atonement! On this principle, then, Christ's atonement would be resolved *into MERE SOVEREIGN APPOINTMENT, the NECESSITY for His atonement would be destroyed,* and it could not with propriety be said, "It became Him, for whom are all things, and by whom are all things, in bringing many sons unto glory, to make the Captain of their salvation perfect through sufferings" (Heb. 2:10).

If a holy God demanded less in atonement for sin than the real punishment sin deserved, there could be no satisfaction made to divine justice by such an atonement. It would be improper to represent the great atonement, the great work of redemption, as a kind of commercial transaction between a creditor and his debtor; yet the satisfaction of justice in all cases of offence requires that there be an expression of the displeasure of the offended against the conduct of the offender, equal to what the nature of the offence is in reality. The design of Christ's atonement is to express displeasure against disobedience.

The first sin was the sin of disobedience. Adam deliberately disobeyed God because he did not fully believe what God had said. God clearly told Adam what to do, He told him *the one thing he was NOT to do,* and plainly spelled out the penalty for disobedience. But Adam did not fully believe what God told him. He disobeyed God, thereby offending God and breaking the perfect fellowship that had existed between God and man.

The object of punishment is not the horrible misery, the excruciating pain of the offender, but the general good accomplished. Its design is to express displeasure against disobedience; and where punishment is inflicted according to the true desert of the offence, *justice is satisfied.* Jesus completely satisfied God as having to do with man's offence against Him. One man offended God—and through his offence all men became offenders. One Man—the Lord Jesus Christ—*satisfied God* because He met every requirement God demanded. He suffered all the agony "the wages of sin" required. The punishment inflicted upon Jesus was in perfect accord with the desert of the sinner. Therefore justice is satisfied in the eyes of a holy God and now God can be just and yet justify the sinner who believes in the shed blood and finished work of the Lord Jesus Christ.

An atonement made by a substitute in any case requires that the same end be answered as if the guilty party had actually suffered. I believe Jesus actually suffered all of the agony, misery, and pain that the sinner could suffer throughout eternity in the lake of fire, separated from God. When Jesus cried out, "My God, my God, why hast thou forsaken me?" He *was forsaken* by God the Father. God cannot look on sin, and at that moment Jesus was bearing all the sin of all the world in His own body on the cross. It was when God forsook Him that He suffered an eternity of separation *from* God—the eternity the sinner will suffer if he rejects the finished work of the Lord Jesus Christ.

The law of God thunders out, "The soul that sinneth, it shall die!" (Ezek. 18:4). Sin is transgression of God's law (I John 3:4). The law of God is the Word of God. He spoke to Adam, but Adam broke God's law and through his disobedience sin and death moved upon all men (Rom. 5:12—21). Since God's law demands death for sin, it was necessary that Jesus suffer what sin demanded in every detail—otherwise His atonement would have been a failure. He fulfilled every jot and tittle of the law (Matt. 5:17). He finished the work He came to do, He glorified God in everything He did (John 17:4). Therefore God can now be righteous and just and holy—and yet justify all who believe on Jesus (Rom. 3:21—28).

In the atonement, God the Eternal Father—holy, righteous, unchanging—is said to have set Jesus forth to be a propitiation for sin, to declare God's righteousness (Rom. 3:25,26). There are those who place the virtue of the atonement in the *appointment* of God; but if this be so, then I ask, *Why was it "not possible that the blood of bulls and of goats should take away sins"* (Heb. 10:4), since they *also* were God-appointed through Moses and penned down in the books of the law?

When Abraham would have sacrificed Isaac, a substitute was provided and Abraham's son was spared (Gen. 22:1—14). But there was no substitute for *God's* Son. It was necessary that God be wrapped in a body of humiliation, that His blood pulsate through the veins of the Son of man and be shed on a cross—

the most shameful manner of death in that day. Does
it not stand to reason that if any other gift of God
could have answered for an atonement He would have
spared His only begotten Son? But there could *be*
no substitute. It had to be Jesus, God in flesh:

"What shall we then say to these things? If God
be for us, who can be against us? He that spared
not His own Son, but delivered Him up for us all,
how shall He not with Him also freely give us all
things? Who shall lay anything to the charge of God's
elect? It is God that justifieth" (Rom. 8:31–33).

The Deity and Atonement of Christ Are Inseparable

It is impossible to separate the deity of Christ and
His atonement. All major Bible doctrines proceed
from or originate in His deity and His atonement.
The Person of the Lord Jesus Christ is without any
doubt the foundation upon which the Church of the
living God is built:

"When Jesus came into the coasts of Caesarea Phi-
lippi, He asked His disciples, saying, Whom do men
say that I the Son of man am? And they said, Some
say that thou art John the Baptist: some, Elias; and
others, Jeremias, or one of the prophets. He saith
unto them, *But whom say ye that I am?*

"And Simon Peter answered and said, *Thou art
the Christ, the Son of the living God.* And Jesus answered and said unto him, Blessed art thou, Simon
Bar-jona: for flesh and blood hath not revealed it
unto thee, but my Father which is in heaven. And I
say also unto thee, That thou art Peter, and *upon
this rock I will build my Church;* and the gates of
hell shall not prevail against it" (Matt. 16:13–18).

The Apostle Paul (to whom God revealed the mystery of the Church) did not mince words when he
rebuked the Galatians: "I marvel that ye are so soon

removed from Him that called you into the grace of Christ unto another gospel: which is not another; but there be some that trouble you, and would pervert the Gospel of Christ. *But though we, or an angel from heaven, preach any other gospel unto you than that which we have preached unto you, let him be ACCURSED.* As we said before, so say I now again, *If any man preach any other gospel unto you than that ye have received, LET HIM BE ACCURSED"* (Gal. 1:6—9). To be accursed from Christ is to burn in hell forever—and when the Holy Spirit repeats the same words in no more than two verses you may rest assured that the repeated statement is of utmost importance!

In Galatians 5:12 Paul said, "I would they were even cut off which trouble you." In other words, Paul said, *"I wish those who pervert the Gospel—*mixing law and grace or works and grace—*were dead."* The ministers to whom Paul referred taught that justification was by the works of the law, and Paul declared if men could be justified by the works of the law, then Christ died in vain. If men could be justified through the works of the law, then Christ's horrible death on Calvary was the greatest tragedy of the ages! He laid His life down to make a ransom for poor, lost sinners; and if lost, totally depraved sinners can be saved through the works of the law, then Jesus truly died in vain.

To teach that Christ was just a good man or an extraordinary teacher is to render His sufferings void and of none effect. If the deity of Christ be a divine truth—*and it IS*—then it cannot reasonably be denied that it is of equal importance with the doctrine of justification by His righteousness. If to reject the doctrine of justification by faith without the deeds of the law was declared a perversion of the Gospel, then nothing less can be said concerning the rejection of the deity of Christ.

The atonement concerns three parties: (1) God the Father; (2) the sinner who sinned against a holy God; (3) the Mediator who made possible the atonement through His shed blood.

God is the Judge of all. The sinner who sinned against God stands before the judgment seat of God—not in an impenitent state of mind, but as Job stood before God when he cried out, "Behold, I am vile; what shall I answer thee? I will lay mine hand upon my mouth" (Job 40:4). The sinner will stand before a holy God with the spirit David had when he cried out, "I acknowledge my transgressions: and my sin is ever before me. Against thee, thee only, have I sinned, and done this evil in thy sight: that thou mightest be justified when thou speakest, and be clear when thou judgest" (Psalm 51:3,4).

When the sinner stands before God with the spirit of Job or David, then the Lord Jesus Christ the Mediator takes over and pleads for the sinner (who could never be heard for himself, could never be pardoned in his own name or through his own righteousness).

Jesus gave a parable which perfectly illustrates this: "He spake this parable *unto certain which trusted in themselves that they were righteous, and despised others:*

"Two men went up into the temple to pray; the one a Pharisee, and the other a publican. The Pharisee stood and prayed thus with himself: *God, I thank thee, that I am not as other men are,* extortioners, unjust, adulterers, or even as this publican. I fast twice in the week, I give tithes of all that I possess.

"And the publican, standing afar off, would not lift up so much as his eyes unto heaven, but smote upon his breast, saying, *God be merciful to me a sinner.*

"I tell you, this man went down to his house justi-

fied rather than the other: for every one that exalteth
himself shall be abased; and he that humbleth himself shall be exalted" (Luke 18:9—14).

The Pharisee was a self-righteous religionist who
trusted in himself, depending on his good works and
the sinful things he *had NOT done;* but the poor publican, realizing his lost estate and his hopeless condition, would not so much as *look* toward the mercy
seat, but cried out, "God, be merciful to me *a sinner!*"
This man went home justified, rather than the religious
Pharisee who trusted in his own righteousness.

Concerning our Mediator, the Apostle Paul said:
"Wherefore in all things it behoved Him to be made
like unto His brethren, that He might be a merciful
and faithful high priest in things pertaining to God,
to make reconciliation for the sins of the people. For
in that He Himself hath suffered being tempted, He
is able to succour them that are tempted" (Heb. 2:17,
18).

Our Mediator, in pleading our case before God,
must have an interest with the Judge before whom
He pleads for the sinner, and He must be interested
in the sinner for whom He pleads. He must condemn
sin, not attempting to cover the sin even though He
is interceding for the sinner. He must also be fully
acquainted with the case, and He must have something to plead which will effectually overbalance the
unworthiness of the sinner. Now let us see if we can
find, in the Word of God, qualifications that meet
these requirements as applying to Jesus our Mediator
and Advocate with the Father:

Did He have an interest with God the Righteous
Judge? I declare that He had the highest possible
interest in the favor of the Judge because He was the
only begotten Son who dwelleth in God's bosom, and
He never offended God at any time in any way. He
did always those things that pleased the Father:

"Then said Jesus unto them, When ye have lifted up the Son of man, then shall ye know that I am He, and that I do nothing of myself; but as my Father hath taught me, I speak these things. *And He that sent me is with me: the Father hath not left me alone; FOR I DO ALWAYS THOSE THINGS THAT PLEASE HIM*" (John 8:28,29).

Did Jesus really do always those things that pleased God? The answer is found in the Scripture. God the Father was so pleased with the obedience of His Son that He "hath highly exalted Him, and given Him a name which is above every name: that at the name of Jesus every knee should bow, of things in heaven, and things in earth, and things under the earth; and that every tongue should confess that Jesus Christ is Lord, to the glory of God the Father" (Phil. 2:9—11).

John 3:35 tells us, "The Father loveth the Son, and hath given all things into His hand."

Prophecy also speaks concerning Jesus. In Psalm 2:8 God the Father said of His Son, "Ask of me, and I shall give thee the heathen for thine inheritance, and the uttermost parts of the earth for thy possession."

In view of these truths from God's infallible Word, who could doubt the success of a cause placed in the hands of a Mediator so completely qualified to make atonement?

But what about Jesus and His interest in sinners? He is deeply interested in saving the lost; it is not His will that any should perish (II Pet. 3:9). His invitation is, "Come unto me, all ye that labour and are heavy laden. . . . Him that cometh to me, I will in no wise cast out. . . . Whosoever shall call upon the name of the Lord shall be saved!" On one occasion, as He wept over Jerusalem He cried out, "O Jerusalem, Jerusalem, thou that killest the prophets, and stonest them which are sent unto thee, *how often*

*would I have gathered thy children together, even as
a hen gathereth her chickens under her wings, AND
YE WOULD NOT!"* (Matt. 23:37).

When Moses cried out to God for forgiveness for
Israel, he prayed, "Yet now, if thou wilt forgive their
sin—; and if not, *blot me, I pray thee, out of thy book
which thou hast written"* (Ex. 32:32). Moses demonstrated the spirit of a true advocate, and he was suc-
cessful: God heard his prayer. But the Lord Jesus
Christ *our* Mediator went a step further: He did not
simply *offer* to die for us, *He DID die in our stead;*
and His death alone is the propitiation for our sins,
and for the sins of the whole world (I John 2:2).

Yet while Jesus pleads for sinners He does not
attempt to cover sin. He pleads the case of the sinner, but He condemns sin. He hates sin with the
same holy hatred with which God the Father hates
sin. As He prayed in the Garden of Gethsemane,
Satan hurled all hell against Him. And when Jesus
saw the cup that contained the bitter dregs of sin
He cried out to the Father, "O my Father, if it be
possible, let this cup pass from me: nevertheless not
as I will, but as thou wilt" (Matt. 26:39). These words
are proof sufficient that Jesus hated sin. If that were
not true He would never have said, in effect, "If it
is not possible to make atonement except I drink the
cup, then I will drink it!" Yes, He hates sin, and
He never attempts to cover the sin of the sinner.

Jesus was made in the likeness of sinful flesh, yet
He never sinned. He left the bosom of the Father,
took a body of humiliation, lived among sinners; yet
in character He was "holy, harmless, undefiled, separate from sinners . . ." (Heb. 7:26). While advocating
the cause of the sinner, He did so in His own proper
character of *"Jesus Christ the righteous"* (I John 2:1).
Because of His proceeding on these just and honorable
principles, God the Father approved and honored Him:

"Thou lovest righteousness, and hatest wickedness: therefore God, thy God, hath anointed thee with the oil of gladness above thy fellows" (Psalm 45:7).

Is the Lord Jesus Christ acquainted with the case of the sinner? Yes, indeed He is! John 2:24,25 tells us that Jesus *"knew all men, and needed not that any should testify of man: for He knew what was in man."* Yes, our Mediator knows all about us, He knows the worst that is in us.

In Luke 7:36—50 we see a magnificent picture of our Lord's understanding of sinners. In the house of Simon the Pharisee, a sinful woman washed the feet of Jesus with her tears and dried them with her hair. Jesus did not rebuke the woman for her actions, and Simon, seeing this, said to himself, "This Man, if He were a prophet, would have known who and what manner of woman this is that toucheth Him: for she is a sinner." But even though Simon did not *speak* his thoughts, Jesus knew exactly what he was thinking, and after revealing this fact to Simon He proceeded to plead the cause of the poor, penitent, sinful woman. Her sins were scarlet and they were many; but Jesus forgave her—and in so doing He justified Himself in His actions. Our Mediator knows all about us, He knows all about our sins, our needs, and our wants.

Jesus said to Peter, ". . . behold, Satan hath desired to have you, that he may sift you as wheat: but I have prayed for thee, that thy faith fail not . . ." (Luke 22:31,32). He knew the exact temptation that would bring about Peter's denial, and He prayed for Peter before it happened. I am so thankful that the same Saviour who prayed for Peter also prays for believers today—even for you and me. In John 17:20 we read, "Neither pray I for these alone, *but for them also which shall believe on me through their word."*

All believers have this assurance from God's Word:

"There hath no temptation taken you but such as is common to man: but God is faithful, who will not suffer you to be tempted above that ye are able; but will with the temptation also make a way to escape, that ye may be able to bear it" (I Cor. 10:13).

In the sinner Jesus finds no worthiness whatsoever on which to ground His plea *for* the sinner; but *He* has that to plead which effectually overbalances all of the unworthiness of the one for whom He pleads.

Genesis chapter 44 records Judah's plea to Joseph on behalf of his younger brother Benjamin. It is remarkable that Judah did not declare Benjamin innocent, neither did he plead for mercy on the grounds that Benjamin did not know the silver cup was in his sack and had no knowledge of how it got there. In other words, Judah did not plead from the standpoint of Benjamin's offence, but rather pleaded for mercy for Benjamin on the grounds of his father's love for him and his own obligation to bring the boy back to his father.   (Read Genesis chapters 42 through 45 and feel the depth of this moving true story.) The charges against Benjamin were mysterious and extremely doubtful; and since Judah could not prove his brother's innocence, *he admitted his guilt.*

Our guilt is beyond any shadow of doubt.   We have all sinned, we have all come short of the glory of God.   Therefore our Advocate, in pleading for us before a holy God, rests His plea on the propitiation provided through His blood; and *in consideration* of that propitiation our unworthiness is passed over and our sins are forgiven for Christ's sake (Eph. 4:32).   It is *only* for Christ's sake that God passes over our sins, forgives us, and redeems us unto Himself.   The Man Christ Jesus, seated at the right hand of God the Father, is our Advocate *with* the Father on the grounds of His propitiation: "For *Christ also hath once suffered for sins, the JUST for the UNJUST,* that He might bring us to God . . ." (I Pet. 3:18).

Through Christ's Atonement
Believers Are Reckoned Righteous

"What shall we say then that Abraham our father, as pertaining to the flesh, hath found? For if Abraham were justified by works, he hath whereof to glory; but not before God. For what saith the Scripture? *Abraham believed God, and it was counted unto him for righteousness.*

"Now to him that worketh is the reward not reckoned of grace, but of debt. But to him that worketh not, but believeth on Him that justifieth the ungodly, his faith is counted for righteousness. Even as David also describeth the blessedness of the man, unto whom God imputeth righteousness without works, saying, Blessed are they whose iniquities are forgiven, and whose sins are covered. Blessed is the man to whom the Lord will not impute sin" (Rom. 4:1—8).

What is meant by *"imputation"*? In general, the term signifies "to charge, to reckon, or to place to account," depending on the different objects to which it is applied. It has a *primary* (or proper) meaning, and also a *figurative* meaning. The primary meaning of "imputation" is the *charging, or reckoning, or placing to the account* of persons and things that which properly *belongs* to them. It is used in this sense in the following Scriptures:

In I Samuel 1:13, concerning Hannah as she prayed in the temple, we read, "Eli thought she had been drunken."

In I Corinthians 4:1, *"Let a man so ACCOUNT of us,* as of the ministers of Christ, and stewards of the mysteries of God."

In II Corinthians 10:11, *"Let such an one THINK THIS,* that, such as we are in word by letters when we are absent, such will we be also in deed when we are present."

In Romans 8:18, *"For I RECKON that the suffer-ings of this present time* are not worthy to be com-pared with the glory which shall be revealed in us."

"Reckoning" or "accounting" in the Scriptures given here means *judging persons and things according to what they really are or what they appear to be.* Therefore, to "impute sin" in this sense is simply to charge guilt upon the guilty person in a judicial way with a view to punishment. We find an illustration of this in II Samuel 19:18—20 when Shimei requested of David that his iniquity might not be imputed to him:

"And Shimei the son of Gera fell down before the king, as he was come over Jordan; and said unto the king, *Let not my lord impute iniquity unto me,* neither do thou remember that which thy servant did per-versely the day that my lord the king went out of Jerusalem, that the king should take it to his heart. For thy servant doth know that I have sinned: there-fore, behold, I am come the first this day of all the house of Joseph to go down to meet my lord the king."

It was also in this sense that Paul prayed that the sin of those who deserted him might not be laid to their charge: "At my first answer no man stood with me, but all men forsook me: *I pray God that it may not be LAID TO THEIR CHARGE"* (II Tim. 4:16).

It is thus that the term "imputation" is ordinarily used in everyday life.   To *impute a crime* to a man is the same thing as *charging* him with having *com-mitted* the crime, and the charge is made in view of his being punished accordingly.

The *figurative* meaning of imputation is "to charge, reckon, or place to the account of" persons and things *that which does not properly BELONG to them as though it DID belong to them.*   The term is used in this sense in the following passages:

Numbers 18:27: "And this your heave-offering *shall be RECKONED unto you, AS THOUGH IT WERE* the corn of the threshingfloor, and as the fulness of the winepress."

Job 13:24: "Wherefore hidest thou thy face, *and HOLDEST me* for thine enemy?"

Romans 2:26: "Therefore if the uncircumcision keep the righteousness of the law, shall not his uncircumcision *be COUNTED for* circumcision?"

Philemon 18: "If he hath wronged thee, or oweth thee ought, *put that on mine ACCOUNT.*"

It is in this latter sense that I understand the term "impute" when it is applied to justification: "Abraham *believed God,* and it was *COUNTED unto him* for righteousness. Now *to him that WORKETH* is the reward not reckoned of grace, but of debt. But to him *that WORKETH NOT, but BELIEVETH on Him that justifieth the ungodly, his faith is COUNTED for righteousness*" (Rom. 4:3—5).

The counting or reckoning in these instances is not a judging of things *as they really are,* but as they *are NOT* as though *they WERE.* "Faith" here means *believing*—not as a virtuous exercise of Abraham's mind which God consented to accept instead of perfect obedience, but *as having RESPECT to the promised Messiah and His righteousness* as the grounds of acceptance.

Here, *justification* is ascribed to faith in the same manner that *healing of the body* in the New Testament is frequently ascribed to faith. On more than one occasion Jesus said, "Thy faith hath made thee whole," or "According to thy faith be it unto you." In such cases, faith is not used as that from which the virtue proceeds, but as that which receives from the Saviour's fulness. Paul declares this truth in Colossians 2:9,10:

"For in Him (Christ) dwelleth all the fulness of the

Godhead bodily. And ye are complete in Him, which is the head of all principality and power."

However, if it were true that *faith* (in Romans 4:3,5) *should* really mean the object believed in, it still remains that this was not Abraham's *own* righteousness and therefore could not be properly *counted* by Him who judges of things as they are, but it was RECK-ONED unto Abraham *as if it WERE his own.* Therefore the effects or benefits of faith were actually *imparted TO him*, although Abraham *did not* become meritorious nor did he cease to be *unworthy.* The righteousness he possessed was imputed (or reckoned) unto him, just as with believers today— *"Christ in you, the hope of glory"* (Col. 1:27).

Apart from Christ, we have no righteousness whatsoever because "we are all as an unclean thing, and all our righteousnesses are as filthy rags . . ." (Isa. 64:6). But hallelujah! *"Of Him are ye in Christ Jesus, who of God is made unto us wisdom, and RIGHT-EOUSNESS, and sanctification, and redemption:* That, according as it is written, He that glorieth, let him glory in the Lord" (I Cor. 1:30,31).

Covered by the blood of Jesus, saved by God's grace for Jesus' sake, *the believer is righteous*—but only because of the obedience of Christ, which obedience is imputed to the believer as if it were his own. Only in Jesus can we stand before God acceptable. *Apart* from Jesus man is strengthless, helpless, hopeless, and hell-bound!

It was in this sense that the sin of the world was imputed to Christ. He was accounted in the Divine Administration *as if He were*—or had been—a sinner, in order that those who believe on Him and trust in His shed blood might be accounted as if they were *righteous.* To be justified in the sight of God is to be just as though we had never sinned. When we are in Christ we are righteous, spotless, without wrinkle.

IN CHRIST we are as just as Jesus is just, and that is the only way we can enter heaven.

In Revelation 21:27 we read, *"And there shall in no wise enter into it* (the Holy City) *any thing that defileth, neither whatsoever worketh abomination, or maketh a lie:* but they which are written in the Lamb's book of life."

Jesus Did More Than Pay a Debt

The Word of God clearly teaches that the blood of Jesus is the price of redemption (Eph. 1:7); *but sin is more than a debt.* Sin is a *crime,* and satisfaction before God *concerning* sin had to go beyond pecuniary principles. Sin's penalty as having to do with a holy and righteous God had to be satisfied *on MORAL principles.* Thus we have the enlightening Scripture in I Peter 1:18—20:

"Forasmuch as ye know that *ye were not redeemed with corruptible things, as silver and gold,* from your vain conversation received by tradition from your fathers; *but with the PRECIOUS BLOOD OF CHRIST,* as of a lamb without blemish and without spot: who verily was foreordained before the foundation of the world, but was manifest in these last times for you."

In verses 18 and 19 of Paul's letter to Philemon we find a perfect illustration of imputation. Concerning Onesimus, Philemon's former slave, Paul wrote: *"If he hath wronged thee, or oweth thee ought, PUT THAT ON MINE ACCOUNT;* I Paul have written it with mine own hand, *I will repay it . . . ."*

Had Philemon accepted that part of Paul's offer which pertained to *property* and placed to Paul's account whatever Onesimus had *taken,* he could not have been said to have *remitted* the debt. But the Scripture indicates that Onesimus had *"wronged"* Philemon in a greater way than embezzling his money or goods. Perhaps he had corrupted his master's children

or gravely injured his character. Therefore, for Philemon to accept *that* part of Paul's offer would be quite
different from accepting the *monetary* restitution. In
the one case he would have been accepting money
representing the financial loss. In the other case, he
would have suffered a *moral* loss. Satisfaction in the
first instance (to satisfy the monetary loss) would
annihilate the idea of remission on Philemon's part,
but it would have nothing to do with the *moral injury.*

Whatever satisfaction Paul *as a mediator* might render to Philemon respecting the injury inflicted upon
his character and honor would not cause to be set
aside the necessity of pardon being sought by Onesimus (the offender), and in return, pardon freely bestowed by Philemon (the offended).

Jesus (*our* Mediator) satisfied the Father concerning
the debt we owe because of our sin, but that does
not do away with the necessity of *our* coming to God
and asking His forgiveness and pardon.

The reason for this difference can be easily understood if we consider that *debts are transferrable,* while
crimes are *not* transferrable. By way of illustration,
if you should owe me a debt which you could not
pay, but which a third party—perhaps your brother
or your father—paid *for* you, the debt would be can-
celled. Even though *you* did not pay it, another paid
it for you, thereby cancelling it.

But a third party can never cancel a *crime*—he can
only obliterate the effects of it. The desert of *the one
who committed the crime* remains. A *debtor* is accountable to his creditor as a private individual, and
that individual has the power of accepting a surety
or, if he be pleased to do so, he has the power to
remit the debt *without any satisfaction* being given.
In the former, he would be *just.* In the latter he
would be *merciful.* But no place is afforded by either
the debtor or his creditor for the *combination* of justice

and mercy in the same proceeding.

However, in the case of one who has committed a crime, the criminal is accountable to the judge or magistrate—not as a private individual, but *as a public person.* In such a case the judge or magistrate cannot remit the punishment without invading the law and destroying justice, nor can he allow a third person to stand in the criminal's place and accept the criminal's penalty.

In the case of a debtor, when the debt is paid, justice demands that the debtor be completely discharged from responsibility to his creditor. But in the case of a criminal, the law can be satisfied and justice can be meted out to the criminal—*but the CRIME remains!* The man who commits murder can be found guilty and sentenced to die in the electric chair. The law is satisfied when the man is pronounced dead—but the crime is not erased because the man he murdered remains dead, the wife whose husband was killed is still a widow.

Cases like that of Philemon and Onesimus represent, in a sense, the redemption of Christ, but the atonement Christ made for us is a work which stands alone and without parallel simply because it is *a work of God*—a perfect work which leaves all the petty concerns of poor, finite mortals infinitely behind it. Any comparison we might use in an effort to illustrate God's work in the atonement provided through Jesus could do no more than give some idea of *the principle on which it proceeds.*

God said to Adam, "The day thou eatest thereof *thou shalt SURELY die.*" He did not say, "*You* shall die—or someone will die *on your behalf.*" Had God's law literally taken its course, *every child of mortal man must have perished!* Therefore the sufferings of the Lord Jesus Christ in our stead were not a punishment inflicted in the ordinary course of justice, but an *extraordinary interposition* of the infinite wisdom and love of Almighty God.   This is not contrary to the law, but rather *ABOVE the law*—that is, deviating from the letter of the law but preserving the spirit thereof.   Sin is the transgression of God's law.   We have all broken that law because we have all sinned. In God's sight all sinners are criminals; but through Christ's atonement, in the redemption we have through His blood, *God has forgotten that we ever sinned and has reckoned us always righteous:*

"This is the covenant that I will make with them after those days, saith the Lord, I will put my laws into their hearts, and in their minds will I write them; *and their sins and iniquities will I remember no more. NOW WHERE REMISSION OF THESE IS, THERE IS NO MORE OFFERING FOR SIN*" (Heb. 10:16—18).

Facts We Need to Face

The covenant God made with Adam was *"Obey and LIVE.   SIN and DIE!"* Jesus obeyed the Father in all things, He learned obedience through the things He suffered, and He satisfied God in every respect of the law.   But His obedience to the law of God alone could not have paid sin's debt in full and would have afforded no expression of His displeasure against sin. Therefore, after spending His earthly life in doing the will of God, doing at all times the things that *pleased* God, it was a divine necessity that He lay His life down.   It was not possible that the "cup" should pass from Him:

"Therefore doth my Father love me, because I lay down my life, that I might take it again" (John 10:17).

Obedience would have been insufficient without the sufferings of Jesus, and His sufferings would have been insufficient without His obedience.   In truth, obedience was *preparatory* to His suffering:

"Wherefore He is able also to save them to the uttermost that come unto God by Him, seeing He ever liveth to make intercession for them. For such an high priest became us, who is *holy, harmless, undefiled, separate from sinners,* and made higher than the heavens" (Heb. 7:25,26).

As Mediator between a holy God and man depraved, it was necessary that Jesus should be an enemy to sin, and that He declare and manifest that enmity. This was a divine necessity before He could plead for sinners. The Lord Jesus Christ *did* hate sin, He *displayed* that hatred, and this endeared Him to His Father:

"Thou hast loved righteousness, and hated iniquity; therefore God, even thy God, hath anointed thee with the oil of gladness above thy fellows" (Heb. 1:9).

Therefore it is "by the righteousness of One" — and *only* by His righteousness — that we partake of "justification of life" (Rom. 5:18).

In Christ's atonement for sinners, the paramount ends designed before the foundation of the world were to express God's love of righteousness and His hatred of unrighteousness. These ends are answered completely by the obedience and the vicarious sufferings of the Lord Jesus Christ; and because of the dignity of the character of Jesus they are answered in a higher degree than if man had kept the law or could have suffered the penalty. Christ's death included both obedience and suffering; therefore His death gloriously and minutely answered every detail of moral government and opened the way by which God could not only pardon the sinner who should believe on Jesus, but also go beyond pardon and bestow upon the believer *eternal life:*

"As many as received Him, to them gave He power to become the sons of God, even to them that believe on His name: *which were born,* not of blood, nor of the will of the flesh, nor of the will of man, *but of GOD"* (John 1:12,13).

The Scriptures clearly teach that eternal life and everything the believer possesses in Christ are ours because of His mediation. *IN CHRIST the believer possesses ALL things;* but without Christ man is an eternal pauper: "Therefore let no man glory in men. *For ALL THINGS are your's;* whether Paul, or Apollos, or Cephas, or the world, or life, or death, or things present, or things to come; all are your's; *and YE ARE CHRIST'S; and Christ is GOD'S"* (I Cor. 3:21—23).

"For whosoever will save his life shall lose it: and whosoever will lose his life for my sake shall find it. *For what is a man profited, if he shall gain the whole world, and lose his own soul?* or what shall a man give in exchange for his soul?" (Matt. 16:25,26).

The position of a born again believer is glorious:

We are *IN Christ Jesus* (Rom. 8:1).

Christ is in the believer (Col. 1:27).

We are *"hid with Christ in God"* (Col. 3:3).

We *"sit together in heavenly places* in Christ Jesus" (Eph. 2:6).

But let us ever keep in mind the solemn truth that what we *have* in Christ is because of the atonement. What we *are* in Christ we are because we believe and trust in Him. We have faith in His shed blood and finished work. All that we have—and all that we *will* have—in Christ, God has given us *"for Christ's sake"* (Eph. 4:32).

There is no sinner so great and no sin so black but that God can and will forgive—for Christ's sake.

There is no blessing so rich, so wonderful and marvelous, but that God will bestow it upon the believer who trusts and obeys.

There is no service so insignificant but that God will reward it, even if it be only a cup of cold water given to a disciple in the name of Jesus and for His sake.

"For the Lord God is a sun and shield: the Lord will give grace and glory: no good thing will He withhold from them that walk uprightly" (Psalm 84:11). God graciously blesses all who walk uprightly, all who will trust and obey. This proves His love to Christ, His love to the believer, and His regard and love for righteousness.

Since the Scriptures clearly teach that the deity of Christ is divine truth, then we know it is God's will that all men honor Jesus the Son in the same sense and to the same degree that they honor God the Father. Since the deity of Christ is divine truth, then we know Jesus is the only One in whom the sinner can trust. I do not mean that the unbeliever must trust Jesus as a witness from God such as John the Baptist was; but we must *trust IN Him.* He is the *object* of our trust *as God* because He *WAS GOD IN FLESH* (II Cor. 5:19), and only in God do we find salvation. It was God the Father who set Jesus forth that He might be a propitiation for sin, and Matthew 12:21 declares, "In His name shall the Gentiles trust."

The Apostle Paul declared, *"I know WHOM I have believed,* and am persuaded that He is able to keep that which I have committed unto Him against that day"* (II Tim. 1:12). Paul did not say, *"I know WHAT I have believed,"* but "I know *whom* I have believed—*I know a PERSON,* the Lord Jesus Christ."

The Deity of Christ is one of the great doctrines of Christianity, and it is a divine imperative that one *believe* in His deity in order to be saved. Those who declare that He was "just a good man," or "just a great teacher" cannot be saved, for those who deny the Son do not possess the Father: *"Whosoever transgresseth, and abideth not in the doctrine of Christ, hath not God. He that abideth in the doctrine of*

Christ, he hath both the Father and the Son" (II John 9).

The death of Jesus is the only atoning sacrifice which makes a way for sinners to be saved: "And almost all things are by the law purged with blood; and *WITHOUT shedding of blood is NO REMISSION"* (Heb. 9:22).

"Neither is there salvation in any other: for there is none other name under heaven given among men, whereby we must be saved" (Acts 4:12).

The only grounds on which God saves and forgives is that of the atoning sacrifice made by Jesus in laying down His own life and giving His blood for the remission of sins. Those who deny that His blood is the only means by which sinners can be saved, cannot—and certainly will not—be saved!

The doctrine of atonement by the cross of the Lord Jesus Christ is divine truth, it is the very substance of the Gospel. It is also the grand and glorious peculiarity of Christianity and it occupies a very large part of the Scriptures. It is related to all major doctrines of the Word of God. Therefore it is absurd to think that anyone could be accepted by God the Father in any other way save through the atonement made by the Son of His love.

The Scripture declares that Jesus was "delivered for our offences" (Rom. 4:25), He was wounded for our transgressions . . . bruised for our iniquities . . . the Lord hath laid on Him the iniquity of us all . . . It pleased the Lord to bruise Him, He hath put Him to shame, and made His soul an offering for sin. He poured out His soul unto death . . . He was numbered with the transgressors . . . He bare the sin of many (Isa. 53:5—12).

Paul declared, "We preach *Christ crucified,* unto the Jews a stumblingblock, and unto the Greeks foolishness; but unto them which are called, both Jews and Greeks, Christ the power of God, and the wisdom of God" (I Cor. 1:23,24).

Jesus came into the world to take away the sin of the world (John 1:29).

He made peace through the blood of His cross, and by His death on Calvary He reconciled us to God (Col. 1:20,21).

He redeemed us and washed us from our sins in His own blood (Rev. 1:5).

It was by His blood that He obtained eternal redemption for us (Heb. 9:12).

"Take heed therefore unto yourselves, and to all the flock, over the which the Holy Ghost hath made you overseers, to feed the Church of God, *which He hath purchased WITH HIS OWN BLOOD*" (Acts 20:28).

The doctrine of the cross of the Lord Jesus Christ is not simply a New Testament "doctrine," nor is it just an important part of the Gospel. *The Cross IS the Gospel.*

The Apostle Paul declared to the Corinthian Christians, *"I determined not to know any thing among you, save Jesus Christ, AND HIM CRUCIFIED"* (I Cor. 2:2).

The cross is to the universe of Bible doctrine what the sun is to nature. If it were possible to extinguish the sun, this earth would become void, a universe of death. Just so, apart from the cross of Calvary, the Bible would be a book void and empty, holding out no hope whatsoever to poor, helpless, hell-bound humanity!

Genesis 1:1 declares, *"In the beginning—GOD...."* John the Beloved adds, *"In the beginning was THE WORD, and the Word was with God, and the Word WAS God"* (John 1:1).

God changes not. He is the same yesterday, today, and forever (Heb. 13:8). His Word changes not—*"For*

ever, O Lord, thy Word is settled in heaven" (Psalm
119:89). God's Word is His law, and His law thunders
out, *"The soul that sinneth, IT SHALL DIE!"* (Ezek.
18:4). And since all men are sinners, the law of God
stops every mouth:

"Now we know that what things soever the law
saith, it saith to them who are under the law: *that
every mouth may be stopped, AND ALL THE WORLD
MAY BECOME GUILTY BEFORE GOD.* Therefore
by the deeds of the law there shall no flesh be justified in His sight: for by the law is the knowledge
of sin" (Rom. 3:19,20).

Yes, every mouth is stopped and the whole world
stands guilty before a holy, righteous, and unchanging
God! The only possible way for sinners to approach
God is in the name of the Lord Jesus Christ, because
He is the only One in heaven or on earth who can
be heard in our behalf.

The *law* of God *stops* every mouth, but the *grace
of God opens* every mouth that will call in the right
name:

"And the Word was made flesh, and dwelt among
us, (and we beheld His glory, the glory as of the only
begotten of the Father,) *full of GRACE and TRUTH"*
(John 1:14). Jesus is grace, Jesus is truth; and His
name is the only name "under heaven given among
men whereby we must be saved" (Acts 4:12).

To the Apostle Paul God revealed the door to
heaven, and under inspiration of the Holy Spirit, Paul
penned these marvelous words:

*"If thou shalt confess with thy mouth the Lord
Jesus, and shalt believe in thine heart that God hath
raised Him from the dead, thou shalt be saved. For
with the heart man believeth unto righteousness; and
with the mouth confession is made unto salvation"*
(Rom. 10:9,10).

You have HEARD. Now BELIEVE. Believe on

the Lord Jesus Christ, trust in His shed blood, call
on God the Father and He will save you *for Jesus'
sake.*

Chapter Four

GOD THE FATHER AND THE ATONEMENT

"In the beginning GOD . . ." (Gen. 1:1). God is *infinite,* man is *finite.* God created man from the dust of the ground, breathed into his nostrils the breath of life—and man became a living soul (Gen. 2:7). This universe and everything in it was created by Almighty God, and the Creator is greater than that which He created; yet His greatness includes His ability (and His deep desire) to care for *the smallest detail* of His creation! The God who created this universe numbers the hairs of our head, and not even one little sparrow falls to the ground without His knowledge of its fall.

Jesus said to His disciples, "Are not two sparrows sold for a farthing? and one of them shall not fall on the ground without your Father. *But the very hairs of your head are all numbered.* Fear ye not therefore, ye are of more value than many sparrows" (Matt. 10:29–31).

God is a great and powerful God. However, His *greatest achievement* is seen in the atonement—His provision for the eternal salvation of poor, lost sinners who would otherwise be *condemned forever* by God's infinite holiness and untainted righteousness. In the words of Jesus, *"What is a man profited, if he shall gain the whole world, and lose his own soul? or what shall a man give in exchange for his soul?"* (Matt. 16:26). Therefore, according to the words of Jesus, the atonement which makes possible the redemption of sinners is of more value than all else of God's creation.

God Is Sovereign

God is sovereign, supreme over all. He is the Creator of all things and He is over all things. He yields to no other power, authority, or glory:

"See now that I, even I, am He, and there is no god with me: I kill, and I make alive; I wound, and I heal: Neither is there any that can deliver out of my hand. For I lift up my hand to heaven, and say, I live for ever! If I whet my glittering sword, and mine hand take hold on judgment; I will render vengeance to mine enemies, and will reward them that hate me. I will make mine arrows drunk with blood, and my sword shall devour flesh; and that with the blood of the slain and of the captives, from the beginning of revenges upon the enemy. Rejoice, O ye nations, with His people: for He will avenge the blood of His servants, and will render vengeance to His adversaries, and will be merciful unto His land, and to His people" (Deut. 32:39—43).

There is no other being throughout the universe who can compare with God. He is perfect to an infinite degree in every aspect of His being. Our God has never been surprised, He has never been uncertain, He has always been sure about everything. He has never been defeated—nor will He ever *be* defeated.

However, when God created man and breathed into him the breath of life, man did not become God's *puppet:* he became "a living soul," and it pleased God to release to him some measure of freedom of choice. Therefore man is a free moral agent—God allows him to choose, *but He also holds him responsible for his decisions.*

In Adam's case, God made it very clear what he

was to do and what he was not to do—and at the
same time He made known to Adam the penalty for
disobedience. And today, through His WORD God
has also made clear what man is to do—and what he
is not to do—and plainly stated the results if *we* dis-
obey His Word.

For Adam, God Himself provided a covering at the
sacrifice of the innocent animals whose blood was
shed and their skins used to cover Adam's sin. Very
shortly thereafter God promised the Redeemer (Gen.
3:15), and "in the fulness of the time" the Lamb of
God came as promised (Gal. 4:4,5). It was God who
"so loved the world that He gave His only begotten
Son" (John 3:16).

But the Word of God clearly declares that the
natural man does not turn to God except the moving
of the Holy Spirit prompt him to do so: "No man
can come to me, *except the Father which hath sent
me draw him . . ."* (John 6:44).

In John 16:7—11 Jesus said to His disciples, "Nevertheless I tell you the truth: It is expedient for you
that I go away: for if I go not away, the Comforter
will not come unto you; but if I depart, I will send
Him unto you. *And when He (the Holy Spirit) is
come, HE WILL REPROVE THE WORLD OF SIN,
AND OF RIGHTEOUSNESS, AND OF JUDGMENT:*
of sin, because they believe not on me; of righteousness, because I go to my Father, and ye see me no
more; of judgment, because the prince of this world
is judged."

The Scriptures also teach very clearly that when
the Holy Spirit troubles the heart of man and draws
him toward God, man must believe on the Lord Jesus
Christ in order to become a child of God. *There IS
no other way.* There are many "ways" that *seem*
right, "but the end thereof are the ways of death"
(Prov. 16:25). In the Son of His love, God provided

the only way to be saved.

It is further written in God's Word that when the Holy Spirit draws us to God and we believe on the Lord Jesus Christ, it is *God* who works in our heart "both to will and to do of His good pleasure" (Phil. 2:13). "As many as received Him, to them gave He power to become the sons of God, even to them that believe on His name: which were born, not of blood, nor of the will of the flesh, nor of the will of man, BUT OF GOD" (John 1:12,13).

Then in Ephesians 2:8−10 we read, "*For BY GRACE are ye saved through faith; and that not of yourselves: it is the gift of God: Not of works, lest any man should boast. For we are HIS WORKMAN-SHIP*, created in Christ Jesus unto good works, which God hath before ordained that we should walk in them."

When man believes unto salvation, the Holy Spirit comes into the inner man (Rom. 8:9); and then in Romans 12:1,2 we read, "I beseech you therefore, breth-ren, by the mercies of God, that ye *present your bodies A LIVING SACRIFICE, holy, acceptable unto God, which is your REASONABLE service.* And be not conformed to this world: but be ye transformed by the renewing of your mind, that ye may prove what is that good, and acceptable, and perfect, will of God."

Since God is sovereign He knows all things. He knew the end in the beginning, He knows everything that lies *between* the beginning and the end; and you may rest assured that when the history of man and of the universe is completed, all things purposed and planned in the beginning will have been wrought out according to His will.

The Attributes of God

The Scriptures reveal certain qualities which belong

to God, but He in no sense *acquired* these attributes: *they are what God IS,* what He always has been and always will be. He is the *beginning,* the *source,* and the *fountain* of each and all of His attributes. Let us look at just a few passages from both the Old and the New Testaments which reveal a few of the attributes of God:

God is eternal: "Before the mountains were brought forth, or ever thou hadst formed the earth and the world, even from everlasting to everlasting, thou art God" (Psalm 90:2).

God is a Spirit: "God is a Spirit; and they that worship Him must worship Him in spirit and in truth" (John 4:24).

God is life: "But the Lord is the true God, He is the living God, and an everlasting king . . ." (Jer. 10:10).

God is self-existent: "And God said unto Moses, I AM THAT I AM: and He said, Thus shalt thou say unto the children of Israel, I AM hath sent me unto you" (Ex. 3:14).

God is infinite: "Great is the Lord, and greatly to be praised; and His greatness is unsearchable" (Psalm 145:3).

God is truth: "He is the Rock, His work is perfect: for all His ways are judgment: a God of truth and without iniquity, just and right is He" (Deut. 32:4). "Sanctify them through thy truth: thy Word is truth" (John 17:17).

God is immutable: "Thou art the same, and thy years shall have no end" (Psalm 102:27). "For I am the Lord, I change not..." (Mal. 3:6). "Every good gift and every perfect gift is from above, and cometh down from the Father of lights, *with whom is no variableness, neither shadow of turning*" (James 1:17).

God is holy: ". . . it is written, Be ye holy; *for I am holy*" (I Pet. 1:16). "This then is the message which we have heard of Him, and declare unto you, that *God is light, and in Him is no darkness at all"* (I John 1:5).

God is love: "He that loveth not knoweth not God; for *God IS love"* (I John 4:8).

God is omnipotent: "Jesus beheld them, and said unto them, With men this is impossible; but *with God all things are possible"* (Matt. 19:26).

God is omniscient: "He telleth the number of the stars; He calleth them all by their names. Great is our Lord, and of great power: *His understanding is infinite"* (Psalm 147:4,5).

God is omnipresent: "Whither shall I go from thy spirit? or whither shall I flee from thy presence? If I ascend up into heaven, *thou art there:* if I make my bed in hell, behold, *thou art there"* (Psalm 139:7,8). "Can any hide himself in secret places that I shall not see him? saith the Lord. Do not I fill heaven and earth? saith the Lord" (Jer. 23:24).

Paul, under inspiration of the Holy Ghost, said this about our God: "O the depth of the riches both of the wisdom and knowledge of God! How *unsearchable* are His judgments, and His ways *past finding out!* For who hath known the mind of the Lord? or who hath been His counsellor? Or who hath first given to Him, and it shall be recompensed unto him again? For of Him, and through Him, and to Him, are all things: to whom be glory for ever. Amen" (Rom. 11:33—36).

God has allowed man to share in many things; but there are certain divine undertakings in which He never has allowed—and never *will* allow—any other being to share, whether it be men or angels. In His sovereign wisdom and power, *Deity alone* wrought creation, the preservation of all things, His providence, His unconditional covenants, the dispensations, and His grace. God was in the beginning, and He created all things by and for the Lord Jesus Christ. God is over all, blessed forever. He preserves all things, His providence cannot be altered, His covenants are eternal and cannot be changed. He has marked out certain periods of time wherein He deals with certain groups, as with Israel under the law, and the Gentile bride He is calling out for His Son during this Dispensation of Grace. The dispensations were set by God and they cannot be altered by man. God's grace is His alone. Jesus brought God's grace down to man. There is nothing man can do to attain or merit grace, nor to *add to it.* Jesus came from the bosom of the Father (John 1:18), and He was "full of grace and truth" (John 1:14).

For His Name's Sake

Everything God the Father does or has done has Himself eternally as its goal. Whatsoever God has done in the past, whatsoever He will do until time is no more, He does "for His name's sake" (Psalm 23:3). God is *the Absolute One.* He is the "blessed God" (I Tim. 1:11). He exists on His own account and He eternally suffices for Himself.

But *God is love* (I John 4:8), and love by the necessity of its nature needs a beloved. It is true that God's beloved Son, the Lord Jesus Christ, was present with Him in the beginning; but God's great love desired many sons, and in His own wisdom *He willed* that many sons make up the heavenly family. Therefore He created the universe, placed man on this earth, *and loved him.* Also in His wisdom and love He provided an *atonement* for man, that man should become a son of God, a possessor of divine nature and, in the end, should have a body like the glorious resurrection body of Jesus.

There are those who ask, "If God is omnipotent, omniscient, and omnipresent, why is He concerned with *men*?'' The Scripture answers:

"What is man, that thou art mindful of him? or the son of man, that thou visitest him? Thou madest him a little lower than the angels; thou crownedst him with glory and honour, and didst set him over the works of thy hands: thou hast put all things in subjection under his feet. For in that He put all in subjection under him, He left nothing that is not put under him. But now we see not yet all things put under him. But we see Jesus, who was made a little lower than the angels for the suffering of death, crowned with glory and honour; that He by the grace of God should taste death for every man. *For it became Him, for whom are all things, and by whom are all things, in bringing MANY SONS unto glory, to make the Captain of their salvation perfect through sufferings*'' (Heb. 2:6—10).

It was necessary for God to provide atonement for sinners because "all have sinned, and come short of the glory of God" (Rom. 3:23). It was God's love that caused Him to set forth Jesus to be a propitiation for sins—"for God *so loved* the world, that He gave His only begotten Son, that whosoever believeth in Him should not perish, but have everlasting life" (John 3:16).

Since God is sovereign, since He knows the end in the beginning and all that lies *between* the beginning and the ending, *He knew man would sin.* Therefore Deity agreed that the blood of Jesus would atone for sin (I Pet. 1:18—20).

Do not ask me to explain all this. I am but a poor finite creature saved by God's grace. God is the eternal, Infinite One, and as such He should never be the thought problem of poor, finite human beings. The idea of God transcends all human means of thought. *God IS*—so let us accept Him simply because the Bible declares that *He is God:*

"For my thoughts are not your thoughts, neither are your ways my ways, saith the Lord. *For as the heavens are higher than the earth, so are my ways higher than your ways, and my thoughts than your thoughts"* (Isa. 55:8,9).

"Wherefore, as by one man (Adam) *sin entered into the world, and death by sin; and so death passed upon all men, for that all have sinned"* (Rom. 5:12). Since the first Adam completely disobeyed God and through his disobedience sin entered into the world—and death by sin—how could God be sure that *the last Adam* (the Lord Jesus Christ) would completely fulfill the demand required to make an atonement? *God* knew because He is *sovereign;* but for our instruction these words are written: "The *first man* Adam was made *a living soul;* the *last* Adam was made *A QUICKENING SPIRIT. . . .* The first man is of the earth, earthy: *the second Man is the Lord from heaven"* (I Cor. 15:45,47).

I have pointed out several times in this study that what God demanded, only God could provide, and He did provide (in flesh) *blood that was holy and undefiled,* blood that made perfect atonement for sin:

"God was in Christ, reconciling the world unto Himself . . ." (II Cor. 5:19). The blood of Christ was the blood of God. We read in Acts 20:28 that God purchased the Church *"with His own blood."* Therefore the blood of Christ makes complete atonement:

"God commendeth His love toward us, in that, while we were yet sinners, Christ died for us. Much more then, being now justified by His blood, we shall be saved from wrath through Him. For if, when we were enemies, we were reconciled to God by the death of His Son, much more, being reconciled, we shall be saved by His life. And not only so, but we also joy in God through our Lord Jesus Christ, BY WHOM WE HAVE NOW RECEIVED THE ATONEMENT"

(Rom. 5:8—11).

It was foreordained before the foundation of the world that the precious blood of Christ, as of a lamb without spot or blemish, would redeem lost souls; and in the fulness of time God sent forth Jesus, born of the Virgin Mary, "to be a propitiation through faith in His blood, to declare His righteousness for the remission of sins that are past (sins from Adam to Calvary), through the forbearance of God" (Rom. 3:25).

The righteousness of God which is by faith in Jesus Christ is for all who will believe. God imputes righteousness to all who believe on Jesus, and they are born into God's family:

"As many as received Him, to them gave He power to become the sons of God, even to them that believe on His name: which were born, *not of blood, nor of the will of the flesh, nor of the will of man, BUT OF GOD*" (John 1:12,13).

Jesus said to Nicodemus, "Except a man be born of water and of the Spirit, he cannot enter into the kingdom of God" (John 3:5). Some teach that the "water" in this verse speaks of baptism, but the Scriptures are clear concerning the meaning of water as used in connection with the birth of the spirit. Jesus said to His disciples, "Now ye are clean *through the WORD* which I have spoken unto you" (John 15:3). *Paul* tells us in Ephesians 5:25,26 that Christ loved the Church and gave Himself for it, "that He might sanctify and cleanse it *with the washing of water BY THE WORD.*" Therefore we see that the "water" in John 3:5 is the Word of God.

Further proof of this is found in I Peter 1:23: "Being born again, not of *corruptible* seed, but of *incorruptible, BY THE WORD OF GOD*, which liveth and abideth for ever."

When Jesus saved the Samaritan woman He did not *baptize* her. He gave her the *Word*—He spoke seven words to her: "I that speak unto thee am He" (John 4:26); and when she heard His words she left her waterpot and ran into the city, and gave testimony that she had met the Messiah, the Christ. Through the Word of God she was born into God's family. Faith comes by hearing the Word, and all who are born of God are born by hearing the Word and receiving the Lord Jesus Christ *by faith.* When one hears and believes the Word, the Holy Ghost unites that person to the body of Christ.

Jesus was God in flesh. His flesh was given to Him by Mary, but the spirit and *the blood* of Jesus were God's. Therefore when we hear and receive the engrafted Word which is able to save our souls (James 1:21) we actually receive *God,* because "in the beginning was the Word, and the Word was with God, *and the Word WAS God*" (John 1:1). When we hear, believe, and receive the Word of God, the Word "borns" us into God's family through the miracle of the life-giving Spirit of God.

One of the most difficult things for any true minister of the Gospel to do is to bring men to the place where they will admit that salvation is of God, provided and presented by Him, and all that sinners can do to become sons of God is to receive what God has already finished in providing atonement for sinners. All one can do to come into possession of a gift is to receive it from the giver; and the very moment one believes on the Lord Jesus Christ he becomes a son of God:

"Beloved, *NOW are we the sons of God,* and it doth not yet appear what we shall be: but we know that, when He shall appear, we shall be like Him; for we shall see Him as He is" (I John 3:2).

The very moment we are saved, we are baptized into the body of Christ: "For as the body is one, and hath many members, and all the members of that one body, being many, are one body: so also is Christ. For by one Spirit are we all baptized into one body, whether we be Jews or Gentiles, whether we be bond or free; and have been all made to drink into one Spirit" (I Cor. 12:12,13).

The moment we are saved we become possessors of divine nature: "Whereby are given unto us exceeding great and precious promises: that by these ye might be partakers of the divine nature, having escaped the corruption that is in the world through lust" (II Pet. 1:4).

When one becomes a believer he becomes a possessor of the Holy Spirit, and "if any man have *not* the Spirit of Christ, he is none of His" (Rom. 8:9).

Christ takes up His abode in the believer's heart (Col. 1:27), and thus we are "hid with Christ in God" (Col. 3:3)—and praise His saving, keeping name, we are sealed by the Holy Spirit of God "unto the day of redemption" (Eph. 4:30).

Since salvation is of God and we are born into the family of heaven by God's power through the miracle of the incorruptible seed and the operation of the Holy Spirit, we have the assurance that we are *"more than conquerors through Him,"* and that *"neither death, nor life, nor angels, nor principalities, nor powers, nor things present, nor things to come, nor height, nor depth, NOR ANY OTHER CREATURE, shall be able to separate us from the love of God, which is in Christ Jesus our Lord"* (Rom. 8:37–39).

The question may be asked, "Why would a holy, all-powerful God do so much for man who deliberately disobeyed God and sinned against Him—and then hid from God's presence?" The answer is simply that God has done and is doing all of this for believers for His own honor and glory, *"that in the ages to come He might shew the exceeding riches of His grace in His kindness toward us through Christ Jesus"* (Eph.

2:7). In other words, what God does for us He does *for Jesus' sake* (Eph. 4:32).

Everything God does, has done, or will do has Himself eternally as its goal. Whatsoever has come to pass or *will* come to pass is *for His name's sake,* and for Himself throughout; *"that we should be to the praise of His glory,* who first trusted in Christ." The Holy Spirit is "the earnest of our inheritance until the redemption of the purchased possession, *unto the praise of (God's) glory"* (Eph. 1:12,14).

All of this is true in order "that God may be *all in all"* (I Cor. 15:28). God is the highest perfection in wisdom, in holiness, in righteousness, in purity, in all things. Therefore by virtue of His perfection He must always wish the highest and will the highest; and since there is none like Him He must always have that which is within His own nature as the goal of His perfect will. Therefore God's work must be so ordered that all of His work may *lead TO Him* and all of His doings have their end *IN Him.* Therefore God's purpose in creating all things consists in the unfolding, setting forth, and putting on display *THE GLORY OF GOD.*

God is the *beginning,* He is the *ending,* He is the *middle,* and He is the *ultimate objective.* He is the first and the last—He is the Alpha and the Omega:

"For of Him, and through Him, and to Him, are all things: TO WHOM BE GLORY FOR EVER. Amen" (Rom. 11:36).

"For by Him were all things created, that are in heaven, and that are in earth, visible and invisible, whether they be thrones, or dominions, or principalities, or powers: all things were created by Him, and for Him" (Col. 1:16).

"God, who at sundry times and in divers manners spake in time past unto the fathers by the prophets, hath in these last days spoken unto us by His Son, whom He hath appointed heir of all things, by whom also He made the worlds" (Heb. 1:1,2).

God's Eternal Goal

". . . God is love" (I John 4:8). God is *perfect* love: "We have known and believed the love that God hath to us. God is love; and he that dwelleth in love dwelleth in God, and God in him" (I John 4:16).

God called this world into existence in order that He might *love* the world (John 3:16), "for God sent not His Son into the world to condemn the world; but that the world through Him might be saved" (John 3:17). Therefore the world should love God in return.

God's goal evermore is to lead the world to an eternal share in the joy of His holiness and His love, thereby leading all creation to such blessedness and glory as only God in His holiness can know. But *apart from the atonement* it is divinely impossible for man to share in the enjoyment of God's holiness and love. Heaven is a prepared place for a prepared people, and *the only way* to prepare for heaven is to be created in Christ Jesus (Eph. 2:10). In that glorious moment when time shall be no more, we can say, *experimentally,* that "the sufferings of this present time are not worthy to be compared with the glory which shall be revealed in us" (Rom. 8:18).

Jesus on Calvary was God's love on display, and the revealing of that perfect love was a divine necessity in order to bring many sons into glory. Because of God's nature this self-displaying, eternal plan of Almighty God must be perfect. Therefore it must unfold itself—not only in God's omnipotence, omnipresence, and omniscience, but also in His righteousness, His love, and His truthfulness.

The omnipotence, omniscience, and omnipresence

of God has been displayed in the creation of the universe. No one but Almighty God could speak a world into existence, place the stars in their sockets, and guide them through the lanes of outer space. The Psalmist declared, "The heavens declare the glory of God; and the firmament sheweth His handywork" (Psalm 19:1).

But in order for God to reveal His righteousness, His perfect love, and His truth untainted, it was necessary that He create man in His own image and make him a being of morally free personality in whom a spiritual kingdom could exist. Thus when one believes on the Lord Jesus Christ, the kingdom of God comes into that person:

When the Pharisees asked Jesus when the kingdom of God would come, He answered, "The kingdom of God cometh not with observation: neither shall they say, Lo here! or, lo there! for, behold, *the kingdom of God is WITHIN YOU*" (Luke 17:20,21).

The Apostle Paul declared, "The kingdom of God is not meat and drink; but righteousness, and peace, and joy in the Holy Ghost" (Rom. 14:17).

Because holiness is the nature of God, in His world-plan the higher purpose of the material must lie in the moral realm; and the chief ground for the very creation of the universe must be the magnifying of the moral qualities of God as the Holy One, the blessed and all-wise God by the creation of morally free personalities. Only in personalities can God perfectly display His glory in creation. He did not create this earth *waste*, nor did He create it to be covered with thorns and thistles. He did not create the *animal* kingdom for its inhabitants to devour each other, and there is a day coming when not only *man*, but *all creation*, will be completely delivered from the penalty, the power, and the presence of sin:

"For the earnest expectation of the creature waiteth

for the manifestation of the sons of God. For the
creature was made subject to vanity, not willingly,
but by reason of Him who hath subjected the same
in hope. Because the creature itself also shall be delivered from the bondage of corruption into the glorious
liberty of the children of God. *For we know that the
whole creation groaneth and travaileth in pain together
until now. And not only they, but ourselves also,
which have the firstfruits of the Spirit, even we ourselves groan within ourselves, waiting for the adoption,
to wit, the redemption of our body"* (Rom. 8:19—23).

Isaiah describes the earth and the animal kingdom
when all creation shall have been delivered from the
curse:

"The wolf also shall dwell with the lamb, and the
leopard shall lie down with the kid; and the calf and
the young lion and the fatling together; and a little
child shall lead them. And the cow and the bear
shall feed; their young ones shall lie down together:
and the lion shall eat straw like the ox. And the sucking child shall play on the hole of the asp, and the
weaned child shall put his hand on the cockatrice'
den. They shall not hurt nor destroy in all my holy
mountain: for the earth shall be full of the knowledge
of the Lord, as the waters cover the sea" (Isa. 11:6—9).

True morality is not only an outward objective
carrying out a law to meet legal demand, thereby
producing legal freedom from sin and guilt. True morality goes deeper, even to a personal, organic par-
ticipation in the moral life of Deity. By His perfect
right, God the supreme Lawgiver has appointed the
moral ordering of the world according to His nature—
and His nature is *love and pure holiness.* Therefore
the moral appointment of God's created free creatures
must also be *an appointment to love;* and the supreme,
final purpose of the creation of the world must consist
in the self-unfolding and the self-display of God *as*

He IS—perfect, holy, *the Loving One.*

In that glorious moment when Satan will be in the lake of fire to be tormented with the beast and the false prophet forever and ever; when all the enemies of God have become Christ's footstool; when the world and its works shall be burned up and we have a new heaven, a new earth, and the Pearly White City; in that glorious moment when time shall cease and eternity shall unfold before our eyes, *the establishment of a divine fellowship of life and divine love between the Creator and the creature will have come to pass.* This is God's ultimate goal in the atonement provided through the shedding of the blood of His only begotten Son, the Lamb without spot. God called this world into existence in order to love it. He created man in order to love man. God created all things for His own glory—*and one day all things WILL glorify the Creator!*

"By His Blood"

"Being justified freely by His grace through the redemption that is in Christ Jesus: whom God hath set forth to be a propitiation through faith in His blood, to declare His righteousness for the remission of sins that are past, through the forbearance of God" (Rom. 3:24,25).

It is "in His blood" (the original Greek reads *"BY His blood"*) that we have a propitiation through faith. It was in the shedding of the blood of the Lamb of God that the essence of the atonement was exhibited on the cross. The *perfect life* of Jesus was necessary; but His perfect life could never have provided the atonement. While He tabernacled among men His life, His miracles, and all of His labors of love *led UP TO Calvary;* but Calvary itself was the culminating act of His coming into the world, and it was Calvary that brought *into reality* an atonement for sin.

"Whom God hath set forth . . . ." Here, God is
an exhibitor. The cross is the culmination of the specific purpose of Christ's coming into the world, and
from the cross proceeds unmistakeable truth that makes
men free. Jesus said, *"Ye shall know the TRUTH,
and the truth shall make you free. . . .* If the Son
therefore shall make you free, ye shall be free indeed"
(John 8:32,36). He also said, *"I am truth"* (John 14:6).

Jesus on the cross was God's perfect *love,* His perfect *light,* and His perfect *truth* on display. Calvary
was not an *accident*—it was the culmination of God's
eternal plan. Calvary was the moment when God displayed love that was in the beginning before the world
was, when it was agreed among the Persons of the
Godhead that Jesus would shed His blood for the
remission of sin (I Pet. 1:18—20).

The *love* of God was in the beginning; the *blood*
to provide the atonement was in the beginning; *but
Calvary was the focal point* (the time and place) when
God's love, God's light, and God's truth were put on
display and the blood was shed, making the atonement possible.

Did God the Father *know about Calvary* in the
beginning? He not only *knew* about it, but it was
planned. Calvary was part of God's plan to bring
about His ultimate goal for all creation. God the
lawgiver is also God the Christ-giver. God who thundered out the law on Mount Sinai is the same God
who *set forth His Son* to be a propitiation for sin!

The atonement provided in Jesus does not persuade
God to have mercy on sinners, but rather *liberates
God's love* along the lines of His wonderfully satisfied
righteousness and holiness. The cross of Jesus so
completely satisfied God's holy law and His righteousness that He gave His Son the highest seat in heaven—
at His own right hand.

God had a *purpose* in Calvary. He had a purpose

in the death of His only begotten Son on the cross. He knew all about it *in the beginning.* This does not remotely suggest, however, that either God or Jesus *enjoyed* the cross; but Calvary was a divine necessity if atonement for sin was to be made:

"Wherefore seeing we also are compassed about with so great a cloud of witnesses, let us lay aside every weight, and the sin which doth so easily beset us, and let us run with patience the race that is set before us, *looking unto Jesus the author and finisher of our faith; who for the joy that was set before Him ENDURED the cross, DESPISING THE SHAME, and is set down at the right hand of the throne of God"* (Heb. 12:1,2).

Christ's Death on the Cross Acquainted Man with God's Love

"But God commendeth His love toward us, in that, while we were yet sinners, Christ died for us" (Rom. 5:8).

The Greek word here translated "commendeth" is translated "stood with" in Luke 9:32 when Moses and Elijah appeared with Christ on the Mount of Transfiguration: "But Peter and they that were with him were heavy with sleep: and when they were awake, they saw His glory, and the two men that *stood with* Him."

In Galatians 2:18 the same Greek word is rendered "make": "For if I build again the things which I destroyed, I *make* myself a transgressor."

In Romans 16:1, II Corinthians 7:11 and 10:18 the same word is used in the sense of approving another in commending that person to favorable notice.

The deeper meaning in each of these instances is that one person is so closely identified with another that the two stand together, as when David assured

Abiathar that his life was safe as long as he abode
with him: "Abide thou with me, fear not: for he
that seeketh my life seeketh thy life: but with me
thou shalt be in safeguard" (I Sam. 22:23).

In Christ's death on the cross—death demanded
by the wages of sin (Rom. 6:23)—God the Eternal Father in His love *associated Himself* with the death of
His only begotten Son. Romans 5:6—8 shows the
striking contrast between man and God, in that man
may (though not as a rule) sacrifice himself for a
"good" man; *but GOD in His love sacrificed Himself
for BAD men.* God was in Christ, reconciling the
world unto Himself (II Cor. 5:19); and the death of
Jesus on the cross *commends the FACT of God's love.*
His death *proves* God's love, for only pure, *divine*
love would make such a sacrifice. Therefore the glorious message of the Gospel of God's grace is the message of truth concerning the act of God in which He
commended His love toward us. Even when we were
unworthy, hopeless, hell-deserving sinners *Christ DIED
for us!* God not only *declared* His love for sinners,
He *proved* that love *in the death of His only begotten
Son.*

God the Father Sent Jesus the Son Into the World
to Perform a Stipulated Service

What *was* God's stipulated service in the death of
the Lord Jesus Christ? Jesus came to do what no other being in heaven or on earth *could* do. Even the
law of God, holy and powerful though it is, could
not do what Jesus came to do:

"For what the law could not do, in that it was
weak through the flesh, God sending His own Son in
the likeness of sinful flesh, and for sin, condemned
sin in the flesh: that the righteousness of the law
might be fulfilled in us, who walk not after the flesh,

but after the Spirit" (Rom. 8:3,4).

The *atonement* explains the *Incarnation*—that is, the Incarnation took place in order that the sin of the world might be put away by the offering of the Lord Jesus Christ: "By the which will we are sanctified through the offering of the body of Jesus Christ once for all" (Heb. 10:10).

Though Jesus was the Son of God, "yet learned He obedience by the things which He suffered" (Heb. 5:8). The obedience of Christ, like *all* obedience, has a definite *moral value.* It has a value for Himself, but *its redemptive value for US* belongs to it—not simply as obedience, but as *obedience to the will of God the Father,* which required the Redeemer of the sinner to take upon Himself in death the full responsibility of the sin of the world. In order to satisfy the holiness and righteousness of God, it was a divine necessity that Jesus as our Redeemer take upon Himself *the full wages of sin* and pay the sin-debt in full; and the only possible way for Him to pay that debt was to *die!*

The Incarnation of the Lord Jesus Christ does not explain His substitution for sinners, but His substitution for sinners explains His Incarnation. The divine purpose in the Incarnation was that the Son of God, in the likeness of sinful flesh, should do what *the law of God* was *unable* to do because of the weakness of the flesh.

Suppose we use this illustration: I am now speaking into the microphone of a dictaphone. The dictaphone is recording my voice because I press a little button which turns on the electric power by which the dictaphone operates. But to make this possible, there must be a wire which is connected to the dictating machine in my office and also to the power plant where the electricity originates. The wire, then, is *the MEANS by which* electricity reaches the little recording instrument I am using. Thus the purpose of the wire.

So is *the END of the Incarnation.* The substitutionary sacrifice made by the Lord Jesus Christ in His death on the cross proves the necessity of the means to that end. That is, it was a divine necessity that Jesus the Son of God become flesh and take upon Himself the *likeness* of men in order to *die* for men. God is an Eternal Spirit, therefore God cannot die (John 4:24; Psalm 90:1,2). But *God was IN Christ,* reconciling the world unto Himself (II Cor. 5:19).

The Apostle Paul declares that Christ was in the *form* of God, that He considered it not robbery to be *equal* with God, yet He "made Himself of no reputation, and took upon Him the form of a servant, and was made in the likeness of men: and being found in fashion as a man, He humbled Himself, and became obedient unto death, even the death of the cross" (Phil. 2:6–8).

God SENDING His Son into the world pinpoints the *origin* of the provision God made for us *through* His only begotten Son. "Sending" here refers to the Sender (God the Father) who commissioned and sent His only begotten Son, and points not to God's sending Jesus *to earth,* but points rather *to the place from whence He came*—the bosom of the Father.

In John 3:17 Jesus declared, "For God sent not His Son into the world to condemn the world; but that the world through Him might be saved." The Greek word *here translated* "sent" is different from the word so translated in Romans 8:3. In John 3:17 it signifies a *"fitting out" for a mission.* Therefore what Jesus actually said was, "God the Father *fitted out* His Son and sent Him into the world—not to *condemn* the world, but to SAVE the world." Jesus came on a mission of salvation, not destruction. When He comes again "in flaming fire" (II Thess. 1:8), He will judge and destroy the wicked; but God sent Him into the world "fitted out" to *save* the world and give His life a ransom for many (Matt. 20:28).

In I Timothy 2:5,6 Paul tells us, "There is one God, and one Mediator between God and men, the Man Christ Jesus; *WHO GAVE HIMSELF A RANSOM FOR ALL,* to be testified in due time."

We find an interesting passage in Luke 9:51−56. Jesus "stedfastly set His face to go to Jerusalem," and He sent His disciples on before Him to make ready for Him. They entered a village of the Samaritans, but the inhabitants there refused to receive Jesus "because His face was as though He would go to Jerusalem." In other words, He was a Jew, and the Jews had no dealings with the Samaritans (John 4:9). This rejection of their Lord angered James and John, and they asked, *"Lord, wilt thou that we command fire to come down from heaven, and consume them, even as Elias did?"* (See II Kings 1:10.)

But Jesus turned to His disciples "and rebuked them, and said, *Ye know not what manner of spirit ye are of. FOR THE SON OF MAN IS NOT COME TO DESTROY MEN'S LIVES, BUT TO SAVE THEM.* And they went to another village."

God the Father "fitted out" His Son for His mission in the world, and sent Him forth to be condemned for poor, lost, depraved, hell-deserving sinners. No wonder the Apostle Paul, under inspiration of the Holy Spirit, exclaimed: *"Thanks be unto God FOR HIS UNSPEAKABLE GIFT!"* (II Cor. 9:15).

In Christ's Death on the Cross, God the Father Dealt with Sin

Because God's nature is holy and righteous, He must condemn sin. He cannot condone sin—and in the language of the Bible He "will not at all acquit the wicked" (Nah. 1:3).

When God created Adam and breathed into him the breath of life, Adam became a living soul. God then placed him in the most beautiful garden this world has ever known and gave him *a perfect wife* to be his helpmate and companion. God gave Adam a perfect diet—and in the midst of the perfection that surrounded him, Adam faced one negative stipulation from God: *He was not to eat of the fruit of the tree of the knowledge of good and evil.* He knew God's command, he understood it perfectly. But he deliberately disobeyed God—and when he sinned *he died spiritually.*

God could have annihilated Adam right then and there. He could have destroyed the first man and woman from the face of the earth. But remember— Adam bore the image of God, and *God is LOVE.* So instead of annihilating Adam and Eve, He *loved* them and provided a covering for the shame of their nakedness. In slaying the innocent animals to provide the coats of skins, God condemned the actions of Adam and Eve, and through the suffering of an innocent substitute He provided a covering to hide their nakedness. But neither the coats of skins nor the blood of the innocent animals could satisfy God's holiness, "for it is not possible that the blood of bulls and of goats should take away sins" (Heb. 10:4).

A scarlet line runs from Eden to Calvary, and *only God* knows how many tens of thousands of turtle doves, lambs, bullocks, and other animals died, their blood shed in sacrifice. But even though a river of blood flowed down through the centuries, God in His holiness and righteousness found no pleasure in the blood of those sacrifices:

"In burnt-offerings and sacrifices for sin *thou hast had no pleasure.* Then said I, Lo, I come (in the volume of the book it is written of me,) to do thy will,

O God.   Above when He said, Sacrifice and offering
and burnt-offerings and offering for sin thou wouldest
not, *neither hadst pleasure therein;* which are offered
by the law" (Heb. 10:6—8).

Even though God allowed the sacrifices from Eden
to Calvary (and it was "through the forbearance of
God" that those who offered them *in faith* were declared righteous before God), such sacrifices could
never deal a death-blow to sin.   It was a divine necessity that sin be judged by One who was *without* sin.
Therefore, what Deity demanded, only Deity could
provide.   God had to condemn sin in a specific way—
that is, He sent Christ into the world to take the sinner's place, *and then judged CHRIST for US.*   I again
point you to II Corinthians 5:19,21:

"To wit, that God was in Christ, reconciling the
world unto Himself . . . *For He* (God) *hath made Him*
(Christ) *to be sin for us* (for you and for me), *who
knew no sin* (Christ knew no sin); *that we might be
made the righteousness of God in Him."*

In the book of Leviticus God gives details concerning the walk, worship, and service of His people.
Some Bible scholars say that Leviticus is the "Hebrews" of the Old Testament and Hebrews is the "Leviticus" of the New Testament.   It is there that we
find the tabernacle, from which God spoke and in
which He dwelt in the midst of His people in the Old
Testament era.   It is in the book of Leviticus that
God gave instructions to His people concerning offerings and ceremonies which would exalt His holiness
in their approach to and communion with Himself.

"Holiness" is the key-word in Leviticus, and it
occurs there eighty-seven times.   The same Hebrew
word is used for "sin" and "sin-offering," and that
word occurs in Leviticus more than *seventy* times.
Chapter 4 speaks of the sin-offering, and the word
occurs over and over again.   Therefore, the typical

significance of sin and the sin-offering being one and the same, sin is identified with the offering and the offering is identified with the sin for which it is offered.

In the Old Testament economy the tabernacle, the offerings, the holy days, the ceremonies and all things in worship were typical of the Lamb of God and pointed to Him when He should come to take away the sin of the world. And the fact that "sin" and the "sin-offering" mean one and the same is also typical of Christ; because on the cross He identified Himself with the believer's sin, and the believer in exercising faith in the shed blood of Christ is identified *with* Christ:

"Beloved, *NOW are we the sons of God,* and it doth not yet appear what we shall be: but *we know that, when He shall appear, we shall be like Him;* for we shall see Him as He is" (I John 3:2).

"There is therefore NOW no condemnation to them which are in Christ Jesus . . ." (Rom. 8:1).

". . . Christ in YOU, the hope of glory" (Col. 1:27).

Christ gave Himself an offering for sin, and *IN CHRIST the believer has answered for his sins;* but no man can answer for his sin *apart* from being in Christ by faith in His shed blood by which we have the atonement. Jesus took our sins and bore them in His own body on the cross, that we might possess God's righteousness.

Peter declared that Christ "did no sin, neither was guile found in His mouth: who, when He was reviled, reviled not again; when He suffered, He threatened not; but committed Himself to Him that judgeth righteously: *who His own self bare our sins in His own body on the tree, that we, being dead to sins, should live unto righteousness: by whose stripes ye were healed.* For ye were as sheep going astray; but are now returned unto the Shepherd and Bishop of your souls" (I Pet. 2:22—25).

God the Eternal Father equipped Jesus for the specific mission of dealing with sin and sent Him forth, wrapped up in the likeness of sinful flesh, *"and for sin, CONDEMNED sin in the flesh."*

"Condemned" is a powerful and forceful word; it suggests three things: (1) a crime committed; (2) a verdict declared; (3) a punishment meted out. Two examples of this are found in the experiences of Noah and of Lot:

Genesis 6:8 tells us that Noah "found grace in the eyes of the Lord," and Hebrews 11:7 declares *"BY FAITH Noah, being warned of God of things not seen as yet, moved with fear, prepared an ark to the saving of his house; by the which he CONDEMNED the world, and BECAME HEIR OF THE RIGHTEOUS-NESS WHICH IS BY FAITH."*

Grace allowed Noah to build the ark — and by building the ark he saved his household and *condemned the world.* The sin of the people in Noah's day caused God to repent that He had made man, "and it grieved Him at His heart. And the Lord said, *I will destroy man whom I have created from the face of the earth; both man, and beast, and the creeping thing, and the fowls of the air; for it repenteth me that I have made them"* (Gen. 6:6,7).

The sin committed by the people of Noah's day caused God to declare — and carry out — judgment against them. Because of God's holy nature He must — and does — condemn sin!

Genesis chapter 19 gives the account of the destruction of Sodom; but the Scripture declares that God could not touch the city until Lot was safely outside its wicked boundaries (Gen. 19:22); for in spite of the fact that Lot had grievously backslidden and disgraced God, in spite of the fact that he had lost the respect of family and friends, he was still *a "just"*

man who was "vexed with the filthy conversation of
the wicked. *For that RIGHTEOUS MAN dwelling
among them, in seeing and hearing, vexed his RIGHT-
EOUS SOUL from day to day with their unlawful
deeds"* (II Pet. 2:7,8).

God sent heavenly messengers at evening to warn
Lot to flee from the city. They said, "We will destroy
this place, because the cry of them is waxen great
before the face of the Lord; and the Lord hath sent
us to destroy it" (Gen. 19:13).

But when morning came, Lot was still in the city—
and there is no doubt that he spent the night pleading
with his children to leave with him—"but he seemed
as one that mocked" (Gen. 19:14). In other words,
they looked upon him as a crazy old man. The angels
then "laid hold upon his hand, and upon the hand
of his wife, and upon the hand of his two daughters;
the Lord being merciful unto him: and they brought
him forth, and set him without the city. . . . *Then
the Lord rained upon Sodom and upon Gomorrah
brimstone and fire from the Lord out of heaven; and
He overthrew those cities, and all the plain, and all
the inhabitants of the cities, and that which grew
upon the ground"* (Gen. 19:16—25 in part).

Sin brings condemnation, destruction, and death.
In both instances—Noah and Lot—we see the sin
which called forth the sentence of judgment, and we
see the execution of that judgment in the subsequent
condemnation; *but the Lord Jesus Christ was UN-
JUSTLY condemned* because *He did no sin.* Yet we
see the same three things: He was charged with blasphemy; He was tried and condemned; He was put to
death. In Mark 14:64 we read, *"Ye have heard the
blasphemy: what think ye? AND THEY ALL CON-
DEMNED HIM TO BE GUILTY OF DEATH."*

Because of man's sins, God condemned the old
world with the judgment of the flood; and because of

the sins of the people of Sodom and Gomorrah He condemned those cities and burned them to ashes. *He condemned His Son for US.* Thus the heart-rending cry, "My God! My God! *WHY HAST THOU FORSAKEN ME?"* Because of God's holy nature He *had* to forsake Jesus the Son, for at that moment Jesus in His humiliation was bearing the sin of the world, and at that moment God condemned sin in the flesh, that we through the shed blood of His Son might possess the righteousness of God by faith.

I pray that God will help me to see—as far as my poor, finite mind can be *allowed* to see—Jesus hanging on the cross, suffering agony such as mortal language can never describe, paying the ransom for my sin! Jesus did not sin; but *I sinned,* and He took my suffering, He took my condemnation, He paid my penalty. He died on the cross for *my* sin, and thank God, through faith in His shed blood and finished work, *I have redemption through HIS atonement!*

God Spared Not His Own Son

"What shall we then say to these things? If God be for us, who can be against us? He that spared not His own Son, but delivered Him up for us all, how shall He not with Him also freely give us all things?

"Who shall lay anything to the charge of God's elect? It is God that justifieth. Who is he that condemneth? It is Christ that died, yea rather, that is risen again, who is even at the right hand of God, who also maketh intercession for us" (Rom. 8:31—34).

It was not possible for God to spare His Son if atonement was to be made. The very nature of God demanded the death of Jesus if sin was to be condemned, sin's wages met and remission of sin procured. There was no other in all the universe who could satisfy God's holiness, His righteousness, and His law concerning sin. He is a just and righteous God, and it is impossible for Him to do wrong. He would have done wrong had He spared Jesus because the Scripture plainly declares that before the world was, the Trinity foreordained that God's Son should die for the remission of sin (I Pet. 1:20). Therefore, God "spared not His own Son, *but delivered Him up for us ALL.*"

God did not spare Adam and Eve. He warned Adam concerning sin and gave him a command; but Adam disobeyed that command. Therefore God put a curse on the man and his wife, He drove them from the Garden of Eden and condemned them to till the ground and earn their bread by the sweat of their brow (Gen. 3:14—24).

God did not spare Cain. Cain knew the kind of offering God required, but he brought an offering of his own choosing and God rejected it. "And Cain was very wroth, and his countenance fell" (Gen. 4:5); but God gave him a second chance, assuring him that if he would bring the right offering he would be accepted. But Cain refused to bring a blood offering, he later murdered Abel and then lied to God about it, and God put a curse on him which caused him to cry out, "My punishment is greater than I can bear!" (Gen. 4:13).

God did not spare *Pharaoh* and his armies when they attempted to overtake Moses and the children of Israel as they crossed the Red Sea. In Exodus 14:27,28 we read, ". . . the Lord overthrew the Egyptians in the midst of the sea. And the waters returned, and covered the chariots, and the horsemen, and all the host of Pharaoh that came into the sea after them; there remained not so much as one of them!"

God did not spare the angels who left their first estate and followed Lucifer in his rebellion against God. II Peter 2:4 tells us that they were delivered "into chains of darkness, to be reserved unto judgment."

Therefore, God could not spare His own Son if sin was to be condemned in the flesh. Jesus knew no sin, but God made Him to be sin for us. He was made to be our sin-offering, that through faith in His shed blood we might escape the damnation of hell. *Sin must be dealt with,* and the only possible way for a holy God to deal with sin was in the death of a holy Substitute—and Jesus was that Holy One. There was no other way, and since Jesus left the bosom of the Father and the glories of heaven and came to earth on a specific mission (to settle the sin-question once and forever) it was impossible for God to spare Him.

"All we like sheep have gone astray; we have turned every one to his own way; *and the Lord hath laid on JESUS the iniquity of us ALL. . . .* It pleased the Lord to bruise Him; He hath put Him to grief: when thou shalt make His soul an offering for sin, He shall see His seed, He shall prolong His days, and the pleasure of the Lord shall prosper in His hand. He shall see of the travail of His soul, and shall be satisfied: by His knowledge shall my righteous Servant justify many; *for He shall bear their iniquities*" (Isa. 53:6−11 in part).

Shall we face it? It was GOD who struck the death-blow to His only begotten Son who hung on the cross paying your sin-debt and mine! He was "SMITTEN OF GOD" (Isa. 53:4). Malachi 3:17 declares that "a man spareth his own son that serveth him," yet *God smote HIS Son*—and certainly God's Son served Him well! It was not possible for God the Father to spare His Son, because He was made to be *our substitute.* God sent Him forth to be born of a virgin, and in the fulness of time (as foreordained of God) His blood was shed for the remission of sin. If you and I were to be spared the eternal condemnation of hell, God *could not* spare His Son! Therefore, because God's stroke fell on *Him* we can be delivered from eternal damnation when we put our faith in His shed blood and finished work, receiving Him as our Saviour on the terms of the Gospel.

For Whom Did Jesus Die?

God "spared not His own Son, but *delivered Him up* for us all." Rest assured that the hands of wicked men could never have taken Jesus and crucified Him *by force* had not God the Father delivered Him up! On several occasions during His earthly ministry the enemies of Jesus attempted to take His life.

In John 8:59, after He had declared, "Before Abraham was, I AM" they took up stones to stone Him— "but Jesus hid Himself, and went out of the temple, going through the midst of them, and so passed by."

In John 10:30,31 He declared, "I and my Father are one," and they again took up stones to stone Him. In verse 39 of the same chapter "they sought again to take Him: but He escaped out of their hand."

When He preached in the synagogue at Nazareth the people became so angry they put Him out of the synagogue and out of the city, and attempted to push Him over a precipice, "but He passing through the midst of them went His way" (Luke 4:28–30).

On another occasion the chief priests and Pharisees sent their best officers to arrest Jesus; but when the officers returned without Him and the religious leaders asked, "Why have ye not brought Him?" they replied, *"Never man spake like THIS Man!"* (John 7:45,46).

On the night Judas led a band of men and officers into the Garden of Gethsemane to arrest Him, Jesus, "knowing all things that should come upon Him, went forth, and said unto them, *Whom seek ye?*" They replied, "Jesus of Nazareth." Jesus then said, "I AM

HE"—and as soon as He spoke those three words "they went backward, and fell to the ground!"

Imagine the feeling in the hearts of the disciples as they witnessed the power of His Word! He then asked a second time, "Whom seek ye?" and again they replied, "Jesus of Nazareth." He then assured them that *He* was Jesus of Nazareth, and added, "If therefore ye seek *me,* let these (disciples) go their way" (John 18:2—8). Then the band of officers took Him and led Him away.

Do you see what I mean? Only moments before, Jesus had spoken but three words and his enemies fell prostrate on the ground. Then they bound Him and led Him away to be brought to trial. *Why?* The moment had come when the Son of God was fore-ordained to be "delivered up for us all." I repeat: *no man* could have taken the life of Jesus, no man could have handcuffed Him and led Him to trial, no man could have taken Him and crucified Him *by force.*

No one but God could have delivered up His only begotten Son, and the only reason the hands of wicked men took Him, bound Him, tried and condemned Him and nailed Him to a cross was *because GOD "delivered Him up for us all!"* God gave the worthy Son of His love for worthless sons of men, for sinners going astray, that we might be "returned unto the Shepherd and Bishop of our souls" (I Pet. 2:25).

God for Us

In this chapter we have studied the atonement from God's standpoint. *It was GOD who "so loved the world* that He gave His only begotten Son, that whosoever believeth in Him should not perish, but have everlasting life" (John 3:16).

It was GOD who set Jesus forth "to be a propitiation through faith in His blood, to declare His righteousness for the remission of sins that are past, through the forbearance of God" (Rom. 3:25).

It was GOD who "commendeth His love toward us, in that, while we were yet sinners, Christ died for us" (Rom. 5:8).

It was GOD who sent His own Son "in the likeness of sinful flesh, and for sin, condemned sin in the flesh, that the righteousness of the law might be fulfilled in us . . ."* (Rom. 8:3,4).

It was GOD who "spared not His own Son, but delivered Him up for us ALL . . ." (Rom. 8:32).

Thus we see from God's holy Word that what He did in the atonement *was done for US;* and we are led to ask with the Apostle Paul:

"What shall we then say to these things? *If GOD be FOR us, who CAN be against us?* He that spared not His own Son, but delivered Him up for us all, *how shall He not WITH HIM also FREELY GIVE US ALL THINGS?*

"*WHO shall* lay anything to the charge of God's elect? *It is GOD that justifieth.* Who is he that *condemneth?* It is *CHRIST* that *died,* yea rather, that is risen again, who is even at the right hand of God, who also *maketh intercession for us.*

"Who shall *separate* us from the love of Christ? Shall *tribulation, or distress, or persecution, or famine, or nakedness, or peril, or sword?* As it is written, For thy sake we are killed all the day long; we are accounted as sheep for the slaughter.

"*NAY, in ALL THESE THINGS we are MORE than conquerors through Him that loved us. For I am persuaded, that neither death, nor life, nor angels, nor principalities, nor powers, nor things present, nor things to come, nor height, nor depth, NOR ANY OTHER CREATURE, shall be able to separate us from the love of GOD, which is IN CHRIST JESUS our Lord"* (Rom. 8:31—39).

Precious truth! Blessed assurance given by these inspired questions and answers! Since God loved us so much that He allowed His only begotten Son to come into the world to suffer and die for us, *truly He WILL freely give us all things in Jesus' name and for His sake.* Since God justified us through the atonement made for us by the shed blood of Jesus, then who on earth, in heaven, or in hell could *condemn* us? Christ died for us, but death could not hold Him. He rose again, and He sits today at the right hand of God as our Mediator, to make intercession for us. Therefore *He certainly* will not bring accusation against us, for He died and rose again to *free* us from condemnation (Rom. 8:1).

The death of the Lord Jesus Christ on Calvary's cross proclaims God's gift of His only begotten Son, and in His vicarious sufferings and death Christ gave to God that which met God's righteousness and satisfied God's holiness. But all Christ *gave* and all He *did* are the giving and doing of God Himself, for God was in Christ, reconciling the world unto Himself.

All this clearly brings out the divine fact that the paramount and crowning act of revelation is the act of God's infinite love in the death of His only begotten Son:

"Herein is LOVE, not that we loved GOD, but that HE LOVED US, and sent His Son to be the propitiation for our sins" (I John 4:10).

God did "see of the travail of His soul," and His holiness and righteousness were satisfied (Isa. 53:11). At the cross of Jesus, sin was dealt with, sin's penalty was satisfied, sin's debt was paid in full. Every darkness sin brought is now dispelled. Every question is answered, every enemy of the soul is defeated. Every fear is forever quelled. Every hunger is satisfied, every hope is completely and fully met, and every longing of man's heart is fulfilled. Yes, every promise from

Genesis through Malachi has been kept!

For *in Christ* "dwelleth all the fulness of the God-head bodily. *AND YE ARE COMPLETE IN HIM*, which is the head of all principality and power: In whom also ye are circumcised with the circumcision made without hands, in putting off the body of the sins of the flesh by the circumcision of Christ: Buried with Him in baptism, wherein also ye are risen with Him through the faith of the operation of God, who hath raised Him from the dead. And you, being dead in your sins and the uncircumcision of your flesh, hath He quickened together with Him, having forgiven you all trespasses; *blotting out the handwriting of ordinances that was against us, which was contrary to us, and took it out of the way, nailing it to His cross; AND HAVING SPOILED PRINCIPALITIES AND POWERS, HE MADE A SHEW OF THEM OPENLY, TRIUMPHING OVER THEM IN IT*" (Col. 2:9—15).

Chapter Five

WHAT DID CHRIST TEACH
CONCERNING HIS ATONEMENT?

"Therefore doth my Father love me, because I lay down my life, that I might take it again. No man taketh it from me, but I lay it down of myself. I have power to lay it down, and I have power to take it again. This commandment have I received of my Father" (John 10:17,18).

In our last chapter we studied *God's* part in the atonement—the fact that He so loved the world that He gave Jesus to be a propitiation for our sins, and that because of God's holy nature He could not spare His only begotten Son, but delivered Him up to pay the sin-debt for us all.

But what about the Son? Did the Lord Jesus Christ willingly leave the bosom of the Father? Did He willingly leave the glories of heaven to come into earth's sorrow—*and did He know WHY He was coming into the world?* Did He fully understand His mission? What did He Himself make known concerning His coming into the world? Did He know that He would die on a cross, *crucified for the very men who demanded His death?*

The Lord Jesus Christ was in the beginning with the Father (John 1:2). In the fulness of time (*and according to promise*) He left the Father's bosom, took a body of flesh, and came into the world to declare

God (John 1:18). He tabernacled among men for approximately thirty-three and one-half years, the last three and one-half years being given to His public ministry. During those years He declared that God is life, God is love, and that it is not God's will that men perish eternally, but that they have eternal life through faith in the shed blood and finished work of His only begotten Son. He made known the truth that God had not sent Him into the world to condemn the world, but that through Him the world might be saved.

During the last months and weeks of our Lord's life on earth, He taught His disciples the truth concerning His earthly mission—that He came to die on the cross, and in death take away the sin of the world. He spoke very plainly to them. In Luke 12:50 He told them, *"I have a baptism to be baptized with; and how am I straitened till it be accomplished!"*

To Nicodemus He declared, "As Moses lifted up the serpent in the wilderness, *even so must the Son of man be lifted up:* that whosoever believeth in Him should not perish, but have eternal life" (John 3:14,15).

In Luke 13:33 He spoke of *a goal that He must reach:* "Nevertheless I must walk to day, and to morrow, and the day following: for it cannot be that a prophet perish out of Jerusalem."

He taught His disciples that He must *suffer:* "The Son of man must be delivered into the hands of sinful men, and be crucified, and the third day rise again" (Luke 24:7).

On several occasions He spoke of an *"hour"* which must strike. In John 12:27 He said, "Now is my soul troubled; and what shall I say? Father, save me from this hour: but for this cause came I *unto* this hour."

In Mark 14:41, to the sleeping disciples He said, "Sleep on now, and take your rest: it is enough, *the hour is come;* behold, the Son of man is betrayed into the hands of sinners."

In John 10:11 He declared Himself "the Good Shepherd," and said, "The Good Shepherd *giveth His life* for the sheep."

He taught the disciples that in Him the Scripture would be fulfilled: "And He said unto them, These are the words which I spake unto you, while I was yet with you, that *all things must be fulfilled, which were written in the law of Moses, and in the prophets, and in the Psalms, concerning me*" (Luke 24:44).

He spoke of *the cup* which He must drink: "Then said Jesus unto Peter, Put up thy sword into the sheath: the cup which my Father hath given me, shall I not drink it?" (John 18:11).

He made known to them the fact that His blood would be shed: "And He took bread, and gave thanks, and brake it, and gave unto them, saying, This is my body which is given for you . . . Likewise also *the cup* after supper, saying, *This cup is the new testament in my blood*, which is shed for you" (Luke 22:19,20).

He taught them concerning the death He would die: "And Jesus answered them, saying, The hour is come, that the Son of man should be glorified. Verily, verily, I say unto you, *Except a corn of wheat fall into the ground and die, it abideth alone:* but if it die, it bringeth forth much fruit" (John 12:23,24).

He told the disciples of *a vicarious act He would perform:* ". . . the Son of man came not to be ministered unto, but to minister, and to give His life a ransom for many" (Matt. 20:28).

He made known to them *a gift He would bestow:* "I am the living bread which came down from heaven: if any man eat of this bread, he shall live for ever: and the bread that I will give is my flesh, which I will give for the life of the world" (John 6:51).

He taught of *a remission He would secure for men:*

"And He took the cup, and gave thanks, and gave it to them, saying, Drink ye all of it; for this is my blood of the new testament, which is shed for many for the remission of sins" (Matt. 26:27,28).

He taught of *a power He would communicate:* "He that believeth on me, as the Scripture hath said, out of his belly shall flow rivers of living water. But this spake He of the Spirit, which they that believe on Him should receive: for the Holy Ghost was not yet given; because that Jesus was not yet glorified" (John 7:38,39).

He assured His disciples that *victory would be His:* "Now is the judgment of this world: now shall the prince of this world be cast out. And I, if I be lifted up from the earth, will draw all men unto me" (John 12:31,32).

Just before His ascension, the Son of God clearly taught His disciples that through His suffering, death, and resurrection, remission of sin would be granted to all who believe on His name among all nations: "Thus it is written, and thus it behoved Christ to suffer, and to rise from the dead the third day: and that repentance and remission of sins should be preached in His name among all nations, beginning at Jerusalem. And ye are witnesses of these things" (Luke 24:46—48).

Just before He walked the last mile to Golgotha, He said to His disciples: "These things I have spoken unto you, that in me ye might have peace. In the world ye shall have tribulation: but be of good cheer; I have overcome the world" (John 16:33).

Then He turned His eyes heavenward and spoke to the heavenly Father from whence He had come:

"Father, *the hour is come;* glorify thy Son, that thy Son also may glorify thee: As thou hast given Him power over all flesh, that He should give eternal life to as many as thou hast given Him. And this is life eternal, that they might know thee the only true God, and Jesus Christ, whom thou hast sent. *I have glorified thee on the earth: I have finished the work which thou gavest me to do.* And now, O Father, glorify thou me with thine own self with the glory which I had with thee before the world was" (John 17:1–5).

Did Christ know the significance of the mission for which He came into the world? *Indeed He did know!* Not only did He know the fulness of His mission when He left the Father's bosom to be born of Mary, but He was present at the council of the Holy Trinity before the world was, before there was a sinner who needed the salvation provided by Christ's atonement! Yes, He knew perfectly well that He would leave the glories of heaven and take up His abode in a body of humiliation in which body He would suffer and die for the sins of the world!

The Baptism of Jesus and His Cross

What did Jesus mean when He said to His disciples, *"I have a baptism to be baptized with"*? Certainly He was not speaking of His baptism in the river Jordan, because that had happened months before. He was speaking of His baptism on Calvary, of which His baptism in Jordan was a symbol.

In Matthew chapter 3 we read of the ministry of John the Baptist when he was preaching in the wilderness of Judaea, and his message was, "Repent ye: for the kingdom of heaven is at hand. For this is he that was spoken of by the prophet Esaias, saying, The voice of one crying in the wilderness, Prepare ye the way of the Lord, make His paths straight" (vv. 1–3).

In verses 5 and 6 we read, "Then went out to him Jerusalem, and all Judaea, and all the region round about Jordan, *and were baptized of him in Jordan,*

CONFESSING THEIR SINS."

Many of the Pharisees and Sadducees came to
John to be baptized, but because they had not repented
of their sins (vv. 7—12) he refused to baptize them.
But in verses 13 through 17 we read:

"Then cometh Jesus from Galilee to Jordan unto
John, to be baptized of him. But John forbad Him,
saying, I have need to be baptized of thee, and comest
thou to me? And Jesus answering said unto him,
Suffer it to be so now: for thus it becometh us to fulfil all righteousness. Then he suffered Him.

"And Jesus, when He was baptized, went up
straightway out of the water: and, lo, the heavens
were opened unto Him, and he saw the Spirit of God
descending like a dove, and lighting upon Him: and
lo a Voice from heaven, saying, This is my beloved
Son, in whom I am well pleased."

"THEN cometh Jesus . . . ." What time in the
life of Christ does the word *"then"* pinpoint? What
was John the Baptist doing *"then"*? He was baptizing
people in the river Jordan, people who came *"confessing their SINS"* (v. 6).   But why did *Jesus* come to
John to be baptized *"then"*? He had *no sin* to confess, He was the Sinless One.   John knew who Jesus
was and why He had come into the world, and he
knew He was *sinless.*   Therefore John was justified
when he said, *"I have need to be baptized of THEE,
and comest thou to ME?"*

It is true that Christ had no personal sin to confess. He did not sin in thought, word, or deed. But
he had sins *representatively*—He had come into the
world to take *the sinner's place,* to represent the sinner
in death in order that the sinner might have life eternally.

In Psalm 69:1—21 the Psalmist speaks of *"my* sins
. . . *my* reproach . . . *my* shame . . . *my* dishonour"—
but the words are prophetic; they speak of the suffer-

ings of Jesus. He took *my* sins, my *reproach*, my *shame*. He represented *me*. Therefore He had sins representatively. God made Him to be sin for us.

Do not misunderstand me—God did not make Jesus *commit* sin. II Corinthians 5:21 clearly states that God made Jesus *TO BE* sin *FOR us*, that we might be made the righteousness of God in Him. Jesus could not have said *personally* "my sins...my reproach... my shame," but *representatively* it was true.

In Hebrews 1:3 we read that Jesus was the brightness of God's glory, "and the express image of His person, and upholding all things by the word of His power, *when He had by Himself purged our sins*, sat down on the right hand of the Majesty on high." (One outstanding Greek scholar translated, "when He had made *purification for Himself.*") Jesus is the head of the Church, and *in that capacity* He acted for His mystical body in answering for the sin of the members of that body (Eph. 5:23,30).

In the intrinsic worth of Christ's personality there was no need for Him to make purification because He was co-equal with God in holiness, in righteousness, and in purity. But as *the SON of God* representing the *sons* of God, He acted for us; and thus in *His* action, *WE acted*.

Jesus overruled John's objection to baptizing Him in Jordan. He said, *"Suffer it to be so NOW: for thus it becometh us to fulfil ALL righteousness."* I again point out that *as God the Son*, in the intrinsic worth of Christ's personality there was no righteousness *to BE fulfilled;* but as the representative of all believers *He acted FOR* the "sons" of God, and in *His* action, *all believers* acted. Therefore Jesus said to John, "It is necessary that I be baptized of you in Jordan in order to fulfill a divine requirement concerning me and my mission on earth. *Thus it becometh us to fulfil ALL righteousness.*"

Jesus came into the world to take away the sin of the world, and He is the propitiation for our sins (John 1:29; I John 2:2). He met the claim of righteousness when He died on the cross for sinners. Since He died in our stead and in His death took the sinner's place, the believer can now claim the righteousness of God which is by faith in the finished work and shed blood of the Lord Jesus Christ. Righteousness cannot be attained, merited, or earned through good works. *Righteousness is IMPUTED:*

"For what saith the Scripture? *Abraham believed God, and it was COUNTED unto him for righteousness"* (Rom. 4:3). In the Greek, "counted unto" means *reckoned, imputed,* or *put to the account of.* What did Abraham do to be accounted righteous? Did he work? Did he give a sum of money? The Word of God tells us *"Abraham BELIEVED GOD,"* and *because* he believed God (because he exercised faith) God imputed *His OWN righteousness* to Abraham.

Then in Romans 4:5 we read, "But to him that worketh not, but *believeth on Him that justifieth the ungodly,* his *faith* is counted for righteousness." In other words, when the unbeliever hears the message of salvation by grace through faith in the finished work of Jesus *and believes on Him* as Saviour, *that person is justified and righteousness is IMPUTED to him.* "Even as David also describeth the blessedness of the man unto whom God *imputeth righteousness without works"* (Rom. 4:6).

Jesus was very God in flesh, *unimpeachable God;* yet the Scriptures make it clear that He was *"numbered with the transgressors;* and He bare the sin of many" (Isa. 53:12). Jesus Himself declared, "I say unto you, *that this that is written must yet be accomplished in me,* And He was reckoned among the transgressors: for the things concerning me have an end" (Luke 22:37).

When John the Baptist was baptizing in Jordan, surely he would have been pleased beyond words if Jesus had come to him and said, *"Let me baptize YOU."* But instead of offering to baptize John, Jesus took His stand with the people who had come to John to be baptized, and in so doing He identified Himself with sinners. Certainly He did not need to be baptized for the remission of sins, for *He HAD no sin*— and the Scriptures do *not* teach that water *washes away* sin! It is *the blood of Jesus* (not the water in the baptistry) that cleanses from sin (I John 1:7). But our Lord took His place with the multitudes who were confessing their sins, and as far as baptism could express it, *He made all that was theirs, HIS.*

Christ's baptism in Jordan was no small act on His part. It demonstrated His loving, tender communion with the sinner's unloveliness and misery. He was numbered with the transgressors; and *because* He was numbered with us, *when we believe in His shed blood and finished work WE are numbered WITH HIM* in His merit and in His accomplished mission on earth:

We "sit together *in heavenly places* in Christ Jesus" (Eph. 2:6).

We are "hid *with Christ* in God" (Col. 3:3).

We are *"heirs of God, and joint-heirs with Christ"* (Rom. 8:17).

It was not by accident that John the Baptist was the one who baptized Jesus in Jordan. John was called before he was born. He was commissioned of God to announce the coming of the Messiah. He was the representative of the majesty of Almighty God in God's holy law. He was the last of the prophets under the old dispensation. Jesus said of him, "He was a burning and a shining light" (John 5:35). In contrasting John the Baptist with believers He said, "Among them that are born of women there hath not risen a greater than John the Baptist: notwithstanding *he that is least in the kingdom of heaven is greater than he"* (Matt. 11:11). He did not mean that a believer is greater *in character* than John was. He meant that we are greater *in privilege.* We live in the most glorious age this world has ever known!

On the banks of the river Jordan, two men stood— John the Baptist, and God's only begotten Son—each with a mission, a ministry to perform. *John's* part was that of Almighty God's holy law which cannot be altered or changed.

Christ's part was "to put away sin by the sacrifice of Himself" (Heb. 9:26). His part was to be made sin and a curse for us (II Cor. 5:21; Gal. 3:13). His part was to suffer for our sins. Sin and suffering are inseparable—"Sin, when it is finished, bringeth forth death" (James 1:15). Therefore it was *an absolute MUST* that Jesus suffer sin's penalty, "the Just for the unjust, *that He might bring us to God,* being put to death in the flesh, but quickened by the Spirit" (I Pet. 3:18).

Believers are delivered from the penalty and the power of sin by union with Christ in death and resurrection. Paul said to the believers in Rome, "Know ye not, that *so many of us as were baptized into Jesus Christ were baptized into His death?* Therefore we are *buried with Him by baptism into death:* that like as Christ was raised up from the dead by the glory of the Father, even so *we also should walk in newness of life"* (Rom. 6:3,4).

To believe on the Lord Jesus Christ is to come into possession of all that He accomplished for us in His finished work. To the Galatian Christians Paul wrote, "*I am crucified with Christ:* nevertheless I live; yet not I, but Christ liveth in me: and the life which I now live in the flesh I live by the faith of the Son of God, who loved me, and gave Himself for me" (Gal.

2:20).

What did Paul mean by saying, *"I am crucified with Christ"*? Certainly he was not nailed to a cross with Christ, but when Jesus died *He died FOR ALL;* therefore when Paul believed on Jesus and received Him as his personal Saviour, he came into possession of all that Jesus accomplished for sinners in His vicarious atonement!

Continuing his instructions to the believers in Rome, Paul said, "If we have been planted together *in the likeness of His death,* we shall be also in the likeness of *His resurrection:* Knowing this, that our old man is crucified with Him, that the body of sin might be destroyed, that henceforth we should not serve sin. For he that is dead is freed from sin.

"Now *if we be dead with Christ, we believe that we shall also LIVE with Him:* Knowing that Christ being raised from the dead *DIETH NO MORE;* death hath no more dominion over Him. *For in that He died, He died unto sin ONCE: but in that He liveth, He liveth unto God.*

"Likewise reckon ye also yourselves to be dead indeed unto sin, but alive unto God THROUGH JESUS CHRIST OUR LORD" (Rom. 6:5—11).

The baptism of Jesus was definitely a type of His death on Calvary, His burial in the garden tomb, and His resurrection from the dead. When believers are baptized in the name of the Father, and of the Son, and of the Holy Ghost, our immersion in water signifies our death, burial, and resurrection with Christ: *"Therefore if any man be in Christ, he is a new creature: old things are passed away; behold, ALL things are become NEW"* (II Cor. 5:17).

I believe *and teach* that every born again believer should be baptized; but I do not teach that baptism has anything to do with redemption from sin. Water *cannot* wash away sin, but water baptism *does* denote

death, burial, and resurrection. When we believe on
Jesus, the Holy Spirit takes up His abode in our heart,
and we walk in newness of life *because we ARE new
creations in Christ.*

The place where John was *"THEN" baptizing* is
not without significance. He could have been baptizing in the Sea of Galilee—or in any of several other
locations; but the Scripture tells us he was baptizing
in the river Jordan, very near Jericho—and Jericho is
very near the spot where most outstanding Bible ar-
cheologists believe the cities of Sodom and Gomorrah
stood when the terrible judgment struck them in the
days of Lot.

Like most things in Palestine, the river Jordan has
a typical meaning—and this is certainly true as relating
to the baptism of Jesus. The river lies far below sea
level. It issues from the Sea of Galilee, and in its
onward flow it plunges ever downward, lower and
lower, until it empties into the Dead Sea (which ar-
cheologists believe to be the grave of the wicked cities
of Sodom and Gomorrah). Most assuredly the Dead
Sea is one of the most *unusual* things on earth. It is
a giant chasm of salt, potash, nitrate, pitch—and
desolation! Its surface lies 1,300 feet below sea level.

I believe the river Jordan is a type of penal death,
death issuing into the bottomless pit. The name of
the river comes from a root word meaning "downward
plunger," and as I have already stated, the stream does
plunge downward—it makes twenty-seven distinct de-
scents before it finally reaches the Dead Sea. Jesus
was baptized in "the river of judgment"—or, "the
downward plunger."

In the Word of God, raging (or troubled) waters
are frequently used as an example of God's wrath.
One of the Hebrew words used in describing the wrath
of God literally means "to wash thoroughly... to drown
. . . to overflow." Isaiah used this word in describing

the woe and judgment that would come upon Ephraim: "Behold, the Lord hath a mighty and strong one, which as a tempest of hail and a destroying storm, *as a flood of mighty waters overflowing,* shall cast down to the earth with the hand" (Isa. 28:2).

David used the same Hebrew word in speaking prophetically of the Lord Jesus Christ: "I sink in deep mire, where there is no standing: *I am come into deep waters, where the floods overflow me*" (Psalm 69:2).

The same word is translated "drown" in The Song of Solomon 8:7: "Many waters cannot quench love, *neither can the floods drown it . . . .*"

When Jesus was baptized by John in the river Jordan, He was "drowned" beneath the waters of judgment for you and for me—but thank God, those waters of judgment could not drown nor even dampen *His love* for us! and because Jesus went beneath the waters of judgment for us, we have the assurance that those waters will never overflow or drown us:

"When thou passest through the waters, I will be with thee; and through the rivers, they shall not overflow thee: when thou walkest through the fire, thou shalt not be burned; neither shall the flame kindle upon thee" (Isa. 43:2).

When Jesus said to His disciples, "I have a baptism to be baptized with; and how am I straitened till it be accomplished" (Luke 12:50), He knew He was to face the baptism of death on Calvary. He knew that every minute detail of judgment sin demanded would be His. He knew He would be plunged beneath the floods of wrath because He was taking the sinner's place. Yes, the Lord Jesus Christ knew full well what it would cost Him to make the atonement— yet knowing all that He faced, knowing every minute detail of suffering, anguish, disappointment and humiliation that lay ahead of Him, He willingly left the

Father's bosom and laid His life down that *we* might
have life. His baptism in the river Jordan is definitely
a type of the baptism of death which He suffered for
us.

The Corn of Wheat

"Verily, verily, I say unto you, Except a corn of
wheat fall into the ground and die, it abideth alone:
but if it die, it bringeth forth much fruit" (John 12:24).

Here Jesus again declared the divine necessity of
His death if atonement for sin was to be made and if
sinners were to be saved. He said, *"EXCEPT a corn
of wheat fall into the ground and die...."* In John's
Gospel, the word *"except"* lays down the unalterable
rule that a condition must be fulfilled before the end
can be attained.

This is also shown in John 3:2, when Nicodemus
came to Jesus "by night, and said unto Him, Rabbi,
we know that thou art a teacher come from God: *for
no man can do these miracles that thou doest, EX-
CEPT God be with him."* No ordinary man could do
what Jesus was doing.

In the same way, the new birth is the divine qualification for entering the kingdom of God. In John 3:3,5
Jesus declared, *"EXCEPT a man be born again,* he
cannot see the kingdom of God. ... *EXCEPT a man
be born of water and of the Spirit,* he cannot enter
into the kingdom of God."

In verse 27 of that same chapter John the Baptist
declared, *"A man can receive nothing, EXCEPT it
be given him from heaven."*

Man cannot "born" himself into the kingdom of
God. It is "not of blood, nor of the will of the flesh,
nor of the will of man" that we are born into the
kingdom of God. The spiritual birth is entirely of
God; therefore *the bestowment* of the gift of God is
prerequisite to man's *receiving* the gift of God. It is

God who gives us eternal life, and *EXCEPT He give it we would never possess it!*

Another illustration of this is found in John 6:44 where Jesus said, *"No man can come to me, EXCEPT the Father which hath sent me draw him . . . ."* Some people say, "I will become a Christian when I am ready, or at a more convenient time," but the Word of God clearly teaches that in order to become a possessor of eternal life, man must be drawn by the Holy Spirit. A sinner does not become a Christian when *he* is "ready," or when circumstances and surroundings are favorable. I beseech you, sinner friend, as you read this message if the power of the Holy Spirit draws you, convicts you of sin and convinces you that you need to be born again, *give your heart to Jesus NOW.* Today is the day of salvation, *now* is the accepted time. *"Boast not thyself of to morrow; for thou knowest not what a day may bring forth"* (Prov. 27:1). If God is drawing you today through the convicting power of the Holy Spirit and through this message, fall upon your knees this moment and ask the Lord Jesus Christ to come into your heart and save you right now, for *you cannot come to God EXCEPT the Holy Spirit draw you to Him!*

In John chapter 6, the great chapter on the bread of life, Jesus said to the self-righteous Pharisees, "Verily, verily, I say unto you, *EXCEPT ye eat the flesh of the Son of man, and drink His blood, ye have no life in you"* (John 6:53). Eating is essential to life; if we do not *eat,* we will *die.* Eating is also essential to *eternal life.* Jesus explained what He meant by eating His flesh: "Whoso eateth my flesh, and drinketh my blood, hath eternal life . . . For my flesh is meat indeed, and my blood is drink indeed. *He that eateth my flesh, and drinketh my blood, dwelleth in me, and I in him"* (John 6:54—56).

Jesus was the Word of God *incarnate:* "In the

beginning was the Word, and the Word was with God, and the Word was God. . . . And the Word was made flesh, and dwelt among us . . ." (John 1:1,14). When we appropriate the Word of God, that appropriation brings saving faith: "Faith cometh by hearing, and hearing by the Word of God" (Rom. 10:17). We are born again by the incorruptible seed, the Word of God (I Pet. 1:23). Therefore when we appropriate the Word of God by faith we are eating the flesh and drinking the blood of the Lamb of God. He gave His body to be broken, He shed His blood for the remission of sin; and when we receive "the engrafted Word" (James 1:21) we are saved by God's grace through the shed blood of the Lord Jesus Christ.

Concerning *fruit bearing*, Jesus said to His disciples, "Abide in me, and I in you. *As the branch cannot bear fruit of itself, EXCEPT it abide in the vine; no more can ye, EXCEPT ye abide in ME*" (John 15:4).

In John 12:20−22, Andrew and Philip told Jesus that certain Greeks who had come to Jerusalem to worship at the feast of the Passover had said to them, "We would see Jesus." It was then that Jesus gave the illustration of the corn of wheat, showing that death is necessary to life—that is, before there can be life, there must be death. As long as a grain of wheat or corn remains out of the ground it abides alone; but when it is planted in the earth, the outer shell of the grain decays and dies; but the *heart* of the seed begins to grow, and shortly it brings forth fruit. Thus *one* grain produces many grains—some thirty, some sixty, some a hundredfold.

So it was with Christ. In order that the Greeks (Gentiles, and "whosoever will") might be saved and become part of the family of God, it was necessary that Jesus die, be buried, and rise again, that He might bring forth much fruit, many sons, from *all peoples,* all nations under heaven.

The sinless, holy life of Jesus could never have saved us. His holiness shows us how exceeding sinful man is, but our Lord would have forever walked alone had He not died on the cross for us. It was a divine necessity that He go into the blackness of our death, into the grave we justly deserved, in order that we might share the blessedness of His holiness and have eternal life in Him. *Jesus* went beneath the turbulent waters of *judgment* that *we* might be led beside *the still waters of His peace* through faith in His shed blood. He died that we might have life and have it abundantly. *He IS life,* and only *through Him* can we have life eternal.

The Son of Man Must Be Lifted Up

"As Moses lifted up the serpent in the wilderness, even so must the Son of man be lifted up: that whosoever believeth in Him should not perish, but have eternal life. For God so loved the world, that He gave His only begotten Son, that whosoever believeth in Him should not perish, but have everlasting life" (John 3:14−16).

Jesus not only knew that He came into the world to die for man's sin; He also knew that He, the sinless Son of God, must fulfill the type of the serpent of brass which Moses had lifted up before the children of Israel in the wilderness. (Read Numbers 21:5−9.) He left the glories of heaven with a full understanding of what He must do while He was on earth. Everything He did, every miracle He performed, every step He walked—in other words, all that happened to Him from the moment of His birth until He said, "It is finished"—was divinely necessary. This is proved by the following Scriptures:

"And He (Jesus) began to teach them, that the Son

of man *MUST suffer many things*, and be rejected of the elders, and of the chief priests, and scribes, and be killed, and after three days rise again" (Mark 8:31).

"And He (Jesus) said unto them, How is it that ye sought me? Wist ye not that *I MUST be about my Father's business?*" (Luke 2:49).

"Nevertheless *I MUST walk to day*, and to morrow, and the day following: for *it cannot be that a prophet perish out of Jerusalem*" (Luke 13:33).

"For as the lightning, that lighteneth out of the one part under heaven, shineth unto the other part under heaven; so shall also the Son of man be in His day. *But first MUST He suffer many things*, and be rejected of this generation" (Luke 17:24,25).

"Then came the day of unleavened bread, *when the passover MUST be killed*. . . . For I say unto you, that *this that is written MUST yet be accomplished in me*, And He was reckoned among the transgressors: for the things concerning me have an end" (Luke 22: 7,37).

"*The Son of man MUST be delivered into the hands of sinful men, and be crucified, and the third day rise again*" (Luke 24:7).

"And (Jesus) said unto them, These are the words which I spake unto you, while I was yet with you, that *all things MUST be fulfilled, which were written in the law of Moses, and in the prophets, and in the Psalms, concerning me*. . . . Thus it is written, and thus it behoved Christ to suffer, and to rise from the dead the third day" (Luke 24:44,46).

"As Moses lifted up the serpent in the wilderness, *even so MUST the Son of man be lifted up*" (John 3:14).

"*I MUST work the works of Him that sent me*, while it is day: the night cometh, when no man can work" (John 9:4).

There was no uncertain note in the teaching of the

Lord Jesus Christ concerning His mission on earth. His *coming* was a *MUST*. His *death* was a *MUST*. He prayed, "Father, if it be possible, let this cup pass . . . ." but it was not possible. *He MUST drain the cup to the last bitter dregs* if atonement was to be made and salvation provided for poor, wretched, hell-bound and hell-deserving sinners! If the cup had passed, Jesus could never have said, "It is finished!" God's righteousness and His holy law would not have been satisfied and hell would not have been defeated. But Jesus finished the work the Father sent Him to do, and now "the Spirit and the bride say, *Come.* And let him that heareth say, *Come.* And let *him that is athirst* come. And *WHOSOEVER WILL, let him take the water of life FREELY*" (Rev. 22:17).

His Hour — His Woe — Our Welcome

On different occasions Jesus spoke of a momentous "hour" to which He would eventually come. In John 7:30, His enemies sought to take Him, "but no man laid hands on Him, because *His HOUR was not yet come.*" This is repeated in John 8:20—"No man laid hands on Him; *for His HOUR was not yet come.*"

In John 12:23 Jesus announced, "The hour *is come, that the Son of man should be glorified.*" In John 13:1 we read, "Now before the feast of the passover, *when Jesus knew that His HOUR was come that He should depart out of this world unto the Father*, having loved His own which were in the world, He loved them unto the end."

That dark "hour" was fully known and anticipated by Him, and as its shadows began to close around Him He cried out, *"Father, the HOUR is come! Glorify thy Son, that thy Son also may glorify thee!"* (John 17:1).

In John 12:27 Jesus said, "Now is my soul troubled;

and what shall I say? Father, save me from this hour:
But for this cause came I unto this hour!" It must
have been a very dark and intense hour, because the
soul of Jesus was exceedingly troubled.   Yet in the
midst of such trouble He felt He could not pray, "Father, *deliver* me from this hour," because He knew
that the hour which would soon engulf Him was the
goal of His life. That was the thing for which He had
come into the world. It was settled in the beginning,
foreordained before the foundation of the world, that
He was to *come TO* this terrible hour in order for
poor lost sinners to come to the hour of welcome when
they could hear Him say, "Come unto me, all ye that
labour and are heavy laden, and I will give you rest—
rest for the weary, salvation for the wicked, and everlasting life for those who are dead in trespasses and
sins."

In John 5:25 Jesus declared, "Verily, verily, I say
unto you, *The hour is coming, and now is, when the
dead* (those dead in trespasses and sins) *shall hear the
voice of the Son of God: and they that hear shall
live."*

Christ's Death Was Vicarious

". . . the Son of man came not to be ministered
unto, but to minister, and to give His life a ransom
for many" (Matt. 20:28).

There was no uncertainty in Christ's teaching concerning the fact that His death was *vicarious.*   He
taught that He, the Son of man, left the Father's bosom and came into the world *specifically* to give His
life a ransom for many, to be "cut off" (Dan. 9:26) for
all who will come unto God by Him. The Greek preposition translated *"for"* means "instead of"—that is,
Jesus gave His life "a ransom *instead of* many." Jesus
gave Himself in my stead. I sinned, the wages of sin
is death, therefore I should die; but Jesus took my

place and died on the cross for me.

In Christ's death, everything sin demanded of us was placed on HIM! The vicarious death of the Son of God fulfilled the plan of the Father and provided the atonement for hell-deserving sinners. Jesus went to the place of sacrifice and offered Himself, *the ONE sacrifice* that satisfied God forever:

"But THIS MAN, after He had offered ONE sacrifice for sins FOR EVER, sat down on the right hand of God; from henceforth expecting till His enemies be made His footstool. FOR BY ONE OFFERING HE HATH PERFECTED FOR EVER THEM THAT ARE SANCTIFIED" (Heb. 10:12—14).

Christ's Death Was Voluntary

"Therefore doth my Father love me, because I lay down my life, that I might take it again. No man taketh it from me, but I lay it down of myself. I have power to lay it down, and I have power to take it again. This commandment have I received of my Father" (John 10:17,18).

The only begotten Son of God was not *compelled* to go to Calvary—*the love of God IMPELLED Him to go there.* Jesus was God's love wrapped up in flesh, and it was that love in His heart that impelled Him to lay down His life on the cross. There is no other power in heaven or on earth which moves as mightily as love. No other force is as forceful as *pure* love.

Shortly before His crucifixion Jesus said to His disciples, "I have yet many things to say unto you, but ye cannot bear them now." (They would not have been able to understand them at that time.) "Howbeit when He, the Spirit of truth, is come, He will guide you into all truth: for He shall not speak of Himself; but whatsoever He shall hear, that shall He speak: and

He will shew you things to come. He shall glorify
me: for He shall receive of mine, and shall shew it
unto you. All things that the Father hath are mine:
therefore said I, that He shall take of mine, and shall
shew it unto you" (John 16:12—15).

The following verses which contain the word *"gave"*
will illustrate the ministry of the Holy Spirit in His
testimony concerning the vicarious death of Jesus
Christ:

In Galatians 1:4 Paul speaks of our Lord Jesus
Christ, *"who GAVE Himself for our sins,* that He
might deliver us from this present evil world, according
to the will of God and our Father."

In Galatians 2:20 the Apostle Paul declared, "I am
crucified with Christ: nevertheless I live; yet not I,
but Christ liveth in me: and the life which I now
live in the flesh I live by the faith of the Son of God,
who LOVED me, and GAVE Himself for me."

I Timothy 2:5,6 declares, "There is one God, and
one Mediator between God and men, the Man Christ
Jesus; *who GAVE Himself A RANSOM FOR ALL,
to be testified in due time."*

In Ephesians 5:25 Paul constrains husbands to love
their wives, *"even as Christ also LOVED the Church,
and GAVE Himself for it."*

Christ's intent in giving Himself for us is described
by the Apostle Paul in Titus 2:14: *Jesus "GAVE Himself for us, that He might REDEEM US FROM ALL
INIQUITY, and purify UNTO HIMSELF a peculiar
people, zealous of good works!"*

"It Is Finished!"

The possibility of failure never entered the mind
of the Lord Jesus Christ. Before He left the Father's
bosom—yea, *before the world was*—He knew *victory
would be HIS!* He came to do the Father's will, He

accomplished everything the Father had sent Him to do, therefore He could give the victorious cry, *"IT IS FINISHED!"* (The Greek word could also be rendered "It is accomplished," and it means "to completely *complete . . .* to fulfill, to perfect" —*and Jesus did just that.* He did perfectly and completely all that the Father sent Him to do.

The same Greek word translated *"finished"* in John 19:30 is used in Matthew 10:23 where it is rendered *"gone over"*—"When they persecute you in this city, flee ye into another: for verily I say unto you, *Ye shall not have GONE OVER the cities of Israel, till the Son of man be come."*

In Matthew 17:24 the same word is rendered *"pay"* —"And when they were come to Capernaum, they that received tribute money came to Peter, and said, *Doth not your Master PAY tribute?"*

In Luke 2:39 the same word is translated *"perform"* —"And *when they had PERFORMED all things according to the law of the Lord,* they returned into Galilee, to their own city Nazareth."

In Luke 12:50, 18:31, 22:37, and John 19:28 the same word is translated *"accomplished."*

In James 2:8 it is rendered *"fulfil"*—"If ye FULFIL the royal law according to the Scripture, Thou shalt love thy neighbour as thyself, ye do well."

In Revelation 15:1 the same word is translated *"filled up"*—"And I saw another sign in heaven, great and marvellous, seven angels having the seven last plagues; *for in them is FILLED UP the wrath of God."*

In Revelation 20:7 it is translated *"expired"*—"And *when the thousand years are EXPIRED, Satan shall be loosed out of his prison."*

Then in Revelation 10:7 the same word is rendered *"finished"*—"But in the days of the voice of the seventh angel, when he shall begin to sound, *the mystery*

*of God should be FINISHED, as He hath declared
to His servants the prophets.*"

If we incorporate *ALL of these words* into the
description of Christ's finished work, we begin to understand something of the greatness, the completeness,
and the perfection of His work *for us:*

The Lord Jesus Christ has *"gone over"* all the will
of God on our behalf as poor, depraved sinners: "This
Man, after He had offered *one sacrifice* for sins *for
ever,* sat down on the right hand of God" (Heb. 10:12).

He has *"paid in full"* all the tribute demanded
by God in His righteousness: "Forasmuch as ye know
that ye were not redeemed with corruptible things, as
silver and gold, from your vain conversation received
by tradition from your fathers; *but with the precious
blood of Christ,* as of a lamb without blemish and
without spot" (I Pet. 1:18,19).

He has *"performed"* for us everything the Father
gave Him to do: "I have glorified thee on the earth:
I have finished the work which thou gavest me to
do" (John 17:4).

He has *"accomplished"* all the prophecies concerning Himself: "And He said unto them, These are
the words which I spake unto you, while I was yet
with you, that all things must be fulfilled, which were
written in the law of Moses, and in the prophets, and
in the Psalms, concerning me" (Luke 24:44).

He has *"fulfilled"* all the law of God in its double-
requirement of obedience and death: "And being
found in fashion as a man, He humbled Himself, and
became obedient unto death, even the death of the
cross" (Phil. 2:8). Also in Galatians 3:13 we read,
"Christ hath redeemed us from the curse of the law,
being made a curse for us: for it is written, Cursed
is every one that hangeth on a tree."

Jesus has *"filled up"* all the chaos, havoc, and
emptiness caused by sin in the life of man. (Study

Romans 5:17—21.)

On the cross, He *"expired"* in death—and by death settled sin's debt in full: "For (God) hath made (Jesus) to be sin for us, who knew no sin; that we might be made the righteousness of God in Him" (II Cor. 5:21).

He *"finished"* every detail of God's design, completed the work God sent Him into the world to do: "After this, Jesus *knowing that ALL things were now accomplished, that the Scripture might be fulfilled,* saith, I thirst. Now there was set a vessel full of vinegar: and they filled a spunge with vinegar, and put it upon hyssop, and put it to His mouth. When Jesus therefore had received the vinegar, *He said, IT IS FINISHED: and He bowed His head, and gave up the ghost"* (John 19:28—30).

What the Lord Jesus Christ *began,* all hell could not stop! What He undertook, He consummated. John 1:3 tells us, *"All things* were made by Him; and *without* Him was not any thing made that was made." Thus *in creation* we see the perfection of the skillful *hands* of Jesus; but in the *redemption* He wrought for us we see *the production of His great, loving HEART!*

"WHATSOEVER THE LORD DOETH, IT SHALL BE FOREVER. NOTHING CAN BE PUT TO IT, NOR ANYTHING TAKEN FROM IT, AND GOD DOETH IT, THAT MEN SHOULD FEAR BEFORE HIM" (Eccl. 3:14).

Christ's Last Act Before the Cross

"And when the hour was come, He sat down, and the twelve apostles with Him. And He said unto them, With desire I have desired to eat this passover with you before I suffer: For I say unto you, I will not any more eat thereof, until it be fulfilled in the kingdom of God. And He took the cup, and gave

thanks, and said, Take this, and divide it among yourselves: For I say unto you, I will not drink of the
fruit of the vine, until the kingdom of God shall come.

"And He took bread, and gave thanks, and brake
it, and gave unto them, saying, This is my body which
is given for you: this do in remembrance of me.   Likewise also the cup after supper, saying, This cup is the
new testament in my blood, which is shed for you"
(Luke 22:14—20).

In verse 20, the Greek word translated "shed" is
ekchuno which means *"poured out."* This same Greek
word is used in Luke 5:37 where it is translated
"spilled":   "No man putteth new wine into old bottles; else the new wine will burst the bottles, and be
spilled, and the bottles shall perish."

The same word is used in Acts 1:18 referring to the
death of Judas, and it is there translated *"gushed out"*:
"Now this man purchased a field with the reward of
iniquity; and falling headlong, he burst assunder in
the midst, and all his bowels *gushed out."*

In Acts 10:45 the same Greek word is translated
"poured out," referring to the Holy Spirit when He
came upon the Gentiles in the house of Cornelius.

So—we see the life of Christ was "poured out . . .
spilled . . . gushed out."   His blood was shed for us
and His death was *absolute.* He died the most horrible, shameful death known to man—and it was of
His own free will, for you and for me!

The Old Testament sacrifices were a type of the
offering Jesus made for us when He offered Himself
on the cross, and the term "poured out" was used
often in connection with those sacrifices:

"And thou shalt take of the blood of the bullock,
and put it upon the horns of the altar with thy finger,
*and POUR ALL THE BLOOD beside the bottom of
the altar"* (Ex. 29:12).

"And the priest shall put some of the blood upon

the horns of the altar of sweet incense before the Lord, which is in the tabernacle of the congregation; and shall *POUR ALL THE BLOOD of the bullock* at the bottom of the altar of the burnt-offering, which is at the door of the tabernacle of the congregation" (Lev. 4:7). (See also verses 18, 25, and 30 of this chapter.)

"And he brought the bullock for the sin-offering: and Aaron and his sons laid their hands upon the head of the bullock for the sin-offering. And he slew it; and Moses took the blood, and put it upon the horns of the altar round about with his finger, and purified the altar, *and POURED THE BLOOD at the bottom of the altar, and sanctified it, to make reconciliation upon it*" (Lev. 8:14,15).

"And whatsoever man there be of the children of Israel, or of the strangers that sojourn among you, which hunteth and catcheth any beast or fowl that may be eaten; *he shall even POUR OUT THE BLOOD thereof,* and cover it with dust" (Lev. 17:13).

In all of these offerings, the blood *poured out* was typical of the Lord Jesus Christ whose blood was poured out for us. He *poured out His soul* unto death on our behalf (Isa. 53:10). It is the poured-out life of the Lamb of God which secures for us eternal and abundant life. The death of Jesus *for* sin *saves US from the death OF sin,* for sin and death are synonymous (Rom. 6:23; Ezek. 18:4; James 1:15).

Through the death of the Lord Jesus Christ, we who were *dead IN sin before we believed, are dead TO sin AFTER believing:*

"Who His own self bare our sins in His own body on the tree, *that we, being DEAD TO SINS, should LIVE unto righteousness:* by whose stripes ye were healed" (I Pet. 2:24).

"And you hath He *quickened,* who *were dead in trespasses and sins* . . . But God, who is rich in mercy, for His great love wherewith He loved us, even when we were dead in sins, *hath quickened us together with Christ . . ."* (Eph. 2:1,4,5).

The Words of Jesus: The Declaration of God's Love for the World

"No man hath seen God at any time; *the only begotten Son, which is in the bosom of the Father, HE HATH DECLARED HIM"* (John 1:18).

"Verily, verily, I say unto you, *He that heareth my WORD, and believeth on Him that sent me, hath everlasting life,* and shall not come into condemnation; but is passed from death unto life" (John 5:24).

"It is the Spirit that quickeneth; the flesh profiteth nothing: *the WORDS that I speak unto you, they are spirit, and they are life"* (John 6:63).

"And if any man hear *my WORDS,* and believe not, I judge him not: for I came not to judge the world, but to save the world. *He that rejecteth me, and receiveth not my WORDS, hath One that judgeth him: THE WORD that I have spoken, the same shall judge him in the last day"* (John 12:47,48).

Jesus did not come into the world that there might be *a Gospel to preach—He WAS the Gospel:*

"In the beginning was the WORD, and the Word was WITH God, and the Word WAS God. . . . And the WORD was made FLESH, and dwelt among us, (and we beheld His glory, the glory as of the only begotten of the Father,) full of grace and truth" (John 1:1,14).

John 3:16 has been called "the Gospel in a nutshell"—and rightly so, for in those words of Jesus we find the declaration of the Gospel, God's love for the world, God's gift to mankind, God's invitation to "whosoever," and the plan of salvation through faith in the finished work of the only begotten Son of God. Therefore John 3:16 is the Gospel *in solution:*

Sinners are saved by God's grace. The Gospel is the grace of God in its essence. Jesus was God in flesh, Jesus was full of grace. The *surety* of the Gospel is truth—Jesus said, "Sanctify them through thy truth: thy WORD is truth" (John 17:17). To Thomas He said, "I am truth" (John 14:6).

The *ministry* of the Gospel is mercy: "For God sent not His Son into the world to *condemn* the world; *but that the world through Him might be SAVED*" (John 3:17).

The *source* of the Gospel is love: *"GOD is love"* (I John 4:8).

"Herein is LOVE, not that we loved God, but that He loved us, and sent His Son to be the propitiation for our sins" (I John 4:10).

The Gospel attracts anyone who will allow himself to listen to the Word of God with an open mind and an open heart. *Power* is the Gospel's attractability. Paul said, "I am *not ashamed* of the Gospel of Christ: for it is *the POWER OF GOD unto salvation to every one that believeth;* to the Jew first, and also to the Greek" (Rom. 1:16).

"As many as *received* Him, to them *gave He POWER to become the sons of God,* even to them that believe on His name: which were born, not of blood, nor of the will of the flesh, nor of the will of man, but of God" (John 1:12,13).

The Gospel is the heart, soul, and bloodstream of revelation: *"All Scripture is given by inspiration of God,* and is profitable for doctrine, for reproof, for correction, for instruction in righteousness: *that the man of God may be perfect, throughly furnished unto all good works"* (II Tim. 3:16,17).

All God needs to say *has been SAID* and is recorded in the Word. Christ is rightly *called* the Word because He speaks out in all that He became in taking a body of humiliation, and in that body suffering and

dying as *no mortal* ever suffered and died. He conquered death as no man ever could conquer death.
Therefore in all that He became, in all that He was,
in all that He has done, is doing, and will ever do,
He makes known to us what God IS.

Man Comes Short of the Glory of God

*"For ALL have sinned, and come short of the glory
of God"* (Rom. 3:23).

In His life, in His ministry, in His death, and in
His resurrection Jesus answered for *man,* and for *man's
sin.* He was not only the *sin-offering,* bearing our
sins in His own body, receiving the judgment *we*
should have received because of sin; He was also the
burnt-offering bringing glory to God through the sweet
savor of His perfect life, His perfect obedience even
unto death. Therefore He answered for the sin of
man, and He answered for the sinner in that *man
came short* of the glory of God. Jesus declared, "I
have glorified thee on the earth: I have finished the
work which thou gavest me to do" (John 17:4).

"The heavens declare the glory of God; and the
firmament sheweth His handywork" (Psalm 19:1). The
heavens declare God's glory and the firmament declares His handiwork—*but the glory and the splendor
of God's heart of love was displayed on Calvary!* Jesus
dying on Calvary put on display the glory of God's
love, compassion, wisdom, riches, truth, grace—and
the glory of His worth:

Paul declared, "Unto me, who am less than the
least of all saints, is this grace given, *that I should
preach among the Gentiles THE UNSEARCHABLE
RICHES OF CHRIST"* (Eph. 3:8).

According to the Scriptures, the Lord Jesus Christ
not only knew *why* He had come into the world *(to
die for the SIN of the world),* but death was His goal.

He was *born to die,* and He knew that each step He took brought Him nearer to Calvary.   Many times He taught concerning His death and the *result* of His death.   He pointed to the nature of His death, and to the necessity for His death.   Throughout His earthly ministry that momentous hour loomed before Him when He would pass through the awful suffering for the sins of mankind.   Until that hour was fully come, it was impossible for Jesus to die; but when that hour arrived He knowingly, willingly, freely gave Himself, laying His life down for our sins:

"These words spake Jesus, and lifted up His eyes to heaven, and said, *Father, the hour is come;* glorify thy Son, that thy Son also may glorify thee" (John 17:1).

In John chapter 10, Jesus spoke concerning His death and assuring His disciples that He fully knew He had come to earth to die. (Please study John 10:11, 15, 17, 18.)

It is also in the Gospel of John that we find the triumphant cry of victory: *"IT IS FINISHED!!"* (John 19:30).   In the Greek there is only *one word:* "ACCOMPLISHED!"   It is impossible for the finite mind to fully understand *what* was accomplished in the death of Jesus, but we do know that in His death He satisfied every demand of God in order to make atonement for us.   If He had failed in one single point, if He had stopped one step short of Calvary, His mission on earth would have been in vain.   The Holy Spirit has clearly declared that the *climax* of the ministry of the Lord Jesus Christ was as necessary as its nature: *". . . once in the end of the world hath He appeared to put away sin by the sacrifice of Himself"* (Heb. 9:26).

Chapter Six

THE INCLUSIVENESS
OF CHRIST'S ATONEMENT

"For in Him dwelleth all the fulness of the God-head bodily. And ye are complete in Him, which is the head of all principality and power" (Col. 2:9,10).

"What shall we then say to these things? If God be for us, who can be against us? . . . Who shall separate us from the love of Christ? Shall tribulation, or distress, or persecution, or famine, or nakedness, or peril, or sword? As it is written, For thy sake we are killed all the day long; we are accounted as sheep for the slaughter.

"Nay, in all these things we are more than con-querors through Him that loved us. For I am per-suaded, that neither death, nor life, nor angels, nor principalities, nor powers, nor things present, nor things to come, nor height, nor depth, nor any other creature, shall be able to separate us from the love of God, which is in Christ Jesus our Lord" (Rom. 8:31, 35−39).

". . . He hath said, I will never leave thee, nor forsake thee. So that we may boldly say, The Lord is my helper, and I will not fear what man shall do unto me" (Heb. 13:5,6).

"But my God shall supply all your need according to His riches in glory by Christ Jesus" (Phil. 4:19).

Christ crucified is the center of God's program

from everlasting to everlasting. The atonement of our
Lord and Saviour is the grandest, most glorious, most
distinctive fact in all the Bible.   The atonement is
not only the greatest *divine fact* of Christianity—*the
atonement IS Christianity.*

Christ's atonement is the remover of all human
guilt, it replaces all human sorrow with joy, it answers all of man's questions, and heals man's every
ill.   Christ's atonement is the securer of all divine
glory—yes, in the words Paul wrote to the Colossian
believers, *we are "complete in HIM."* Our every need
is found in Jesus.

At Calvary He paid our sin-debt in full, He settled
the sin-question forever; and now as He sits at the
right hand of God as our Intercessor we can declare
with confidence, *"We are MORE than conquerors
through HIM!"* He died to save us, He lives at the
right hand of the Father to keep us and deliver us,
and one glorious day He is coming to call all born
again believers up to meet Him in the clouds in the
air.   That is our *"blessed hope*—the glorious appearing
of the great God and our Saviour Jesus Christ" (Tit.
2:13).

Christ's atonement is the sum of all knowledge.
To the Corinthian believers Paul declared, "And I,
brethren, when I came to you, came not with excellency of speech or of wisdom, declaring unto you
the testimony of God. *For I determined not to know
any thing among you, SAVE JESUS CHRIST, AND
HIM CRUCIFIED. . . . And my speech and my
preaching was not with enticing words of man's wisdom, but in demonstration of the Spirit and of power:
That your faith should not stand in the wisdom of
men, but in the power of God"* (I Cor. 2:1—5 in part).

When Paul moved into the city of Corinth to declare the Gospel, he did not compose and deliver a
message to gratify the curiosity of the people, nor did

he entertain them with beautiful words and philosophical niceties. His preaching was "not with excellency of speech or of wisdom." Without apology he said, *"I determined not to know ANY THING among you save Jesus Christ—AND HIM CRUCIFIED!"*

Now let us analyze this statement and see what Paul meant:

"I determined not to KNOW . . . ." This does not mean that Paul despised all *other* knowledge (unless such knowledge stood in competition with or in opposition to *the knowledge of Jesus Christ*). What he said was, in essence, "As a result of my most serious inquiries, after having carefully weighed the facts and considered the advantages and disadvantages, after pondering all things fit to come into consideration in the matter, *this is my final determination*: No other knowledge—however profitable or pleasant it may be— is worthy to be compared with *the knowledge of JESUS CHRIST*. I have therefore resolved and determined that the scope and the end of my preaching will be *Jesus Christ, and Him crucified!"*

"I determined not to know ANY THING . . . ." In other words, Paul said, "I am determined to study nothing and teach nothing except *Jesus Christ*—not as a great teacher or a great preacher, but *Christ CRUCIFIED."* It is true that Paul spoke on many other subjects—and in his epistles he wrote on other subjects; but his sermons and his writings all *pointed to* the crucified Christ, and his one determination was to make known the fact of the atonement. To him, this was the most important, the nearest, dearest, and sweetest of all subjects, and anything else, however worthy of time and study, must be second (or in subordination) to the primary responsibility of making Christ known.

"I determined not to know anything among you SAVE JESUS CHRIST AND HIM CRUCIFIED."

Paul singled out this topic from among the excellent truths of Christ, and on it he spent the main strength of his ministry. Thus did he meet and dispose of the vulgar prejudice raised against him on account of the cross of Jesus. He knew that "Christ crucified" was "unto the Jews a stumblingblock, and unto the Greeks foolishness" (I Cor. 1:23); but he loved the Jews, he loved the Greeks, and he knew the only message that would draw them to God was the message of the cross. Therefore "Jesus Christ, and Him crucified" was the predominant theme of his preaching.

In I Corinthians 15:1—4 Paul declared, "Moreover, brethren, I declare unto you the Gospel which I preached unto you, which also ye have received, and wherein ye stand; *by which also ye are saved . . .*

"For I delivered unto you first of all that which I also received, how that *CHRIST DIED FOR OUR SINS* according to the Scriptures; and that *HE WAS BURIED*, and that *HE ROSE AGAIN* the third day according to the Scriptures."

Paul was extremely jealous for the Gospel he preached. To the Galatians he wrote, under inspiration, "I marvel that ye are so soon removed from Him that called you into the grace of Christ unto another gospel: which is NOT another; but there be some that trouble you, and would pervert the Gospel of Christ. But though we, or an angel from heaven, preach any other gospel unto you than that which we have preached unto you, let him be accursed. As we said before, so say I now again: *If any man preach any other gospel unto you than that ye have received, LET HIM BE ACCURSED*" (Gal. 1:6—9).

According to Paul, anything that leaves out the grace of God (Christ crucified) is not Gospel, but a lie; and he was of the definite opinion that anyone who preached *any other* "gospel" should be *"accursed"*—that is, "Let him drop into hell and burn forever!"

The Most Excellent

"But what things were gain to me, those I counted loss for Christ. Yea doubtless, and I count all things but loss for the excellency of the knowledge of Christ Jesus my Lord: for whom I have suffered the loss of all things, and do count them but dung, that I may win Christ, and be found in Him, not having mine own righteousness, which is of the law, but that which is through the faith of Christ, the righteousness which is of God by faith" (Phil. 3:7−9).

"For I would that ye knew what great conflict I have for you, and for them at Laodicea, and for as many as have not seen my face in the flesh; that their hearts might be comforted, being knit together in love, and unto all riches of the full assurance of understanding, to the acknowledgement of the mystery of God, and of the Father, and *of Christ; in whom are hid all the treasures of wisdom and knowledge"* (Col. 2:1−3).

There is no doctrine so excellent (or so necessary) as the doctrine of Christ and Him crucified. All other knowledge—no matter how important it may seem or how much it may be magnified by men—is secondary and commonplace in comparison to the knowledge of Jesus Christ. We will see why this is true as we consider the excellency of the knowledge of Christ, which is the heart, soul, and bloodstream of all Scripture.

1. The knowledge of Christ is the scope and the center of all divine revelation:

The Old Testament *ceremonial law* is filled with Christ. The *Gospel* is filled with Christ. The precious and blessed lines of both the Old and New Testaments meet and harmonize in *Christ and Him crucified,* and *without Christ crucified there IS no har-*

mony between the Testaments.   Therefore I declare
that the knowledge of the unspeakable excellency of
the doctrine of Christ crucified is the key that unlocks
the greatest part of the sacred Scripture from Genesis
through Revelation!   The right knowledge of Jesus
Christ leads to the right knowledge of the rest of the
Scripture, and without the right knowledge concerning
Christ it is impossible to have right knowledge concerning the rest of the Scriptures.

2. *The knowledge of Christ is fundamental to all
graces:*

"And ye are complete in Him, which is the head
of all principality and power" (Col. 2:10).
God created the heaven and the earth in the beginning, and since God is righteous, holy, and perfect
He could not have created an earth without form,
void, and dark.   Yet in Genesis 1:2 we read, "And
the earth was without form, and void; and darkness
was upon the face of the deep."   Therefore we know
that sometime after creation, *judgment struck the earth*
rendering it empty and desolate.   (Study Jeremiah 4:
23—26.)   Then we read, "*And the Spirit of God moved
upon the face of the waters.   And God said, LET
THERE BE LIGHT:*   and there was light" (Gen.
1:2b, 3).
We see then that the first work of the Spirit was
to bring LIGHT, and what was true in the old creation is true in the new—that is, the first work of the
Spirit today is the opening of the eyes of the inner
man: "If our Gospel be hid, it is hid to them that
are lost: *In whom the god of this world hath blinded
the minds of them which believe not,* lest the light
of the glorious Gospel of Christ, who is the image of
God, should shine unto them" (II Cor. 4:3,4).
But when a person is born again he becomes a
new creation in Christ: "Therefore if any man be in

Christ, *he is a new creature: old things are passed away; behold, ALL THINGS are become new"* (II Cor. 5:17).

In II Peter 3:18 we read, "But grow *in grace,* and in *the knowledge* of our Lord and Saviour Jesus Christ . . . ." Here we see how grace and knowledge keep equal pace in the soul of the born again believer—that is, as *one* increases *the other* increases, and to the same degree. But it is impossible for one to believe *without the knowledge of Christ.* In Romans 10:13–17 the Apostle Paul declares, *"Whosoever shall call upon the name of the Lord shall be SAVED"*—but then he explains: "How then shall they *call* on Him in whom they have not believed? and how shall they *believe* in Him of whom they have not heard? and how shall they hear *without a preacher?* and how shall they *preach,* except they be sent? . . . *So then faith cometh by hearing, and hearing by the Word of God."*

Faith is definitely *and assuredly* dependent upon the knowledge of Christ crucified. ". . . *by His knowledge shall MY RIGHTEOUS SERVANT justify many* . . ." (Isa. 53:11).

Hear these words from the "salvation" Gospel: "This is the will of Him that sent me, that every one which seeth the Son" (not with the natural eye but with the eye of the inner man), "and believeth on Him, may have everlasting life: and I will raise him up at the last day" (John 6:40).

3. The knowledge of Christ is fundamental to Christian hope:

The knowledge of Christ brings faith, faith in Christ brings hope; and we hope in God because we have heard the good news of the atonement.

Christ is the *author* of hope: "Blessed be the God and Father of our Lord Jesus Christ, which according to His abundant mercy *hath begotten us again unto a*

LIVELY HOPE (a living hope) by the resurrection of Jesus Christ from the dead" (I Pet. 1:3).

Christ is the *object* of hope: "Which hope we have as an anchor of the soul, both sure and stedfast, and which entereth into that within the veil; whither the forerunner is for us entered, even Jesus, made an high priest for ever after the order of Melchisedec" (Heb. 6:19,20).

Apart from Christ *there IS no hope,* but to His saints God would "make known what is the riches of the glory of this mystery among the Gentiles; which is *Christ in you, the hope of glory"* (Col. 1:27).

Without the knowledge of Jesus Christ and Him crucified, man cannot believe unto salvation, he cannot possess hope in God, he cannot pray acceptably. The only way man can converse with God and have fellowship with Him is in prayer, and the only way man can hope for God to *hear* his prayer is by living faith in Christ, our Mediator. Thus we see just how indispensable is the knowledge of Christ to all who believe, to all who hope, to all who pray, and to all who labor in His vineyard.

4. The knowledge of Christ is fundamental to all comfort:

All the comforts of believers originate in and proceed from this fountain. He is the object of the believer's faith, trust, hope, and joy: "For we are the circumcision, which worship God in the spirit, *AND REJOICE IN CHRIST JESUS,* and have no confidence in the flesh" (Phil. 3:3).

Take away the knowledge of Christ crucified, and believers would be the saddest beings in the world. Our peace, our assurance, our comfort, and our joy proceed from Christ: "Whom having not seen, ye love; in whom, though now ye see Him not, yet believing, *ye rejoice WITH JOY UNSPEAKABLE AND*

FULL OF GLORY" (I Pet. 1:8).

5. *The knowledge of Christ is fundamental to eternal happiness:*

Jesus said, "This is life eternal, that they might know thee the only true God, *and Jesus Christ, whom thou hast sent*" (John 17:3). Since to know Christ is *eternal life*, then it must follow that *NOT to know Him is ETERNAL DAMNATION!* Christ is the door to heaven, and the *knowledge of Christ crucified* is the key that *opens* heaven's door.

Man can attain much through his own effort. Politically, financially—even *religiously*—he may become a man of renown, with great esteem and honor among men. But unless he knows the Lord Jesus Christ he is *hopelessly lost* in spite of all the honorable and noteworthy attainments he may have won. "For after that in the wisdom of God the world *by wisdom knew not God*, it pleased God by the foolishness of preaching to save them that believe" (I Cor. 1:21).

The Lord Jesus Christ "and Him crucified" is the greatest, the most noble, of all subjects, and *all other subjects* are but shadows in comparison. It is boundless as a bottomless ocean—no man can fathom the depth of the knowledge of Christ; there is no way of *measuring* its depth, its height, its length, or its breadth. The Apostle Paul humbly confessed, *"Unto me, who am less than the least of all saints, is this grace given, that I should preach among the Gentiles the UNSEARCHABLE RICHES OF CHRIST"* (Eph. 3:8).

Even eternity itself cannot fully unfold all the wonderful, precious truths about the Lord Jesus Christ, but careful study of the Scripture does reveal many things about Him. The Holy Spirit reveals one fact to one minister, other facts to other ministers, and this has been true in passing generations. Men of God

today understand many things from the Word of God
that were not understood by ministers a century ago—
or even a *generation* ago—secrets which from all eternity lay hidden in the bosom of Almighty God: "No
man hath seen God *at any time;* the only begotten
Son, which is *in the BOSOM of the Father, He hath
declared Him"* (John 1:18).

This is the most glorious age man has known since
God created Adam and breathed into his nostrils the
breath of life. As we study the Scripture, as we feed
upon and appropriate *the living Word,* the Gospel
stamps such heavenly glory upon our lives that men
take notice that we have been with Jesus: "For if the
ministration *of condemnation* be glory, much more
doth *the ministration of righteousness EXCEED in
glory.* . . . But we all, with open face beholding as in
a glass the glory of the Lord, are changed into the
same image from glory to glory, even as by the Spirit
of the Lord" (II Cor. 3:9,18).

The Knowledge of Christ
Compared to All Other Knowledge

". . . no man knoweth the Son, but the Father;
neither knoweth any man the Father, save the Son,
and he to whomsoever the Son will reveal Him" (Matt.
11:27).

All other knowledge is natural, *but the knowledge
of Christ is holy and entirely SUPERNATURAL;* therefore the wisest man on earth could never discover
Christ through mental ability—nor could he find Him
by means of the miracle-machines in use today in the
field of electronics.

Shortly after the Russians placed their first satellite in orbit they boasted that *there IS no God* because
their satellite did not find Him! The fact that the
Russian atheists confess that their miracle-machines

did not make contact with God proves to me that God is exactly what His Word tells us He is. I repeat: The wisest men of this age could never come to know God through their wisdom and knowledge, nor by modern miracle-machines. Only those who have heard God's Word, yielded to the call of the Spirit, and received the Word by faith have acquired the knowledge which is supernatural and definitely the gift of God: *CHRIST "is made unto us wisdom, and righteousness, and sanctification, and redemption"* (I Cor. 1:30).

There are many people who could never master science, mathematics, philosophy, and some other fields of learning, even if they had favorable opportunity; therefore such knowledge is sometimes unattainable. But the mystery and excellency of the knowledge of Christ lies in the fact that the most *unlearned* person can *attain* such knowledge through the teaching of the Holy Spirit. Hear the words of Jesus in Matthew 11:25:

"At that time Jesus answered and said, *I thank thee, O Father, Lord of heaven and earth, because thou hast hid these things from the wise and prudent, and hast REVEALED THEM unto BABES!"*

Then hear the Apostle Paul as the Holy Spirit moved upon him and he wrote to the Corinthian believers:

"For ye see your calling, brethren, how that not many wise men after the flesh, not many mighty, not many noble, are called: But God hath chosen the foolish things of the world to confound the wise; and God hath chosen the weak things of the world to confound the things which are mighty; and base things of the world, and things which are despised, hath God chosen, yea, and things which are not, to bring to nought things that are: *that no flesh* should glory in His presence" (I Cor. 1:26—29).

Though man may attain to *the highest degree of*

knowledge available in this life, such knowledge can never bring him to Christ because *earthly* knowledge is *defective*. We find proof of this in the first chapter of Paul's epistle to the Romans:

The learned heathen became "vain in their imaginations, and their foolish heart was darkened. *Professing themselves to be WISE, they became FOOLS*" (Rom. 1:21,22). Their lusts were stronger than their light, and they held "the truth in unrighteousness" (Rom. 1:18). They "did not like to retain God in their knowledge" (Rom. 1:28). Therefore, *GOD GAVE THEM UP*—"to uncleanness . . . to vile affections . . . to a reprobate mind" (vv. 24, 26, 28). But the powerful influence of the knowledge of *Christ and Him crucified* will change souls into the *image* of that knowledge (II Cor. 3:18). Many *learned philosophers* are burning in hell today, while many *unlearned and illiterate Christians* are in Paradise resting from their labors!

Yes, the Lord Jesus Christ in His atonement is the sum of all knowledge, the hidden and perfect wisdom of God. All pure Bible doctrine leads to the cross, and no ministry is well-pleasing to God unless it leads *men* to the foot of the cross. No attainment of man is praise-worthy, genuine, and vital in God's sight unless it has its root and strength in the cross of Christ.

Saving grace is ours because of Christ's atonement. Jesus was "full of grace and truth" (John 1:14). The grace of God brings salvation—but before we can appropriate the grace of God by faith we must hear His Word, we must be exposed to the knowledge of Christ and Him crucified. The only place to find the truth about Jesus is in the Word of God, and the only way man can appropriate the Word is through the Holy Spirit:

"For the grace of God that bringeth salvation hath appeared to all men, teaching us that, denying ungodliness and worldly lusts, we should live soberly, right-eously, and godly, in this present world; *looking for that blessed hope, and the glorious appearing of the great God and our Saviour Jesus Christ;* who gave Himself for us, that He might redeem us from all iniquity, and purify unto Himself a peculiar people, zealous of good works" (Tit. 2:11—14).

Christ's Atonement Is the Proof of All Prophecy

The Old Testament is filled with prophecies con-cerning the coming of Messiah. From Genesis through Malachi the prophets wrote of the One who would redeem Israel, put down all wickedness, and bring peace on earth with good will toward men. Although they did not *understand* all that they penned down, we know that they wrote under inspiration, for II Peter 1:21 tells us, "The prophecy came not in old time by the will of man: but holy men of God spake *as they were moved by the Holy Ghost.*"

Then in I Peter 1:10,11 we read, "Of which salva-tion *the prophets* have inquired and searched diligent-ly, who prophesied *of the grace that should come unto you:* searching what, or what manner of time the Spirit of Christ which was in them did signify, when it testified beforehand *the SUFFERINGS of Christ, and the GLORY that should follow.*"

The prophets prophesied of Christ's sufferings as well as His glory, and when we study the Old Testa-ment in the light of the sufferings of Christ and His substitutionary work, the Scripture comes alive before us. I suppose the greatest chapter on the atonement *in all of the Old Testament* is Isaiah chapter 53:

"Who hath believed our report? and to whom is the arm of the Lord revealed? For He shall grow up before Him as a tender plant, and as a root out of a dry ground: He hath no form nor comeliness; and

when we shall see Him, there is no beauty that we
should desire Him.

"He is despised and rejected of men; a Man of
sorrows, and acquainted with grief: and we hid as
it were our faces from Him; He was despised, and we
esteemed Him not.   Surely He hath borne our griefs,
and carried our sorrows: yet we did esteem Him
stricken, smitten of God, and afflicted.

*"But He was wounded for our transgressions, He
was bruised for our iniquities: the chastisement of
our peace was upon Him; and with His stripes we are
healed.   ALL we like sheep have gone astray; we have
turned every one to his own way; and the Lord hath
laid on Him the iniquity of us ALL.*

"He was oppressed, and He was afflicted, yet He
opened not His mouth: He is brought as a lamb to
the slaughter, and as a sheep before her shearers is
dumb, so He openeth not His mouth.   He was taken
from prison and from judgment: and who shall declare
His generation? for He was cut off out of the land of
the living: for the transgression of my people was
He stricken.   And He made His grave with the wicked,
and with the rich in His death; because He had done
no violence, neither was any deceit in His mouth.

"Yet it pleased the Lord to bruise Him; He hath
put Him to grief: When thou shalt make His soul an
offering for sin, He shall see His seed, He shall prolong His days, and the pleasure of the Lord shall
prosper in His hand.   He shall see of the travail of
His soul, and shall be satisfied: by His knowledge
shall my righteous servant justify many; for He shall
bear their iniquities.

"Therefore will I divide Him a portion with the
great, and He shall divide the spoil with the strong;
because He hath poured out His soul unto death: and
He was numbered with the transgressors; and He bare
the sin of many, and made intercession for the trans-

gressors" (Isa. 53:1—12).

In this chapter, Christ's atonement is prophesied, proclaimed, and illustrated. Now let us compare this passage with statements found in the New Testament concerning the vicarious sufferings of Jesus and see how He fulfilled every detail of the prophecies recorded by Isaiah:

"Who hath believed our report?" Christ's announcement by John the Baptist was not believed, His own words were not received, and when we study the Gospels—Matthew, Mark, Luke, and John—we readily see that *only a minority* believed Jesus. The masses followed Him only when there were loaves and fishes; *and* (with the exception of John the Beloved) *even the few who were with Him on the night of His arrest forsook Him and fled!*

"He is despised and rejected of men." The religious leaders of Christ's day hated Him from the very outset of His public ministry. They rejected Him, they influenced the multitudes to reject Him, and their hatred of Him deepened until they finally had Him arrested, brought to trial, unjustly convicted, condemned to death—and crucified! Certainly no one would attempt to deny that Christ was "despised and rejected of men"—even by His own people, the Jews (Matt. 27:15—25).

Then in Isaiah 53:4, 12 we read, *"Surely He hath borne our griefs, and carried our sorrows . . . He hath poured out His soul unto death: and He was numbered with the transgressors; and He bare the sin of many, and made intercession for the transgressors."* Yes, He bore our griefs, our sorrows, our sins "in His own body on the tree, that we, being dead to sins, should live unto righteousness: by whose stripes (we) were healed" (I Pet. 2:24).

He "poured out His soul unto death"—and certainly He was numbered with the transgressors, for He was crucified between two thieves (Luke 23:32,33; Matt. 27:38).

And even as He hung on the cross, for whom did He pray? Isaiah prophesied, "He . . . made intercession *for the transgressors,*" and Luke 23:34 records His prayer: *"Father, forgive them; for they know not what they do!"* From the cross He prayed for the very men who crucified Him!

Seven centuries before Christ was born, the Prophet Isaiah wrote, *"He was wounded for our transgressions . . . ."* and as Jesus hung on the cross, His brow pierced with thorns, His face disfigured and covered with blood and spittle, John the Beloved witnessed that horrible sight and penned down, for our admonition and learning, these words: "And *he that saw it* bare record, and his record is *true:* and he *knoweth* that he saith true, *that ye might believe*" (John 19:35).

The Hebrew word translated *"wounded"* literally means "to bore, to torment, to slay." Therefore this verse from Isaiah 53 could read, "He was *pierced,* He was *tormented,* He was *slain* for our transgressions"; and in John 19:37 we read, "And again another Scripture saith, *They shall look on Him whom they pierced.*"

Isaiah wrote, *"He was bruised for our INIQUI-TIES,"* and centuries later, under inspiration Peter wrote, *"Christ also hath once suffered for SINS,* the Just for the unjust, that He might bring us to God, being put to death in the flesh, but quickened by the Spirit" (I Pet. 3:18).

The Hebrew word translated *"bruise"* does not fully describe the suffering of Jesus. The literal meaning is "crushed," and the same word is used in Isaiah 3:15 where it is rendered *"beat to pieces."* The Lord Jesus Christ came to earth to take our place, to become our Substitute and make atonement for sin; but in order for Him to save us it was necessary that He be ground in the mills of God's terrible wrath! He was broken in pieces, crushed, His flesh was torn: "I gave my back to the smiters, and my cheeks to them that plucked off the hair: I hid not my face from shame and spitting" (Isa. 50:6). Christ was sore vexed. His sufferings were real and terrible. His pain was the most excruciating agony man has ever known—*and He WAS MAN*, yet God, bearing our sins in His own body even though He Himself *knew no sin!*

Isaiah wrote, *"The chastisement of our peace was upon Him,"* and in Colossians 1:20 Paul declares, "And, *having made peace* through the blood of His cross, by Him to reconcile all things unto Himself; by Him, I say, whether they be things in earth, or things in heaven." Therefore, we have peace if we have received Jesus by faith. Jesus left a bequest of peace for those who believe on Him. In John 14:27 He said to His disciples, *"Peace I leave with you, MY peace I GIVE unto you:* not as the world giveth, give I unto you. Let not your heart be troubled, neither let it be afraid."

Seven hundred years before the birth of Jesus, Isaiah prophesied, *"With His stripes we are healed."* And centuries later the Apostle Peter *pointed back to Calvary* by declaring that Christ "His own self bare our sins in His own body on the tree, that we, being dead to sins, should live unto righteousness: *BY WHOSE STRIPES YE WERE HEALED!"*

I love the words of Peter here! Jesus took my place, He paid the debt I should have paid in hell forever. He who knew no sin was made to be sin for me (II Cor. 5:21). I *do believe* the record God has given of His Son. I have put my faith and trust in the shed blood of the Lord Jesus Christ; and since I have received Him into my heart by faith, I also share in His death for *I died with HIM!* Paul declared, *"I am crucified with Christ:* nevertheless I live; yet not

I, but *Christ liveth in me:* and the life which I now live in the flesh I live by the faith of the Son of God, who loved me, and gave Himself for me" (Gal. 2:20). With Paul I can say, *"I know WHOM I have believed, and am persuaded that He is able to keep that which I have committed unto Him against that day"* (II Tim. 1:12).

Since Jesus took my place and since I have put my trust in Him, I have received the full wealth of His atonement. He took all of my sorrow, my grief, my misery, pain, and woe and nailed them to His cross. He made atonement for me—and for all who will believe in His shed blood. I have therefore received the riches *of His inclusive atonement.*

Then in verse 6 of Isaiah 53 the prophet declared, *"All we like sheep have gone astray; we have turned every one to his own way; and the Lord hath laid on Him the iniquity of us ALL."* Centuries later John the Baptist announced, "Behold the Lamb of God, which taketh away *the sin of the WORLD"* (John 1:29). In other words, "Behold the One upon whom the God of our fathers has laid *the iniquity of us ALL!"*

Men who have given their lives to the study of the Hebrew language tell us that the Hebrew word translated *"laid"* is entirely too weak in the English. It should read, *"He caused to MEET UPON HIM the iniquity of us all."* God caused *the sin of the world* to meet (to be placed) on Jesus at Calvary.

The same word is used in Amos 5:19 in connection with a bear meeting a man—and you can imagine what would happen under such circumstances, when a bear met a man in a forest. In I Kings 2:25 the same word is used in describing a murder—one man *"fell upon"* another, "that he died."

So you see, when we study this word as it is used in various places in the Old Testament we learn a little of what really happened when God allowed sin to meet Jesus on Calvary. The Lord Jesus Christ was the One upon whom the sin of the world came *crushing down* as a bear would pounce upon a man to wound and kill him. The weight of our sin and iniquity was so terrible that as a cloud it completely hid the face of God when it crushed down upon His dear Son causing Him to cry out, *"My God! My God! WHY hast thou forsaken me!"*

Yes, Jesus *was* oppressed, He was *afflicted.* He was taken "as a lamb to the slaughter"—and as sheep stand dumb before the shearers, "so He openeth not His mouth." These prophecies were penned by Isaiah seven centuries before the birth of Christ, but they were all *literally fulfilled in HIM.*

"He was taken from prison and from judgment," Isaiah declared. This, too, was fulfilled in Jesus. He was arrested and brought before the council of religious leaders among the Jews. He had done nothing wrong, no accusation could be brought against Him in truth; but false witnesses testified against Him, He was judged and condemned to death.

Isaiah then described the death and burial of the Lord Jesus Christ: *"He made His grave with the wicked"* (He died between two thieves) *"and with the rich in His death"* (He was buried in a new tomb provided by Joseph of Arimathaea). Please read Matthew 27:44, 57—61 in connection with this.

There are many other prophecies in the Old Testament which were literally fulfilled in Jesus, but we have not time and space to discuss them in this message. Christ's atonement is *the substantiation of ALL prophecy.* He literally fulfilled every word recorded in the Old Testament Scriptures concerning the coming of Messiah—"that Prophet" foretold by Moses in Deuteronomy 18:15,18.

When we read the Old Testament Scriptures and

then read the Gospels we cannot but wonder how the
Jews missed *seeing* their Scripture fulfilled in Jesus!
How could they have missed His identity? But then—
we look around us and wonder how people miss Him
today. In this great country of America the Lord Jesus
Christ is preached daily, and by means of short-wave
radio and other modern communications His Gospel
is carried to every square foot of this earth! Yet the
vast majority of men still say, "Away with Him!"
By their lives, if not in word, they reject Him and
refuse to let Him become Saviour of their souls and
Lord of their lives.

Christ's Atonement Is the Foundation of His Offices as Prophet, Priest, and Coming King

"In the beginning was the Word, and the Word
was with God, and the Word was God. . . . And the
Word was made flesh, and dwelt among us, (and we
beheld His glory, the glory as of the only begotten of
the Father,) full of grace and truth. . . . For the law
was given by Moses, but grace and truth came by
Jesus Christ. No man hath seen God at any time;
the only begotten Son, which is in the bosom of the
Father, He hath declared Him" (John 1:1, 14, 17, 18).

Almost fifteen centuries before the birth of Jesus,
God spoke through His prophet Moses, saying, "The
Lord thy God will raise up unto thee a Prophet from
the midst of thee, of thy brethren, like unto me; unto
Him ye shall hearken . . . I will raise them up a
Prophet from among their brethren, like unto thee,
and will put my words in His mouth; and He shall
speak unto them all that I shall command Him" (Deut.
18:15, 18).

In Peter's second sermon after Pentecost (recorded
in Acts chapter 3) he reminded the people of this
prophecy: "And He shall send Jesus Christ, which

before was preached unto you: whom the heaven must receive until the times of restitution of all things, which God hath spoken by the mouth of all His holy prophets since the world began. *For MOSES TRULY SAID UNTO THE FATHERS, A Prophet shall the Lord your God raise up unto you of your brethren, like unto me; Him shall ye hear in all things whatsoever He shall say unto you.* And it shall come to pass, that every soul, which will not hear that Prophet, shall be destroyed from among the people" (Acts 3:20—23).

During the Old Testament economy, God spoke to the people through His prophets, but "in these last days" He has spoken to us by "that Prophet"—none other than His own Son, the Lord Jesus Christ (Heb. 1:1,2). Moses instructed the people that from among their own brethren God would raise up a Prophet like unto himself. Then Moses thundered out, *"UNTO HIM YE SHALL HEARKEN!"*

As Prophet, Jesus declared God (John 1:18), and had the Jews *as a nation HEARD His words* they would have received Him as Messiah, instead of nailing Him to a cross. But they refused to hear Him; their refusal of His message led to their rejection of Him as their Messiah—and it is just such unbelief that has damned every soul that burns in hell today! Writing to the Hebrew Christians, Paul said, "Therefore we ought to give the more earnest heed to the things which we have heard, lest at any time we should let them slip. For if the word spoken by angels was stedfast, and every transgression and disobedience received a just recompence of reward; *how shall WE escape, IF WE NEGLECT SO GREAT SALVATION; which at the first began to be spoken BY THE LORD, and was confirmed unto us by them that heard Him;* God also bearing them witness, both with signs and wonders, and with divers miracles, and gifts of the

Holy Ghost, according to His own will?" (Heb. 2:1—4).

The "great salvation" made possible for us through Christ's atonement was first *made known* by Him. He left the Father's bosom, took a body of humiliation, and in that body He did *"what the law could not do in that it was weak through the flesh"* (Rom. 8: 1—4).

Jesus declared the love of God to all men. To Nicodemus He said, "For God so loved the world, that He gave His only begotten Son, that whosoever believeth in Him should not perish, but have everlasting life. For God sent not His Son into the world to condemn the world; but that the world through Him might be saved. He that believeth on Him is not condemned: *but he that BELIEVETH NOT is condemned already, because he hath not believed in the name of the only begotten Son of God"* (John 3:16—18).

Then Jesus explained *why* men refuse to believe and, *because* of their unbelief, are *condemned:* "And *this* is the *condemnation: THAT LIGHT IS COME INTO THE WORLD, AND MEN LOVED DARK-NESS RATHER THAN LIGHT, BECAUSE THEIR DEEDS WERE EVIL.* For every one that doeth evil hateth the light, neither cometh to the light, lest his deeds should be reproved" (John 3:19,20).

Jesus is the Light of the world (John 8:12). God sent the Light into the world—not to condemn the world, but that the world might be saved. But *when the Light appeared,* men chose the darkness and hated the Light because of their evil hearts. They rejected the Son of God and nailed Him to a cross—*and God turned out ALL the lights!* He turned out the sun, the moon, the stars—and the whole world became black as death (Matt. 27:45; Mark 15:33; Luke 23:44). The *physical* lights refused to shine while *the Light of the world* made atonement for sin on the cross!

As Prophet, Jesus clearly and specifically declared the purpose of His mission into this world. He said, "*I am the DOOR of the sheep. . . . I am come that they might have LIFE, and that they might have it more abundantly. I am the GOOD SHEPHERD:* the Good Shepherd *giveth His life for the sheep. . . . I lay down MY LIFE for the sheep. . . .* Therefore doth my Father love me, *because I lay down my life,* that I might take it again. *NO MAN TAKETH IT FROM ME, but I lay it down OF MYSELF.* I have power to lay it down, and I have power to take it again. This commandment have I received of my Father" (John 10:7—18 in part).

The heart of Christ's teaching is that He came into this world on a singular mission: *to give His life a ransom for sinners,* thus making provision for all who will come to God through Him. In the passage just quoted ·from John, He made it plain that His substitutionary work was voluntary, even though He acted under the Father's direction.

Dying was no accident with Jesus; it was *an appointment!* His death revealed His divine purpose on earth. He did everything He could possibly do and said everything He could possibly say to impress upon the minds and hearts of those to whom He ministered *the fact that He had come into the world to die:*

"And He began to teach them, that the Son of man must suffer many things, and be rejected of the elders, and of the chief priests, and scribes, and be killed, and after three days rise again" (Mark 8:31).

". . . He taught His disciples, and said unto them, The Son of man is delivered into the hands of men, and they shall kill Him; and after that He is killed, He shall rise the third day" (Mark 9:31).

". . . He took again the twelve, and began to tell them what things should happen unto Him, saying, Behold, we go up to Jerusalem; and the Son of man shall be delivered unto the chief priests, and unto the scribes; and they shall condemn Him to death, and shall deliver Him to the Gentiles: and they shall mock Him, and shall scourge Him, and shall spit upon Him, and shall kill Him: and the third day He shall rise again" (Mark 10:32b—34).

Day by day—especially in the latter months of His ministry—Jesus taught His disciples of His coming death on the cross; but in spite of all that He said and did, they failed to understand His teaching.

In my studies of the life of Christ as given in the four Gospels, it seems to me that *only one person* (Mary of Bethany) understood *to some extent* the Lord's mission on earth—that is, to die for sinners. In John 12:1—11 we are told that six days before the Passover, Jesus came to Bethany where He attended a supper. "And Martha served: but Lazarus was one of them that sat at the table with Him." Many of the Jews attended the supper—"not for Jesus' sake only," but because they wanted to see Lazarus whom He had raised from the dead only a short time before.

In verse 3 we read, *"Then took MARY a pound of ointment of spikenard, VERY COSTLY, and anointed the feet of Jesus, and wiped His feet with her hair:* and the house was filled with the odour of the ointment."

Judas Iscariot was there, along with others of the disciple band, and he spoke up in criticism of Mary's extravagance. He asked, "Why was not this ointment *sold* for three hundred pence, and given to the poor? This he said, NOT that he cared for the poor; but because he was a thief, and had the bag, and bare what was put therein."

But now hear the Lord's reply to the objection: He said, *"Let her alone! AGAINST THE DAY OF MY BURYING HATH SHE KEPT THIS!"* (v. 7).

When the time came for Jesus to discuss the *deep*

purpose of His visit to this earth, it was necessary for Him to call some of *heaven's* inhabitants in order to be fully understood in what He said concerning His death on the cross—not because of *His inability,* but because of the weakness and lack of faith in those to whom He ministered:

"It came to pass about an eight days after these sayings, He took Peter and John and James, and went up into a mountain to pray. And as He prayed, the fashion of His countenance was altered, and His raiment was white and glistering. *And, behold, there talked with Him two men, which were Moses and Elias: who appeared in glory, AND SPAKE OF HIS DECEASE* (death) *WHICH HE SHOULD ACCOMPLISH AT JERUSALEM"* (Luke 9:28—31).

Christ Our Great High Priest

"For it is evident that our Lord sprang out of Juda; of which tribe Moses spake nothing concerning priesthood. . . . For if He were on earth, He should not be a priest, seeing that there are priests that offer gifts according to the law" (Heb. 7:14; 8:4).

It is extremely important that we understand the difference between Christ's atonement and His priesthood. He did not enter into His office as our great High Priest until after He died and rose again. His death on the cross was *a priestly ACT,* but on the cross He did not act *AS Priest.* On the *cross* He acted as *an offerer*—the Lamb of God offering Himself without spot to God. During His *earthly* ministry He had no *divine right* to act as Priest because He was not of the tribe of *Levi* and He was not of *the house of Aaron.* The Scripture plainly tells us that *Christ* was of the tribe of *Judah.*

We must also keep in mind the fact that Christ's *atonement* speaks of *death;* but His priesthood is a ministry of *life*.

His atonement is *finished* (John 19:30); His priesthood is *continuous:* The Aaronic priests "truly were
many priests, because they were not suffered to continue by reason of death: *but THIS MAN* (Christ),
*because He continueth ever, hath an unchangeable
priesthood.* Wherefore He is able also to save them
to the uttermost that come unto God by Him, seeing
He ever liveth to make intercession for them" (Heb.
7:23—25).

Christ's *atonement* was accomplished here on *earth*
—"as Moses lifted up the serpent in the wilderness,"
Jesus was lifted up on Calvary; His *priesthood* is carried on in heaven, where He now sits at the right hand
of God the Father (Heb. 1:1—3).

His atonement was *for the sinner;* His unending
priesthood is for *believers.*

In the Aaronic priesthood, all priests entered the
holy place with the blood of a turtle dove, a lamb, or
a bullock; but it was *"BY HIS OWN BLOOD"* that
Jesus entered into the presence of the Father to exercise His ministry as *our* great High Priest: *"Neither
by the blood of goats and calves, but by HIS OWN
blood (Jesus) entered in once into the holy place, having obtained eternal redemption for us"* (Heb. 9:12).

Jesus was "holy, harmless, undefiled, separate from
sinners, and made higher than the heavens" (Heb. 7:26)
and it was by means of "His own blood" that He had
the right to enter into the presence of God, to appear
in His presence as our great High Priest. He did not
enter into the holy of holies by virtue of His great love
for sinners, nor by virtue of His great grace. The
priestly office He now occupies at the right hand of
God is based wholly on His death on the cross, by
which we have the atonement.

When Jesus ascended, the Father received Him
and gave Him the highest seat of heaven. This is

evidence that His earthly ministry was *accepted* by
God the Father, and the fact that He *sat down* on
the right hand of God indicates that His redemptive
work is completed.

The fact that Jesus sat down on His *Father's* throne
rather than on His own reveals a truth that should
be emphasized in this day and hour, a truth consistent-
ly taught in the Scriptures—to wit, *that Jesus did not
set up a kingdom on earth at His first advent.* He
did not come to set up a kingdom at that time, but
now He is *"expecting"* until the time when His kingdom *shall* come on earth, when the divine will of God
shall be done "on earth as it is in heaven." The day
will come when the kingdoms of this world will become the kingdoms of our Lord Jesus Christ, and He
will reign forever and ever:

"And the seventh angel sounded; and there were
great voices in heaven, saying, *The kingdoms of this
world are become the kingdoms of our Lord, and of
His Christ; AND HE SHALL REIGN FOR EVER
AND EVER"* (Rev. 11:15).

The day will come when God will give Jesus "the
heathen" for His inheritance and "the uttermost parts
of the earth" for His possession (Psalm 2:8). But the
Scriptures clearly teach that Jesus is not now establish-
ing that kingdom rule on earth. (Please study Matthew 25:31—46.)

At this present time Christ is calling out both
Jews and Gentiles, *a heavenly people* who make up
the New Testament Church; and when the Church
(the body of Christ) is completed, He will appear in
the clouds in the air and call all believers up to meet
Him:

"For the Lord Himself shall descend from heaven
with a shout, with the voice of the archangel, and
with the trump of God: and the dead in Christ shall
rise first: Then we which are alive and remain shall

be caught up together with them in the clouds, to
meet the Lord in the air: and so shall we ever be
with the Lord. Wherefore comfort one another with
these words" (I Thess. 4:16—18). Believers will then
be rewarded for their stewardship (I Cor. 3:12—15;
II Cor. 5:10).

During this time, the Antichrist will reign on earth;
and at the close of His reign (which will last approximately seven years) Jesus will return *with His Church.*
He will set up the tabernacle of David, He will sit
on the throne of David from whence He will reign
over the kingdom of heaven which will be here on
earth.

Before the council at Jerusalem, James testified,
"Men and brethren, hearken unto me: Simeon hath
declared how God at the first did visit the Gentiles,
to take out of them a people for His name. And to
this agree the words of the prophets; as it is written,
After this I will return, and will build again the tabernacle of David, which is fallen down; and I will
build again the ruins thereof, and I will set it up:
that the residue of men might seek after the Lord, and
all the Gentiles, upon whom my name is called, saith
the Lord, who doeth all these things. Known unto
God are all His works from the beginning of the
world" (Acts 15:13—18).

Jesus is a King-Priest "after the order of Melchisedec" (Heb. 5:10; 7:1); but He is now serving as *High
Priest,* not as King of kings. He is now seated at the
right hand of God, "head over all things *to the Church,
which is His body,* the fulness of Him that filleth all
in all" (Eph. 1:22,23). However, when He comes again
He will reign as King of kings and Lord of lords.

As our great High Priest, Jesus ever lives to make
intercession for His own. In John chapter 17 we read
His prayer of intercession (for *believers,* not for unbelievers). In verse 9 we read, *"I pray for them: I*

*pray NOT for the world, but FOR THEM WHICH
THOU HAST GIVEN ME; for they are thine."* (Please
study the entire seventeenth chapter of John's Gospel.)

Christ's ministry of intercession began just before
He left the earth and will continue as long as believers are left in this world. As our Intercessor and
Advocate His work now has to do with our weaknesses, our immaturity as saints. He was *"touched with
the feeling of our infirmities,"* He was *"in all points
tempted like as we are, yet without sin"* (Heb. 4:15).
"Wherefore in all things it behoved Him to be made
like unto His brethren, *that He might be a merciful
and faithful High Priest* in things pertaining to God,
to make reconciliation for the sins of the people. *For
in that He Himself hath suffered being tempted, He
is able to succour them that are tempted"* (Heb. 2:
17,18).

Christ knows our weaknesses, He knows our lim-
itations, He knows that we are made of dust; but He
also knows the power and the strategy of our enemy,
the devil, and as our great High Priest He tenderly
watches over us and listens to our petitions. In Luke
22:31,32 He said to Peter, "Simon, Simon, behold,
Satan hath desired to have you, that he may sift you
as wheat: *BUT I HAVE PRAYED FOR THEE, that
thy faith fail not:* and when thou art converted,
strengthen thy brethren." Jesus cared for Peter, and
He will do the same for His children today.

Under the Old Testament economy the ministry
of the high priest came to an end because of death;
but Christ *"continueth ever."* Because He is *alive
forevermore* He "hath an *unchangeable* priesthood."
Therefore, "He is able also to save them to the uttermost that come unto God by Him, seeing He ever
liveth to make intercession for them" (Heb. 7:23—25).

We who know the Lord Jesus Christ can say with
Paul, "I know WHOM I have believed, and am per-

suaded that He is able to keep that which I have committed unto Him against that day" (II Tim. 1:12). We
can also say with David, "The Lord is my Shepherd;
I shall not want. He maketh me to lie down in green
pastures: He leadeth me beside the still waters. He
restoreth my soul: He leadeth me in the paths of
righteousness *for His name's sake*" (Psalm 23:1–3).

The first epistle of John is God's love-letter to His
"little children," that our joy "may be FULL," and
that we may enjoy our spiritual birthright (I John 1:4).
John also declared, under inspiration, "If we confess
our sins, He is faithful and just to forgive us our sins,
and to cleanse us from all unrighteousness" (I John
1:9).

Even at our very best, we who are believers are
weak and unworthy, we are filled with faults, and we
come short of the glory of God; but notice that John
tells us that *GOD is faithful*, even when we fail Him.
Our great High Priest, the Lord Jesus Christ, assures
us of victory over the world, the flesh, and the devil.
He is our Advocate: I John 2:1,2 declares, "My little
children, these things write I unto you, that ye sin
not. And *if* any man sin, *we have an Advocate with
the Father, JESUS CHRIST THE RIGHTEOUS:* And
He is the propitiation for our sins: and not for our's
only, but also for the sins of the whole world."

An advocate is one who pleads the cause of another
in court, and Christ *our* Advocate is now appearing
in heaven for His own: "For Christ is not entered
into the holy places made with hands, which are the
figures of the true; but *into heaven itself, now to appear in the presence of God FOR US*" (Heb. 9:24).

Some people say that doctrine such as this gives
license to sin and makes it *easy* for Christians to sin;
but the truth is quite to the contrary. The Scriptures
just quoted warn us *NOT to sin,* and born again,
blood-washed believers do not *want* to sin. We "walk

not after the flesh" because the Holy Spirit abides within, and He leads us into paths of right living:

"Ye are not in the flesh, but in the Spirit, if so be that the Spirit of God dwell in you. *Now if any man have NOT the Spirit of Christ, he is none of His. . . . For as many as are led by the Spirit of God, they are the sons of God. . . .* The Spirit itself beareth witness with our spirit, that we are the children of God" (Rom. 8:9, 14, 16).

Jesus is our High Priest, our Advocate, our Intercessor; and this divine fact gives the born again believer unshakeable assurance. We might well ask, *"WHO IS he that condemneth? It is CHRIST that died,* yea rather, that is risen again, who is even at the right hand of God, *who also maketh INTERCESSION for us"* (Rom. 8:34).

Christ the Coming King

"And the angel said unto her, Fear not, Mary: for thou hast found favour with God. And, behold, thou shalt conceive in thy womb, and bring forth a Son, and shalt call His name JESUS. He shall be great, and shall be called the Son of the Highest: and the Lord God shall give unto Him the throne of His father David: and He shall reign over the house of Jacob for ever; and of His kingdom there shall be no end" (Luke 1:30—33).

The throne of David is a historical fact just as surely as the throne of Caesar is a historical fact. Jesus has not yet occupied the throne of David, but one day *He will* sit on David's throne. When His priestly work is finished He will descend into the clouds and will call the Church up to meet Him in the air (I Thess. 4:13—18). He will reward believers for their faithful stewardship, and the marriage of the Lamb will take place:

"And I heard as it were the voice of a great multitude, and as the voice of many waters, and as the voice of mighty thunderings, saying, Alleluia: for the Lord God omnipotent reigneth. Let us be glad and rejoice, and give honour to Him: for the marriage of the Lamb is come, and His wife hath made herself ready. And to her was granted that she should be arrayed in fine linen, clean and white: for the fine linen is the righteousness of saints. And he saith unto me, Write, Blessed are they which are called unto the marriage supper of the Lamb. And He saith unto me, These are the true sayings of God" (Rev. 19:6—9).

Then, along with His Church, Christ will return to earth. We find a vivid description of this event in Revelation 19:11—16:

"And I saw heaven opened, and behold a white horse; and He that sat upon him was called Faithful and True, and in righteousness He doth judge and make war. His eyes were as a flame of fire, and on His head were many crowns; and He had a name written, that no man knew, but He Himself. And He was clothed with a vesture dipped in blood: and His name is called The Word of God. And the armies which were in heaven followed Him upon white horses, clothed in fine linen, white and clean. And out of His mouth goeth a sharp sword, that with it He should smite the nations: and He shall rule them with a rod of iron: and He treadeth the winepress of the fierceness and wrath of Almighty God.

"And He hath on His vesture and on His thigh a name written, KING OF KINGS, AND LORD OF LORDS!"

It is when Jesus returns to the earth with His Church that He will "sit upon the throne of His glory" and judge the nations (Matt. 25:31—46). After this, the Millennial kingdom will run its course for one thousand glorious years.

When Jesus returns to earth with His Church He will destroy the armies of Antichrist in the battle of Armageddon (Rev. 19:17—19).

The beast and the false prophet will be put into the lake of fire (Rev. 19:20).

Satan will be bound and put into the bottomless pit for one thousand years (Rev. 20:1—3).

During this thousand years there will be peace on earth, good will toward men; but at the end of the Millennium, Satan will be loosed for a little season (Rev. 20:3).

Millions of people will be born on earth *during* the Millennium, and those people will not have known temptation because Satan was not free to tempt them. After his release from the pit he will put them to the test. Those who follow him will make up the armies of *Gog;* those who *refuse* to follow him will go into the eternal kingdom. (Please read Revelation 20:7—9.)

Then at the consummation of all things the heavens will pass away with a great noise and the earth will melt with fervent heat. The heavens and the earth will be renovated by fire, and the new heaven and the new earth will appear—along with the Pearly White City as described in Revelation chapter 21. Jesus will then reign as King of kings and Lord of lords.

The Scriptures clearly declare that the purpose of God the Father is to set up a kingdom on earth over which His Son shall reign forever. This promise was given to David through Nathan the prophet: "And thine house and thy kingdom shall be established for ever before thee: thy throne shall be established for ever" (II Sam. 7:16).

God afterward confirmed this promise with an oath, saying, "I have made a covenant with my chosen. I have sworn unto David my servant, Thy seed will I establish for ever, and build up thy throne to all generations. . . . Once have I sworn by my holiness that I will not lie unto David. His seed shall endure for ever, and his throne as the sun before me. It shall be established for ever as the moon, and as a faithful witness in heaven" (Psalm 89:3, 4, 35—37).

This unconditional covenant was reaffirmed to Israel through Jeremiah, "the weeping prophet" (Jer. 33:17—26).

The "Son" which God promised David would reign forever was none other than the Lord Jesus Christ, the Son of God, but God's promise to David did not mean that there would be *an unbroken line of successors* to the throne. This is clear from the fact that after Solomon's reign the kingdom was divided; and in B. C. 587 the last king of Judah was carried captive into Babylon. The promise pointed to *a future King* of David's seed, One who would be raised up to sit on the throne of David. Jeremiah 23:5,6 speaks of this King:

"Behold, the days come, saith the Lord, that I will raise unto David a righteous Branch, and a King shall reign and prosper, and shall execute judgment and justice in the earth. In His days Judah shall be saved, and Israel shall dwell safely: and this is His name whereby He shall be called, THE LORD OUR RIGHTEOUSNESS."

Now compare Jeremiah's prophecy with Isaiah 11: 1,2: "And there shall come forth a rod out of the stem of Jesse, and a Branch shall grow out of his roots: *and the Spirit of the Lord shall rest upon Him, the spirit of wisdom and understanding, the spirit of counsel and might, the spirit of knowledge and of the fear of the Lord."*

Now compare these two prophecies with Luke 2:40: *"And the child grew, and waxed strong in spirit, filled with wisdom: and the grace of God was upon Him."*

Comparing the passage from Jeremiah, the passage from Isaiah, and the passage from Luke, we have no difficulty in identifying the One of whom they spoke.

The Messiah who was to be King and occupy David's throne would not only be of *the lineage of David,* but He was also to be *of divine heritage:* "Therefore the Lord Himself shall give you a sign: Behold, a virgin shall conceive, and bear a Son, and shall call His name Immanuel" (Isa. 7:14).

Later Isaiah declared (as though it had already happened), "For unto us a child is born, unto us a Son is given: and the government shall be upon His shoulder: and His name shall be called Wonderful, Counsellor, The mighty God, The everlasting Father, The Prince of Peace. Of the increase of His government and peace there shall be no end, upon the throne of David, and upon His kingdom, to order it, and to establish it with judgment and with justice from henceforth even for ever. The zeal of the Lord of hosts will perform this" (Isa. 9:6,7).

In Luke 1:26–33 we find the key that unlocks this prophecy: "And in the sixth month the angel Gabriel was sent from God unto a city of Galilee, named Nazareth, to a virgin espoused to a man whose name was Joseph, of the house of David; and the virgin's name was Mary. And the angel came in unto her, and said, Hail, thou that art highly favoured, the Lord is with thee: blessed art thou among women.

"And when she saw him, she was troubled at his saying, and cast in her mind what manner of salutation this should be. And the angel said unto her, Fear not, Mary: for thou hast found favour with God. And, behold, thou shalt conceive in thy womb, and bring forth a Son, and shalt call His name JESUS. He shall be great, and shall be called the Son of the Highest: and the Lord God shall give unto Him the throne of His father David: and He shall reign over the house of Jacob for ever; and of His kingdom there shall be no end."

Matthew, too, wrote under inspiration as the Spirit directed: "Behold, a virgin shall be with child, and shall bring forth a Son, and they shall call His name Emmanuel, which being interpreted is, God with us" (Matt. 1:23).

From these Scriptures we clearly see that Jesus of Nazareth, born of the Virgin Mary, was the promised Son of David. He will one day reign from the throne of David, but His reign as King of kings is yet future. He came the first time as a babe in a manger, the Lamb of God. He was rejected and crucified, but death could not hold Him. He arose from the dead, ascended back to the Father, and now sits at God's right hand until the time when He will come to call His Church to meet Him in the air. Then when He returns to earth with His Church He will sit on the throne of David and will reign in righteousness. It is then that men will "beat their swords into plowshares, and their spears into pruninghooks" (Isa. 2:4).

Under the Millennial reign of Christ this earth will be one great Paradise for one thousand glorious years: "The wolf also shall dwell with the lamb, and the leopard shall lie down with the kid; and the calf and the young lion and the fatling together; and a little child shall lead them. And the cow and the bear shall feed; their young ones shall lie down together: and the lion shall eat straw like the ox. And the sucking child shall play on the hole of the asp, and the weaned child shall put his hand on the cockatrice' den. They shall not hurt nor destroy in all my holy mountain: for the earth shall be full of the knowledge of the Lord, as the waters cover the sea" (Isa. 11:6—9).

Revelation, the last book in our Bible, gives the account of coming glory and righteous judgment. In Revelation we read more about the slain Lamb than in any other book *in* the Bible. In the New Testament, *the Lamb* is mentioned thirty-two times—twenty-eight of these in Revelation.

Chapter 4 of the book of Revelation opens with the description of the Lamb on the throne, and the Lamb on the throne bears the marks of death. Revelation also describes a multitude washed in *the blood* of the Lamb, and speaks of the Lamb slain from the foundation of the world. It tells of a great company of overcomers who won the victory through the blood of the Lamb, and ends by declaring that the Lamb is the light of the New Jerusalem, the Pearly White City. The Lamb is represented as sovereign, the object of all praise in heaven and in earth. He is praised as a Lamb which had been sacrificed, but is now living and victorious over all enemies. He is alive forevermore. It is on the ground of the death of the Lamb and of the redemption made possible by His death that all praise, honor, glory, and worship are ascribed to Him.

Why does Revelation speak so often of the Lamb? What is the Holy Spirit declaring to us? I believe the answer is this:

Everything Christ did and said while He was here on earth pointed to His death on the cross. He knew *why* He came into the world and He came with His eyes fixed on Calvary. "Every good gift and every perfect gift is from above, and cometh down from the Father of lights . . ." (James 1:17), but God's gifts proceed from the cross. If the cross of Jesus had never been, God could never have bestowed one good gift upon us because *all have sinned* and sin does not bring good gifts: *it brings death and everlasting damnation.*

Therefore, all good things given us of God are given *because of Calvary,* and all that Christ is now doing (for both *saints* and *sinners*) is *founded* on the cross. The cross is the foundation of salvation, and had there *been* no cross we would not have a great High Priest—

Mediator and Advocate—seated at the right hand of
God.   All that Christ *will do* as King of kings and
Lord of lords is *secured* by the cross through His atoning sacrifice—the shedding of His blood—by which we
have the atonement.   The cross guarantees His being
crowned King of kings and Lord of lords.   His passion
was the price He paid for the glory that lies ahead
throughout endless eternity!

Christ's Atonement Is the Sum
of All Pure Bible Teaching

It has been previously pointed out that the Gospel
of John is known as *the salvation Gospel:*
"And many other signs truly did Jesus in the presence of His disciples, which are not written in this
book: *But these are written, THAT YE MIGHT BE-
LIEVE THAT JESUS IS THE CHRIST, THE SON
OF GOD; and that believing ye might have life
through His name"* (John 20:30,31).
I would like for us to see several verses in John's
Gospel which prove that Christ in His atonement is
the sum of all pure Bible teaching.   This fact is represented in many different ways:
Jesus is *the Lamb of God* who came to take away
the sin of the world (John 1:29).
He is *the ladder from earth to heaven:*   "Hereafter
ye shall see heaven open, and the angels of God as-
cending and descending upon the Son of man" (John
1:51).
He is *the destroyed temple*—crucified by the hands
of wicked men, buried in a garden tomb, but raised
up *a LIVING temple which none can destroy.*   To the
Jews Jesus said, *"Destroy this temple, and in three
days I will raise it up. . . .* But He spake of the temple of His body" (John 2:19, 21).
He is the *uplifted One* who was represented by

the serpent of brass which was lifted up in the wilderness: "As Moses lifted up the serpent in the wilderness, even so must the Son of man be lifted up" (John 3:14).

He is *the Living Bread:* "I am the living bread which came down from heaven: if any man eat of this bread, he shall live for ever: *and the bread that I will give is my flesh, which I will give for the life of the world.* The Jews therefore strove among themselves, saying, How can this Man give us His flesh to eat? Then Jesus said unto them, Verily, verily, I say unto you, *Except ye eat the flesh of the Son of man, and drink His blood, ye have no life in you"* (John 6:51—53).

Jesus is *the DOOR* to heaven, and all who enter there must enter *by* the Door: "He that entereth not by the door into the sheepfold, but climbeth up some other way, the same is a thief and a robber. . . . The thief cometh not, but for to steal, and to kill, and to destroy: I am come that they might have life, and that they might have it more abundantly" (John 10: 1, 10).

He is *the Good Shepherd* who laid down His life for the sheep: "I am the Good Shepherd: the Good Shepherd giveth His life for the sheep. . . . And I give unto them eternal life; and they shall never perish, neither shall any man pluck them out of my hand" (John 10:11, 28).

He is *the corn of wheat* that fell into the ground and died that it might bring forth much fruit: "*EXCEPT a corn of wheat fall into the ground and die, it abideth alone:* but if it die, it bringeth forth much fruit" (John 12:24).

He came to the hour of hours—the darkest hour known to God or man—and in that hour He bore our sorrows, our iniquities, our sins. He faced a night of anguish such as mortal has never faced. He entered into our night that we might know His light and life.

They nailed Him to the cross, they pierced His hands and His feet; and the pierced Christ is the One of whom the Spirit spoke (in type) in the Old Testament economy.

On that dark night in Egypt when God slew the firstborn in every Egyptian home, the paschal lamb which protected the homes of Israel and the pierced Lamb of God who was nailed to the cross of Calvary are one and the same. The paschal lamb on that night of judgment in Egypt was *a type* of the Lamb of God who came to take away the sin of the world; and from the cross Jesus declared, *"It is finished!"* Yes, Christ in His atonement is the sum of all true Bible teaching.

Christ in His Atonement Is the Unchanging Essence of All True Preaching

"And daily in the temple, and in every house, they ceased not to teach and preach Jesus Christ" (Acts 5:42).

*"*And we declare unto you glad tidings, how that the promise which was made unto the fathers, God hath fulfilled the same unto us their children, in that He hath raised up Jesus again; as it is also written in the second Psalm, Thou art my Son, this day have I begotten thee" (Acts 13:32,33).

The word "preach" occurs more than one hundred times in the New Testament and means *"to proclaim."* The *Greek* word translated "preach" means *"to bear a message or bring tidings."* God calls ministers to preach the Word, to evangelize, to proclaim glad tidings, to tell out the good news that Jesus died for our sins, that He was buried and rose again "according to the Scriptures," and through faith in His finished work we have salvation.

The preachers in the book of Acts pointed people to *Christ on the throne* in resurrection power—but they also pointed them to *Christ on the cross* in substitutionary death. He died—but He is *alive to die no more!* He ever lives to make intercession for us. Therefore Christ's atonement is the substance of all pure Gospel preaching.

Christ in His atonement is the heart of Christianity. Paul said, "I determined not to know any thing among you, save Jesus Christ, and Him crucified" (I Cor. 2:2). Paul preached—*NOT the crucifixion, but CHRIST (THE PERSON) crucified,* through which we have the atonement.

True ministers of the Gospel do not dwell upon "Christ crucified" as an event in centuries behind us, but rather that He was crucified, buried, is risen, ascended, and is now seated at the right hand of God the Father to dispense the blessings which He purchased with His own blood on the cross. Therefore we go to Jesus the Son of God—not on the cross, but seated in the heavenly sanctuary at the right hand of the Majesty, and from Him we receive the gifts of His marvelous grace.

Christ bestows pardon on the sinner when the sinner believes in His shed blood through which the atonement is secured. *All the blessings of the New Testament are ours* because of His shed blood, and He bestows His blessings when we exercise faith in His finished work. This is the only message that brings redemption to the soul of a poor, lost sinner.

Sermon Subjects in Acts

"And daily in the temple, and in every house, they ceased not to teach and preach Jesus Christ" (Acts 5:42).

"Therefore they that were scattered abroad went

every where preaching the Word. . . . When they believed Philip preaching the things concerning the kingdom of God, and the name of Jesus Christ, they were
baptized, both men and women" (Acts 8:4,12).

"Then Philip opened his mouth, and began at the
same Scripture, and preached unto him Jesus" (Acts
8:35).

"The word which God sent unto the children of Israel, preaching peace by Jesus Christ: (He is Lord of
all)" (Acts 10:36).

"And some of them were men of Cyprus and Cy-
rene, which, when they were come to Antioch, spake
unto the Grecians, preaching the Lord Jesus" (Acts
11:20).

(Please read also Acts 14:7,15,21; 15:35; 16:10; and
17:18.)

No wonder the Apostle Paul said to the believers
in Rome, *"I am not ashamed of the Gospel of Christ:
for it is the power of God unto salvation to every one
that believeth;* to the Jew first, and also to the Greek.
For therein is the righteousness of God revealed from
faith to faith: as it is written, The just shall live by
faith" (Rom. 1:16,17).

As we study these passages, we notice that the
message in each of them concerns a *Person,* an *event*
in that Person's life, and the *purpose* of the Person
and the event. We read, *"They ceased not to teach
and preach JESUS . . . They preached Jesus Christ...
They preached unto him JESUS . . . Preaching peace
by JESUS . . . Preaching the Lord Jesus."*

So it is in the book of Acts—and so it should be
in all the messages of every minister of the Gospel.
The preachers in Acts proclaimed a message about
THE Person—the Lord Jesus Christ. The *event* in
His life about which they preached was *His crucifixion*
—He was nailed to a cross and He died there for the
remission of sin. His *purpose* was to die for the sins

of the world—He died that we might live. In a body of humiliation, a body like unto sinful flesh, He did what the law could not do because of the weakness of the flesh, in order that God could bless man through the finished work and the shed blood of God's Son.

"And now abideth faith, hope, charity (love), these three; but the greatest of these is love" (I Cor. 13:13).

FAITH looks back to the cross and sees the Lamb of God as He died there, bearing our sins in His own body.

LOVE looks up to the throne where the Man Christ Jesus sits at the right hand of God. And as we look to the heavenly throne we say, *"We love HIM because He first loved US* and gave Himself for us."

HOPE looks beyond all else, to the glory we will share with Jesus: "The Spirit Himself beareth witness with our spirit, that we are *the children of God:* and if children, then *heirs;* heirs of God, and *joint-heirs with Christ;* if so be that we suffer with Him, that we may be also *glorified together.* For I reckon that *the sufferings of this present time* are not worthy to be compared with *the glory which shall be revealed in us"* (Rom. 8:16—18).

There are many verses in the Word of God that could be used here to illustrate how faith, hope, and love centralize in (and proceed from) the cross, but we will look at only three such passages:

In Romans 3:25 Paul speaks of "Christ Jesus, whom God hath set forth to be a propitiation through faith in His blood, to declare His righteousness for the remission of sins that are past, through the forbearance of God."

John the Beloved wrote, *"We love HIM, because He first loved US"* (I John 4:19).

Then in Titus 2:13, 14, the Apostle Paul declares that we should be "looking for that blessed hope, and the glorious appearing of the great God and our Saviour Jesus Christ; who gave Himself for us, that He might redeem us from all iniquity, and purify unto Himself a peculiar people, zealous of good works."

Christ's Atonement — Faith's Foundation

"Being justified freely by His grace through the redemption that is in Christ Jesus: whom God hath set forth to be a propitiation through faith in His blood, to declare His righteousness for the remission of sins that are past, through the forbearance of God" (Rom. 3:24,25).

"Therefore being justified by faith, we have peace with God through our Lord Jesus Christ" (Rom. 5:1).

Under the law, the mercy seat was the place where atonement was made. The blood was sprinkled—or offered—on the mercy seat. God the Father set forth Jesus the Son to be our propitiation, our mercy seat, the price of expiation. He paid that price through His blood, making possible our redemption through faith in the Expiator—Christ Jesus *crucified.* The *object* of saving faith is the Lord Jesus Christ—not rules, regulations, ceremonies, ordinances. The *foundation* of saving faith is Christ's atonement, but the only possible way for man to know the truth about His atonement is through the Word of God. Therefore the *ground* of saving faith is Christ in the assurance of His unalterable, infallible, eternal Word:

"So then faith cometh by hearing, and hearing by the Word of God" (Rom. 10:17).

Jesus said, "He that heareth *my Word,* and believeth on Him that sent me, hath everlasting life, and shall not come into condemnation; but is passed from death unto life" (John 5:24).

Christ is the author and the finisher of our faith (Heb. 12:2), the beginning and the ending of the faith that brings salvation; but faith *increases* as we feed on the Word—and the only possible way for faith *to* increase is for the believer to appropriate and assimilate the Word of God. Obedience to God is proof that we have exercised faith in Christ, and if we are obedient Christians we will be good stewards, efficient workers in the vineyard of our Lord. "For as the body without the spirit is dead, so faith *without works* is dead also" (James 2:26).

Christ's Atonement Is the Fountain of All Spiritual Blessings

"Therefore being justified by faith, we have peace with God through our Lord Jesus Christ: By whom also we have access by faith into this grace wherein we stand, and rejoice in hope of the glory of God.

"And not only so, but we glory in tribulations also: knowing that tribulation worketh patience; and patience, experience; and experience, hope: and hope maketh not ashamed; because the love of God is shed abroad in our hearts by the Holy Ghost which is given unto us.

"For when we were yet without strength, in due time Christ died for the ungodly. For scarcely for a righteous man will one die: yet peradventure for a good man some would even dare to die. *But God commendeth HIS love toward US, in that, while we were yet sinners, CHRIST DIED FOR US.*

"Much more then, being now justified by His blood, we shall be saved from wrath through Him. For if, when we were enemies, we were reconciled to God by the death of His Son, much more, being reconciled, we shall be saved by His life. And not only so, but *we also joy in God through our Lord Jesus Christ, by whom we have now received the atonement*" (Rom. 5:1—11).

We who are "justified by faith . . . have peace with

God through our Lord Jesus Christ." The only possible way for anyone to be at peace with God is through the finished work of Jesus. He is the author and finisher of faith, therefore He, in His atonement, is the fountain from which the blessing of peace comes. Peace with God is ours when we exercise faith in the shed blood of the Lord Jesus Christ. *HE is the Peacemaker!*

"*By whom* (the Greek reads *through* whom) *we have access by faith INTO this grace wherein we stand.*" Remember—we are studying the *inclusiveness* of Christ's atonement. It is wonderful to know that in this marvelous Dispensation of Grace we are not only *saved* by God's grace, but *His love* fills our hearts, we have *peace WITH God* and *access TO God* through our Mediator, the Lord Jesus Christ. It is no longer necessary to meet God in a certain place on a certain day, nor do we need another man (such as the Old Testament priest) to represent us before God. *We ourselves* commune with the heavenly Father, for every believer is a royal priest (I Pet. 2:9). But we *have* access to God *only through the Lord Jesus Christ.*

Now let us move to verse 9 in our quoted passage: "*Much MORE . . . .*" Paul, under inspiration, uses these two words often in his epistles. We are *justified by faith,* we have *peace with God,* we *commune* with God, and we *rejoice in hope*—all because of Christ's atonement; but there is "*much more*": Being "justified by His blood, we shall be *SAVED FROM WRATH through Him.*"

The wrath of God abides on the unbeliever (John 3:36), and he is "*condemned already,* because he hath not believed in the name of the only begotten Son of God" (John 3:18). But Jesus took the sinner's place, He was made to be sin for us (II Cor. 5:21), He was made a curse for us (Gal. 3:13), He was condemned for us and He "bare our sins in His own body on the tree, that we, being dead to sins, should live unto righteousness . . ." (I Pet. 2:24). Therefore, by means of Him who was condemned for us and who paid our sin-debt on Calvary, believers stand where judgment can never reach us!

It is true that all believers will be judged *according to stewardship,* and we will be *rewarded* according to our *faithfulness* in stewardship; but we will not be judged as to whether we are condemned or saved. For the person who exercises faith in Christ's atonement, *condemnation is removed forever!* God's Word declares, "There is therefore *NOW no condemnation to them which are IN CHRIST JESUS . . .*" (Rom. 8:1). He who has believed on Jesus "SHALL NOT come into condemnation; but IS PASSED from death unto life" (John 5:24).

Thank God for *"much more"!* We are justified, we possess the love of God, we have peace with God, we have access to God, and we hope in God. And "much more"—*we will never suffer the wrath of God* because Jesus suffered that wrath in our stead. So believing on Him and trusting in His shed blood and finished work, we are IN Christ, Christ is in US, and we are "hid with Christ in God" (Rom. 8:1; Col. 1:27; 3:3).

Verse 10 of our text declares still another blessing which is ours through Christ's atonement: "For if, when we were enemies, we were *reconciled to God by the death of His Son, MUCH MORE, being reconciled, we shall be saved BY HIS LIFE.*"

To be *reconciled* means that one's feelings have changed toward another. Jesus did not die on the cross *to reconcile GOD to US,* but to reconcile *us* to *GOD.* This is made clear in II Corinthians 5:19—*"God was in Christ, reconciling the world UNTO HIMSELF."*

Through His death on the cross, Christ brings reconciliation between the sinner and God, because when the sinner *believes*, he changes his mind about God, he turns "face about," and goes in the opposite direction. Thus through faith in the finished work of Jesus he is reconciled to God.

Through the disobedience of Adam, sin moved upon all men. When Adam sinned, the perfect harmony, fellowship, and communion between God and man was broken, and enmity replaced unity. But *in Christ* God's love conquered that enmity and brought about reconciliation to all who will believe in the shed blood and finished work of God's beloved Son.

Sin brings sorrow. *Salvation* brings "joy unspeakable and full of glory" (I Pet. 1:8). But joy—like reconciliation, salvation, and peace with God—comes only through Christ's atonement—". . . *we also JOY IN GOD through our Lord Jesus Christ, BY WHOM we have now received the atonement*" (Rom. 5:11).

Isaiah declared that the Lamb of God would be *"a Man of sorrows, and acquainted with grief"* (Isa. 53:3). He *was* a Man of sorrows and He *did know* grief because He bore *our* sorrows and *our* griefs on Calvary. And only through faith in His finished work can we be delivered from sorrow and the blackness of eternal separation from God.

In Romans 5:17 we read, "For if by *one man's offence* (the first Adam) *death reigned by one; MUCH MORE* they which receive abundance of grace and of the gift of righteousness *shall reign in life by One, JESUS CHRIST* (the last Adam)."

Natural life is union of spirit and body, and when the spirit departs the body, that body ceases to function—in other words, "the body without the spirit is dead" (James 2:26). The same is true in the spiritual life. Eternal life is the union of the Lord Jesus Christ and those who exercise faith in His atonement. We do not need someone to tell us whether or not we are alive *physically*—we KNOW we are alive. We who are alive in Christ *"KNOW whom we have believed"* (II Tim. 1:12). A person may know a lot about "religion" and not have assurance of eternal life; but when one possesses the Spirit of God through faith in Christ's atonement, *that person KNOWS* he has been saved because *"the Spirit Himself beareth witness with our spirit,* that we are the children of God" (Rom. 8:16).

Union between the believer and Christ not only assures present life and present blessings, but *eternal life* and eternal *glory* as well:

"And this is the record, that *God hath given to us ETERNAL LIFE, and this life is in His Son. He that hath the SON hath life; and he that hath NOT the Son of God hath not life.*

"These things have I written unto you that believe on the name of the Son of God; that ye may know that ye have eternal life, and that ye may believe on the name of the Son of God" (I John 5:11—13).

Thanks be unto God for THE INCLUSIVENESS of Christ's atonement! because *through* the atonement believers know God in the fulness of His great love, His rich mercy, His holiness, and His righteousness.

Jesus is the author of eternal salvation (Heb. 5:9).

He is the author and the finisher of our faith (Heb. 12:2).

He is "made unto us wisdom, and righteousness, and sanctification, and redemption" (I Cor. 1:30).

Therefore Christ in His atonement is all we need. His atonement is all-sufficient, it does everything we need done. His blood prevents the judgment of a holy God from falling on us, just as the blood of the paschal lamb in Egypt protected those within the houses where it was applied (Ex. 12:13). Paul said to the believers in Corinth, "Purge out therefore the old leaven, that ye may be a new lump, as ye are unleavened. *For even Christ our Passover is sacrificed for us"* (I Cor. 5:7).

The disease of leprosy is a type of sin. In the Old Testament economy the leper came with an offering, and the blood offered on his behalf by the priest changed the leper's condition and also changed his position. (Read Leviticus 14:1—32, with special attention to verse 14.) Just as the condition and position of the leper were changed by the blood offering, so the condition and position of the sinner are changed when he believes in the shed blood of the Lamb of God. Believers are no longer victims of the leprosy of sin. Through the blood of Jesus we are delivered from sin and become sons of God.

Faith in the blood of Jesus also changes our relationship to the world—*we are IN the world, though no longer OF the world.* We are separated from the world by the redemption which is in Christ Jesus, and our citizenship is in heaven. God said to Pharaoh, "I will put a division between my people and thy people" (Ex. 8:23). The Hebrew word translated "division" means *redemption,* and is so rendered in other passages, as in Psalms 111:9 and 130:7. Therefore God actually said to Pharaoh, "I will put *redemption* between my people and thy people."

Paul bears out this truth in Galatians 6:14 where we read, "God forbid that I should glory, save in the cross of our Lord Jesus Christ, *by whom the world is crucified unto me, and I unto the world!*"

Under the Mosaic economy the blood of the covenant enabled Moses and the elders to draw nigh unto God and fellowship with Him in a very peculiar and personal way:

Moses "sent young men of the children of Israel, which offered burnt-offerings, and sacrificed peace-offerings of oxen unto the Lord. And Moses took half of the blood, and put it in basons; and half of the blood he sprinkled on the altar. And he took the book of the covenant, and read in the audience of the people: and they said, All that the Lord hath said will we do, and be obedient. And Moses took the blood, and sprinkled it on the people, and said, Behold the blood of the covenant, which the Lord hath made with you concerning all these words.

"Then went up Moses, and Aaron, Nadab, and Abihu, and seventy of the elders of Israel: AND THEY SAW THE GOD OF ISRAEL: AND THERE WAS UNDER HIS FEET AS IT WERE A PAVED WORK OF A SAPPHIRE STONE, AND AS IT WERE THE BODY OF HEAVEN IN HIS CLEARNESS" (Ex. 24: 5—10).

Now hear the Apostle Paul as he instructed the *Hebrew* believers: "Having therefore, brethren, boldness to enter into the holiest by the blood of Jesus, by a new and living way, which He hath consecrated for us, through the veil, that is to say, His flesh" (Heb. 10:19,20).

Under the law, when a poor, guilty person brought a sacrifice, the high priest made the sacrifice and offered blood.   The offerer then returned home with assurance, knowing God had pardoned him because he had faithfully met the demands of the law concerning sacrifice for sins. (It would be well to study the entire fourth chapter of Leviticus regarding this.) Now hear *Paul's* declaration to the Colossian believers: "It pleased the Father that in (Jesus) should all fulness dwell; and, *having made peace through the blood of His cross, BY HIM TO RECONCILE ALL THINGS UNTO HIMSELF; by Him, I say, whether they be THINGS IN EARTH, OR THINGS IN HEAVEN"* (Col. 1:19,20).

There is *POWER in the blood of the Lamb of God* who was "slain from the foundation of the world" (Rev. 13:8).   In Revelation 12:7—11 we read where Michael and his angels fought against the dragon and his angels, and the dragon (Satan) and his angels were cast out. Then a loud voice in heaven said, "Now is come salvation, and strength, and the kingdom of our God, and the power of His Christ: for the accuser of our brethren is cast down, which accused them before our God day and night. *And they OVERCAME him by THE BLOOD OF THE LAMB, and by the word of their testimony; and they loved not their lives unto the death"* (Rev. 12:10,11).

In His atonement Christ conquered and overthrew all the powers of hell: "Forasmuch then as the children are partakers of flesh and blood, He (Christ) also Himself likewise took part of the same; *that through death He might DESTROY him that had the power of death, that is, THE DEVIL;* and deliver them who through fear of death were all their lifetime subject to bondage" (Heb. 2:14,15).

"And having spoiled principalities and powers, He made a shew of them openly, triumphing over them in it" (Col. 2:15).

Every blood-washed believer has this assurance: "There is therefore *NOW NO CONDEMNATION* to them which are in Christ Jesus . . ." (Rom. 8:1). Through God's infallible Word we are assured that we are *sons of God NOW*—not when we die, not when we stand in the presence of Jesus, but this very moment—*"NOW are we the sons of God, and it doth not yet appear what we shall be: but we know that, when He shall appear, we shall be like Him; for we shall see Him as He is. And every man that hath this HOPE in him purifieth himself, even as He is pure"* (I John 3:2,3).

The atonement Christ made for us includes all that we need in this life, in death, in judgment, and throughout eternity: *"For in Him dwelleth all the fulness of the Godhead bodily. And (we) are complete IN HIM,* which is the head of all principality and power" (Col. 2:9,10).

Christ's atonement includes all God demands to answer sin. Thus through the atonement believers are saved from the *penalty* of sin, we are saved daily from the *power* of sin, and when Jesus comes to receive His own unto Himself we will be saved from the very *presence* of sin!

Dear reader, *have YOU received Christ's atonement by faith* and put your trust in His shed blood and finished work? If you have not, *accept Him now,* for *NOW is the accepted time, NOW is the day of salvation* (II Cor. 6:2).

"Boast not thyself of tomorrow; for thou knowest not what a day may bring forth" (Prov. 27:1).

". . . it is appointed unto men once to die, but after this the judgment" (Heb. 9:27).

THEREFORE—"Believe on the Lord Jesus Christ, and thou shalt be saved" (Acts 16:31), and you will become God's son NOW!

Chapter Seven

CHRIST'S ATONEMENT
AND ETERNAL GLORY

"And there came unto me one of the seven angels which had the seven vials full of the seven last plagues, and talked with me, saying, Come hither, I will shew thee the bride, the Lamb's wife. And he carried me away in the Spirit to a great and high mountain, and shewed me that great city, the holy Jerusalem, descending out of heaven from God, having the glory of God: and her light was like unto a stone most precious, even like a jasper stone, clear as crystal; and had a wall great and high, and had twelve gates, and at the gates twelve angels, and names written thereon, which are the names of the twelve tribes of the children of Israel: On the east three gates; on the north three gates; on the south three gates; and on the west three gates.

"And the wall of the city had twelve foundations, and in them the names of the twelve apostles of the Lamb. And he that talked with me had a golden reed to measure the city, and the gates thereof, and the wall thereof. And the city lieth foursquare, and the length is as large as the breadth: and he measured the city with the reed, twelve thousand furlongs. The length and the breadth and the height of it are equal. And he measured the wall thereof, an hundred and forty and four cubits, according to the measure of a man, that is, of the angel.

"And the building of the wall of it was of jasper: and the city was pure gold, like unto clear glass. And the foundations of the wall of the city were garnished with all manner of precious stones. The first foundation was jasper; the second, sapphire; the third, a chalcedony; the fourth, an emerald; the fifth, sardonyx; the sixth, sardius; the seventh, chrysolyte; the eighth, beryl; the ninth, a topaz; the tenth, a chrysoprasus; the eleventh, a jacinth; the twelfth, an amethyst. And the twelve gates were twelve pearls; every several gate was of one pearl: and the street of the city was pure gold, as it were transparent glass.

"And I saw no temple therein: for the Lord God Almighty and the Lamb are the temple of it. *And the city had no need of the sun, neither of the moon, to shine in it: FOR THE GLORY OF GOD DID LIGHTEN IT, AND THE LAMB IS THE LIGHT THEREOF.* And the nations of them which are saved shall walk in the light of it: and the kings of the earth do bring their glory and honour into it. And the gates of it shall not be shut at all by day: for there shall be no night there. And they shall bring the glory and honour of the nations into it.

"And there shall in no wise enter into it any thing that defileth, neither whatsoever worketh abomination, or maketh a lie: but they which are written in the Lamb's book of life" (Rev. 21:9—27).

The dictionary defines *glory* as "brilliancy, splendor, celestial bliss." Therefore we might say *glory is the excellency of anything on display.* A diamond "in the rough" is no less a diamond than when it has been cut and polished. In its original state its *glory* is not displayed, but when the hand of the master craftsman, with the tools of his trade, cuts and polishes the stone, the brilliancy, excellency, and glory of the diamond shine forth. By like token, a pearl concealed in the shell of an oyster and buried in the mud at the bottom of the bay is no less a precious jewel than when it is removed and polished. Its glory is not seen and appreciated by man until it is taken from the oyster and brought to lustrous perfection, but that does not alter the fact that it was a *pearl,* a costly gem, before its beauty was made evident. There are glorious things all around us today.

We can see the glory of GOD as clearly as it is *possible* to see Him through natural eyes:

The Psalmist declared, "The heavens declare the glory of God; and the firmament sheweth His handywork" (Psalm 19:1).

The glory of God's holy law declares and displays the excellency of God's righteousness. Hear the words of the Apostle Paul, words written to the believers in Corinth:

"If the *ministration of death,* written and engraven in stones, was glorious, so that the children of Israel could not stedfastly behold the face of Moses for the glory of his countenance; which glory was to be *done away:* how shall not *the ministration of the spirit* be rather glorious? For if the ministration of *condemnation* be glory, *much more* doth the ministration of righteousness *exceed* in glory. For even that which was made glorious had no glory in this respect, by reason of the glory that excelleth. For if that which is done away was glorious, much more that which remaineth is glorious" (II Cor. 3:7—11).

In John 2:11 we read, "This beginning of miracles did Jesus in Cana of Galilee, *and manifested forth His glory;* and His disciples believed on Him."

In John 11:40 Jesus said to Martha, "Said I not unto thee, that, *if thou wouldest believe, thou shouldest see THE GLORY OF GOD?*"

Jesus declared, "I must work the works of Him that sent me, while it is day . . ." (John 9:4), and the glory of the works of Jesus displayed the excellency of His power. He came from the bosom of the Father to declare God (John 1:18), and the glory of His Gospel—the words He spoke—reveals the light of the knowledge of God the Father in the face of Jesus Christ the Son: "For God, who commanded the light to shine out of darkness, hath shined in our hearts, *to give the light of the knowledge of THE GLORY OF GOD in the face of Jesus Christ*" (II Cor. 4:6).

The glory of God's saving grace declares His love for us. To the believers at Ephesus Paul wrote, "Blessed be the God and Father of our Lord Jesus Christ, who hath blessed us with all spiritual blessings in heavenly places in Christ . . . To the praise of *THE GLORY OF HIS GRACE, wherein He hath made us accepted in the Beloved. . . . That we should be to the praise of HIS GLORY*, who first trusted in Christ. In whom ye also trusted, after that ye heard the Word of truth, the Gospel of your salvation: in whom also after that ye believed, ye were sealed with that Holy Spirit of promise, which is the earnest of our inheritance until the redemption of the purchased possession, *UNTO THE PRAISE OF HIS GLORY*" (Eph. 1:3—14 in part).

The heavens which we now behold through mortal eyes declare the glory of God's handiwork and the excellency of His *artistic skill*. God's law declares the excellency of His *righteousness*. The miracles of Jesus (God in flesh) displayed the glory of His *works*, and His works displayed the excellency of His *power*. As Jesus walked and talked among men, the words He spoke revealed the light of the knowledge of God, and His saving grace declares and proves the favor of God's love for us.

Believers are ASSURED of "eternal glory": To young Timothy the Apostle Paul wrote, "Therefore I endure all things for the elect's sakes, that they may also obtain the salvation which is in Christ Jesus *with ETERNAL GLORY"* (II Tim. 2:10).

In I Peter 5:10, 11 we read, "The God of all grace, who hath called us unto His eternal glory by Christ Jesus, after that ye have suffered a while, make you perfect, stablish, strengthen, settle you. *To Him be GLORY AND DOMINION for ever and ever.* Amen."

However, only those who believe on Jesus and put their trust in His finished work will *share* in this eternal glory, because *Christ in the believer is the only HOPE of glory* (Col. 1:27).

It is only through Christ's substitutionary act at Calvary that we can receive the atonement, and those who believe on Him will share His *eternal glory:*

"The Spirit Himself beareth witness with our spirit, that we are the children of God: And if children, then heirs; heirs of God, and joint-heirs with Christ; if so be that we suffer with Him, that we may be also glorified together. For I reckon that *the sufferings of this present time are not worthy to be compared with THE GLORY WHICH SHALL BE REVEALED IN US"* (Rom. 8:16—18).

Christ's Atonement and Glory in Revelation

In the book of Revelation—God's last message to man, given through John the Beloved—we see that the blood of the Lamb of God is closely connected with the eternal glory that awaits the believer—glory *assured* on the *merit* of the blood of Jesus:

". . . Grace be unto you, and peace, from Him which is, and which was, and which is to come; and from the seven Spirits which are before His throne; and from *Jesus Christ,* who is the faithful witness, and the first begotten of the dead, and the prince of the kings of the earth. *Unto Him that loved us, and washed us from our sins in His own blood, and hath*

made us kings and priests unto God and His Father;
*TO HIM BE GLORY AND DOMINION FOR EVER
AND EVER.* Amen" (Rev. 1:4—6).

Christ loved us, and He proved His love on Calvary. It is through His shed blood that we are
washed, cleansed from all sin, and exalted. We are
made "kings and priests unto God." (The Greek
language reads literally, "made us *a kingdom of
priests.*") But the truth set forth here goes further
than the present priesthood of believers: *it speaks of
the reign of believers with Christ* when He reigns as
King of kings and Lord of lords:

"Even He shall build the temple of the Lord; and
He shall bear the glory, and shall sit and rule upon
His throne; and He shall be a Priest upon His throne:
and the counsel of peace shall be between them both"
(Zech. 6:13).

Luke 1:33 tells us, *"He shall reign over the house
of Jacob for ever; and of His kingdom there shall be
no end."*

Our second reference in Revelation is found in
chapter 5, verses 8—10: "And when He had taken the
book, the four beasts and four and twenty elders fell
down before the Lamb, having every one of them
harps, and golden vials full of odours, which are the
prayers of saints. And they sung a new song, saying,
Thou art worthy to take the book, and to open the
seals thereof: *for thou wast slain, and hast redeemed
us to God by thy blood* out of every kindred, and
tongue, and people, and nation; *and hast made us
unto our God kings and priests: and we shall reign
on the earth."*

The Lamb was worthy to open the book because
He was slain at Calvary, and we are redeemed by His
blood, made kings and priests unto God, and we will
reign *with HIM* on the earth.

The same truth is expressed in Revelation 7:9—14

where John saw a multitude so great they could not be numbered, "of all nations, and kindreds, and people, and tongues," arrayed in white robes, and with palms in their hands. This great multitude stood before the throne—before the Lamb of God—and cried, "Salvation to our God which sitteth upon the throne, and unto the Lamb. . . . And one of the elders answered, saying unto me, What are these which are arrayed in white robes? and whence came they? And I said unto him, Sir, thou knowest. And he said to me, *These are they which came out of great tribulation, and have washed their robes, and made them white IN THE BLOOD OF THE LAMB.*"

The fourth reference I would have us notice concerning the blood of the Lamb is found in Revelation 12:10,11: "And I heard a loud voice saying in heaven, Now is come salvation, and strength, and the kingdom of our God, and the power of His Christ: for the accuser of our brethren is cast down, which accused them before our God day and night. *And they OVERCAME him by THE BLOOD OF THE LAMB*, and by the word of their testimony; and they loved not their lives unto the death."

Thus we see that Jesus the Lamb of God loved us and washed us from our sins in His own blood. He is worthy because He, the sinless One, was slain, and through His death on Calvary He redeemed what the first Adam sold to Satan in the Garden of Eden.

In these passages we also see that Jesus not only redeems us and washes our robes white, He also *keeps* them white; and we *overcome* by the blood of the Lamb. Therefore we can say with Paul, *"We are MORE than conquerors THROUGH HIM"* (Rom. 8:37).

The Old Testament Type

"And Aaron shall offer his bullock of the sin-offering, which is for himself, and make an atonement for himself, and for his house. . . . Then shall he kill the goat of the sin-offering, that is for the people, and bring his blood within the vail, and do with that blood as he did with the blood of the bullock, and sprinkle it upon the mercy seat, and before the mercy seat: And he shall make an atonement for the holy place, because of the uncleanness of the children of Israel, and because of their transgressions in all their sins: and so shall he do for the tabernacle of the congregation, that remaineth among them in the midst of their uncleanness.

"And there shall be no man in the tabernacle of the congregation when he goeth in to make an atonement in the holy place, until he come out, and have made an atonement for himself, and for his household, and for all the congregation of Israel. And he shall go out unto the altar that is before the Lord, and make an atonement for it; and shall take of the blood of the bullock, and of the blood of the goat, and put it upon the horns of the altar round about. And he shall sprinkle of the blood upon it with his finger seven times, and cleanse it, and hallow it from the uncleanness of the children of Israel" (Lev. 16:6, 15–19).

On the Day of Atonement in the Old Testament economy, a fivefold atonement was made:

First, the priest made atonement *for himself and his household.*

Second, he made atonement *for the people.*

Third, he made atonement *for the holy place.*

Fourth, he made atonement *for the tabernacle.*

Fifth, he made atonement *for the altar.*

The Old Testament priest was a *type* of our great High Priest, the Lord Jesus Christ. In making an atonement for himself together with his household, he typified Christ in *His* identification with *us.* Jesus left the glories of heaven, took a body of humiliation, and was made exactly as we are (sin apart) in order that He might stand with us as we stand, and that He might taste death for every man (Heb. 2:9).

Through His death, Jesus satisfied the holiness and righteousness of God, fulfilled the law of God, and made it possible for God to "be just, and the justifier of him which believeth in Jesus" (Rom. 3:26).

After the priest made atonement for himself and for his own household he then made atonement for the nation of Israel. Under the Old Testament economy Israel was special in the eyes of God. That nation was God's elect, His chosen people, and Numbers 23:9 tells us that Israel was not "reckoned among the nations." In Exodus 19:5 God said, "Now therefore, if ye will obey my voice indeed, and keep my covenant, then ye shall be *a peculiar treasure* unto me *above ALL people:* for all the earth is mine."

In Abraham God gave Israel specific and special promises regarding the land: "As for me, behold, my covenant is with thee, *and thou shalt be a father of many nations.* Neither shall thy name any more be called Abram, but thy name shall be Abraham; for a father of many nations have I made thee. And I will make thee exceeding fruitful, and I will make nations of thee, and kings shall come out of thee. And I will establish my covenant *between me and thee and thy seed after thee in their generations for an everlasting covenant,* to be a God unto thee, and to thy seed after thee. And I will give unto thee, and to thy seed after thee, the land wherein thou art a stranger, *all the land of Canaan, for an everlasting possession;* and I will be their God" (Gen. 17:4—8).

To David God gave specific and special promises having to do with *the eternal throne* of God: "And when thy days be fulfilled, and thou shalt sleep with thy fathers, I will set up thy seed after thee, which shall proceed out of thy bowels, and I will establish his kingdom. He shall build an house for my name, *and I will establish the throne of his kingdom for ever"* (II Sam. 7:12,13).

BUT—all the promises God made to Abraham, to David, or to any other of His chosen people, find their alpha and omega (their beginning and their ending) in the Lord Jesus Christ, the promised seed (Gen. 3:15) through whom all families of the earth should be blessed:

"Now the Lord had said unto Abram, Get thee out of thy country, and from thy kindred, and from thy father's house, unto a land that I will shew thee: and I will make of thee a great nation, and I will bless thee, and make thy name great; and thou shalt be a blessing: And I will bless them that bless thee, and curse him that curseth thee: *and IN THEE shall ALL FAMILIES OF THE EARTH be blessed"* (Gen. 12:1—3).

Paul tells us in Galatians 3:16, "Now to Abraham and his seed were the promises made. He saith not, And to *SEEDS, as of many;* but as of *ONE,* And to *thy SEED, which is Christ."*

It was to Adam that God made the first promise concerning the seed who would crush the serpent's head (Gen. 3:15). He later *called Abraham,* and in Galatians 4:4,5 we read:

"When the fulness of the time was come, GOD SENT FORTH HIS SON, made of a woman, made under the law, to redeem them that were under the law, that we might receive the adoption of sons."

The Seed promised in Genesis 3:15 (and in the fulness of time born of a woman) was the Babe who was born in Bethlehem—He of whom we read, *"He shall be great, and shall be called the Son of the Highest: and the Lord God shall give unto Him the throne of His father David: AND HE SHALL REIGN OVER THE HOUSE OF JACOB FOR EVER; AND OF HIS*

KINGDOM THERE SHALL BE NO END" (Luke 1:32, 33).

In Luke 2:52 we read of the Babe born in Bethlehem, "Jesus increased in wisdom and stature, and in favour with God and man." This same Jesus marched on to Calvary, and on the cross He died to redeem sinners from sin.

Jesus came into the world to die for the sins of the world (I John 2:2). "For God sent not His Son into the world to *condemn* the world; but that the world *through Him* might be *saved*" (John 3:17).

This does not mean that *all* people will be saved; but Christ's blood shed on Calvary is *retrospective in its benefit* as well as *perspective in its blessing.* Christ died "to redeem them that were under the law" (Gal. 4:5)—which means that every sacrifice offered in the Old Testament economy pointed to the Lamb of God and His sacrifice at Calvary. Had Jesus *not died* on the cross, the blood shed from Eden to Calvary would have availed nothing and every sacrifice offered would have been in vain!

Therefore, every saved person—*from Adam to the end of time and the beginning of eternity*—will be saved through faith in the blood of Jesus! That is why I say His blood is *retrospective* in its benefit (reaching back to those on the other side of Calvary) as well as perspective in its blessings (to those on *this* side of Calvary):

"But now the righteousness of God without the law is manifested, being witnessed by the law and the prophets; even the righteousness of God which is by faith of Jesus Christ unto all and upon all them that believe: for there is no difference: *For ALL have sinned,* and come short of the glory of God; being justified freely by His grace through the redemption that is in Christ Jesus: *Whom God hath set forth to be a propitiation through faith in His blood, to declare*

His righteousness for the remission of sins that are PAST, through the forbearance of God; to declare, I say, at this time His righteousness: that He might be just, and the justifier of him which believeth in Jesus. Where is boasting then? It is excluded. By what law? of works? Nay: but *by the law of faith. THEREFORE WE CONCLUDE THAT A MAN IS JUSTIFIED BY FAITH WITHOUT THE DEEDS OF THE LAW"* (Rom. 3:21—28).

Jesus came "unto the lost sheep of the house of Israel" (Matt. 15:24), but they refused Him and demanded His death. But God has not forsaken His chosen people (Rom. 11:1,2). Christ is coming again to bless Israel, and when the nation looks upon Him they will recognize Him by the scars in His hands and feet:

"And I will pour upon the house of David, and upon the inhabitants of Jerusalem, the spirit of grace and of supplications: *and they shall look upon me whom they have pierced, and they shall mourn for Him, as one mourneth for his only son, and shall be in bitterness for Him, as one that is in bitterness for his firstborn"* (Zech. 12:10).

John the Beloved emphasizes this truth in Revelation 1:7: "Behold, He cometh with clouds; *and EVERY EYE SHALL SEE HIM, AND THEY ALSO WHICH PIERCED HIM:* and all kindreds of the earth shall wail because of Him. Even so, Amen."

Yes, every promise God made to Abraham, to David, and to the Israelite nation as a whole is *secured and assured* in Christ's atonement! His death on the cross is God's guarantee that Israel will be restored to the land of Palestine as promised in Jeremiah 32:37—42:

"Behold, I will gather them out of all countries, whither I have driven them in mine anger, and in my fury, and in great wrath; and I will bring them again unto this place, and I will cause them to dwell safely: And they shall be my people, and I will be their God: and I will give them one heart, and one way, that they may fear me for ever, for the good of them, and of their children after them: And I will make an everlasting covenant with them, that I will not turn away from them, to do them good; but I will put my fear in their hearts, that they shall not depart from me. Yea, I will rejoice over them to do them good, and I will plant them in this land assuredly with my whole heart and with my whole soul.   For thus saith the Lord: *Like as I have brought all this great evil upon this people, so will I bring upon them ALL THE GOOD THAT I HAVE PROMISED THEM!"*

The death of Jesus on Calvary guarantees the fulfillment of God's promise to David, that Christ would sit on his throne in Jerusalem: "And David my servant shall be king over them; and they all shall have *one Shepherd:* they shall also walk in my judgments, and observe my statutes, and do them" (Ezek. 37:24).

Calvary guarantees the reunion of Judah and Israel as prophesied in Ezekiel 37:15—22. (Please read that passage.   Time and space will not allow us to give the full text here.)

Calvary also assures the glory of the Holy City Jerusalem, as set forth in Isaiah 1:26:   "I will restore thy judges as at the first, and thy counsellors as at the beginning: afterward thou shalt be called, *The city of righteousness, the faithful city."* (In connection with this, please read the entire eighth chapter of Zechariah.)

And finally, Calvary guarantees *the salvation of Israel as a nation:* ". . . I will take you from among the heathen, and gather you out of all countries, and will bring you into your own land. Then will I sprinkle clean water upon you, and ye shall be clean: from all your filthiness, and from all your idols, will I cleanse you. *A NEW HEART also will I give you, and A NEW SPIRIT will I put within you:* and I will take away the stony heart out of your flesh, and I will give you an heart of flesh. And *I will put MY SPIRIT within you, and cause you to walk in my statutes, and ye shall keep my judgments, and do them"* (Ezek. 36:24—27).

After the high priest made atonement for himself and his household and for the nation Israel, he made atonement for the holy place (Lev. 16:16). The "holy place" typified the third heaven—God's house—mentioned in Paul's letter to the Corinthian church (II Cor. 12:1—4). The third heaven—the place where God's throne is—could be entered only by means of the blood of Christ the Lamb of God:

"But Christ being come an high priest of good things to come, by a greater and more perfect tabernacle, not made with hands, that is to say, not of this building; *neither by the blood of goats and calves, but by HIS OWN BLOOD He entered in ONCE into the holy place, having obtained ETERNAL REDEMPTION for us"* (Heb. 9:11,12).

The devil is "the prince of the power of the air" (Eph. 2:2), and his kingdom is just above us. The first heaven is literally alive with demons and wicked spirits. But one day the Lord Jesus Christ will *cleanse* the heavens, Satan will be cast down (Rev. 12:7—10), and Jesus will personally bind him, put him into the bottomless pit, "and set a seal upon him" (Rev. 20:1—3). And in the final consummation of all things there will be a *new* heaven and a *new earth* (Rev. 21:1). All of this is assured and guaranteed by the blood of Jesus, shed on Calvary.

The *fourth atonement* offered by the high priest was for the tabernacle (Lev. 16:16). In the Old Testament economy the tabernacle was associated with the earth—i. e., God met the high priest in the holy of holies. No one could enter there *except* God's appointed high priest, and *even he* entered only once each year.

But when the first Adam sinned in the Garden of Eden, *God cursed the earth*—not only the man and woman, but the entire creation; and that curse will remain until Jesus one day *delivers creation* from it (Rom. 8:22,23). Therefore, Jesus took a tabernacle of flesh, and in that tabernacle He did what the law *could NOT do because of the WEAKNESS of the flesh* (Rom. 8:3), and His death on Calvary guarantees *a new heaven, a new earth, the Pearly White City, and eternal glory!* (Read Romans 8:18−23.)

"The earth is the Lord's, and the fulness thereof" (Psalm 24:1), and when the Lord Jesus Christ delivers this earth from the curse, it will be the glorious place God *intended* it to be when He created it. Isaiah chapter 11 describes the Millennial earth, and Isaiah 35:1 further declares, "The wilderness and the solitary place shall be glad for them; *and the desert shall rejoice, and blossom as the rose!*"

Isaiah 55:13 declares, *"Instead of the thorn shall come up the fir tree, and instead of the brier shall come up the myrtle tree: and it shall be to the Lord for a name, for an everlasting sign that shall not be cut off."*

I John 5:19 tells us that *the whole world* "lieth in wickedness," but one day beauty and holiness will replace wickedness, ungodliness, and sin. God's beauty and holiness and glory will *fill* the earth, and the knowledge of the Lord will cover the earth as the waters now cover the sea. Beauty such as only God could create, holiness such as only God could display, will fill all creation.

In Psalm 67 we read, "God be merciful unto us, and bless us; and cause His face to shine upon us... That thy way may be known upon earth, thy saving health among all nations. Let the people praise thee, O God; let all the people praise thee. O let the nations be glad and sing for joy: for thou shalt judge the people righteously, and govern the nations upon earth. . . . Let the people praise thee, O God; let all the people praise thee. *Then shall the earth yield her increase; and God, even our own God, shall bless us. God shall bless us; and all the ends of the earth shall fear Him."*

I believe you will agree with me that even now this earth is a beautiful place; there are some magnificent sights to behold—in the mountains, by the seashore, throughout the earth. If the earth is beautiful now under the curse, think what a glorious place it will be when the curse is removed and the knowledge and glory of God fill the earth as the waters now cover the sea! All of this is guaranteed to the whole creation through Christ's atonement.

The *fifth* atonement the high priest made was for the altar: "And he shall go out unto the altar that is before the Lord, and make an atonement for it; and shall take of the blood of the bullock, and of the blood of the goat, and put it upon the horns of the altar round about" (Lev. 16:18).

The offering was placed on the altar and a fire was placed under the offering. From Eden to Calvary, tens of thousands of innocent animals were slain and their blood sprinkled on the altar. This was typical of the blood of the Lamb of God who shed His blood for the remission of sin, and through His blood we have the atonement.

Do not misunderstand me. I am not suggesting that *animals* are *saved*. They do not have a soul and they are not redeemed as we are. But in the beginning God did not intend for any of His creatures to be killed. Adam and Eve were vegetarians. God *intended* man to be a vegetarian, and *he would have been* had he not sinned. In that glorious day when the curse will be forever removed from the earth, the wolf and the lamb will dwell together, the cow and the bear will feed together, *and "they shall not hurt nor destroy"* (Isa. 11:6—9).

Yes, the new earth will certainly have animals in it. Heaven, the new earth, and the Pearly White City will be all that our God can create that is magnificent, beautiful, and glorious.

Through the Prophet Amos, God declared, "In that day will I raise up the tabernacle of David that is fallen, and close up the breaches thereof; and I will raise up his ruins, and I will build it as in the days of old: that they may possess the remnant of Edom, and of all the heathen, which are called by my name, saith the Lord that doeth this.

"Behold, the days come, saith the Lord, that the plowman shall overtake the reaper, and the treader of grapes him that soweth seed; and the mountains shall drop sweet wine, and all the hills shall melt. And I will bring again the captivity of my people of Israel, and they shall build the waste cities, and inhabit them; and they shall plant vineyards, and drink the wine thereof; they shall also make gardens, and eat the fruit of them. And I will plant them upon their land, and they shall no more be pulled up out of their land which I have given them, saith the Lord thy God" (Amos 9:13—15).

In his second sermon (recorded in Acts 3) Peter said to the Jews, "Repent ye therefore, and be converted, that your sins may be blotted out, *WHEN THE TIMES OF REFRESHING SHALL COME FROM THE PRESENCE OF THE LORD.* And He shall send Jesus Christ, which before was preached unto you: whom the heaven must receive *UNTIL THE TIMES OF RESTITUTION OF ALL THINGS, which God hath spoken by the mouth of all His HOLY*

PROPHETS since the world began" (Acts 3:19—21).

In Romans 8:22 the Apostle Paul declared, "We know that *the whole creation* groaneth and travaileth in pain together until now"—and it will *continue* to groan and travail until Jesus comes and removes the curse. Christ died on the cross "to reconcile all things unto Himself" (Col. 1:20), and the restitution of all things is guaranteed and assured by His atonement.

The Old Testament Prophets Speak of Christ's Coming in Glory As Well As His Death on the Cross

"Behold, my servant shall deal prudently, He shall be exalted and extolled, and be very high. As many were astonied at thee; His visage was so marred more than any man, and His form more than the sons of men: So shall He sprinkle many nations; the kings shall shut their mouths at Him: for that which had not been told them shall they see; and that which they had not heard shall they consider" (Isa. 52:13—15).

This Scripture definitely speaks of Jesus. He *has been* exalted, and He *will be* exalted even more. Paul said to the Philippian believers, "Wherefore (because of His atonement through death on the cross) God also hath highly exalted Him, and given Him a name which is above every name: That at the name of Jesus every knee should bow, of things in heaven, and things in earth, and things under the earth; and that every tongue should confess that Jesus Christ is Lord, to the glory of God the Father" (Phil. 2:9—11).

Then Isaiah declared, "Many were astonied . . . *His visage was so marred more than any man, and His form more than the sons of men.*" During His trial, under the mocking and scourging He endured, Jesus was so mutilated, so bruised and disfigured that the prophet could describe Him as being "marred more than any man . . . more than the sons of men." No man has ever undergone such suffering as was the portion of our Lord as He paid the penalty for our sin.

"So shall He sprinkle many nations." In the Old Testament era, on the Day of Atonement the high priest sprinkled the blood of the sacrifice on (and before) the mercy seat when he made atonement for the sins of the people. Jesus became the atonement — Saviour to the nations of earth who will believe in His shed blood.

In Isaiah 53:10 we read, "Yet it pleased the Lord to bruise Him; He hath put Him to grief: when thou shalt make His soul an offering for sin, He shall see His seed, He shall prolong His days, and the pleasure of the Lord shall prosper in His hand." In this verse Isaiah speaks of the sufferings of Christ on Calvary. On the surface it seems very strange that it would please Jehovah God to bruise Jesus the Lamb; but the last part of the verse makes explanation: *"He shall see His SEED."* Then we remember the words of Jesus in John 12:24:

"Except a corn of wheat fall into the ground and die, it abideth alone: *but if it die, it bringeth forth much fruit."*

It was a divine necessity that the Lamb of God be "bruised" and "put to grief" in order to bring many sons into the family of God. *He came into the world to be bruised,* to lay His life down; and even though the cross was horrible and Jesus despised the shame of it, He endured it because He looked *beyond* Calvary to "the joy that was set before Him" (Heb. 12:2).

Believers are brought into the family of God through the new birth which is made possible through Christ's atonement; and we who are born into the family of God have the divine guarantee that we will be glorified in that day when the glory of God shall fill this earth and all creation.

Isaiah prophesied, *"When thou shalt make His soul an offering for sin . . . He shall prolong His days."* Again the prophet speaks of the sufferings of Jesus and the glory that was sure to follow. When the enemies of Jesus arrested Him and led Him away to be crucified, they thought they had stopped His mouth and put an end to His ministry; but death could not hold Him and He rose from the grave on the third day, just as He had said He would. Seemingly He was cut off—yet His days have been (and will be) prolonged. He conquered not only the world, the flesh, and the devil, but also death, hell, and the grave. He was dead, but He is alive forevermore and He sits at the right hand of God the Father, in the highest seat of heaven.

Yes, He who was made to be sin for us, He who bore our sins in His own body on the cross, now enjoys prolonged glory, and *we shall share that glory* when all things are made new and heaven and earth are filled with the glory of God!

Isaiah further prophesied, "He shall see of the travail of His soul, *and shall be satisfied:* by His knowledge shall my righteous servant justify many; for *He shall bear their iniquities"* (Isa. 53:11). God laid our sins and iniquities on Jesus, and in the first part of this verse the prophet makes known God's satisfaction with the final results of Christ's travail and terrible anguish of body and soul.

The Lamb of God travailed in pain such as man has never known—nor ever *could* know unless he plunged into the lake of fire—because Jesus suffered all the agony, misery, and woe of an everlasting separation from God in the hell that burns with fire and brimstone forever! But God the Eternal Father is well pleased with the result of Calvary. Through

Christ's suffering, through His shed blood and His death on the cross, He satisfied God's holiness and God's righteousness, and He satisfied every jot and tittle of the law. Therefore through His perfect atonement He brought perfect satisfaction to God, to Himself, and to the Holy Spirit concerning the settlement of the sin-question.

". . . *He shall divide the spoil with the strong; because He hath poured out His soul unto death*" (Isa. 53:12). (The literal Hebrew reads, "He shall take the spoil *from* the strong," and this is exactly what Jesus did, and what He will do at the end of time when the devil and evil and all enemies of righteousness are forever destroyed in the lake of fire and brimstone.)

It is *because* Jesus poured out His soul unto death that He will take the spoil from the strong—that is, because of His death on the cross He is King of kings and Lord of lords. Conqueror of the mighty, *He is the ALMIGHTY.* And one day He will personally put the devil into hell and seal him there. Then at the final judgment at the Great White Throne, Satan will be placed in the lake of fire and brimstone with the beast and the false prophet, and with all the wicked, to be tormented forever and ever.

As Jesus talked with the two disciples on the road to Emmaus He asked them, *"Ought not Christ to have suffered these things, and to enter into HIS GLORY?"* (Luke 24:26). Christ's atonement was necessary *for our salvation*—but it was also necessary *for HIS GLORY.*

As — So

"And no man hath ascended up to heaven, but He that came down from heaven, even the Son of man which is in heaven. *And AS Moses lifted up the serpent in the wilderness, even SO must the Son of man be lifted up:* that whosoever believeth in Him should not perish, but have eternal life" (John 3:13—15).

These words were spoken to *Nicodemus*—outstanding teacher in Israel, master in the religion of the Jews—and to him the account of Moses and the serpent of brass was familiar Scripture. He knew that the Israelites who had been bitten by the fiery serpents were instructed to "look and live," and *those who LOOKED, LIVED. Those who REFUSED to look, DIED.* The *lifting up of Jesus* was a divine necessity —there was no other way that God's glorious grace might become ours *through faith IN His "lifting up."* He was lifted up on the cruel cross that *we* might be lifted out of *the miry clay of sin* and that we might become sons of God through faith in the shed blood and finished work of Jesus: "And *AS it is appointed unto men once to die,* but after this the judgment: *SO Christ was once offered to bear the sins of many . . .*" (Heb. 9:27,28).

God made clear to Adam what he should do and what he should not do. He also made clear *the penalty for disobedience.* "The wages of sin is *death"*— always *has* been, always *will be.* Sin and death are synonymous. Through the sin of Adam, death moved upon *all* men. Therefore *all men since Adam* have been born under an appointment with death—and with the exception of Enoch and Elijah, all men since Adam *have* died. God had a very definite purpose in taking those two men out of the world alive.

Men not only *die,* they also stand before God *to be judged:* "For it is written, *As I live, saith the Lord, every knee shall bow to me, and every tongue shall confess to God"* (Rom. 14:11). But just as surely as men have a date with death, just as surely as all men will stand before God to be judged, so Christ died the death sinners should die and bore the judgment sinners should bear. *"Christ was once OFFERED*

. . . ." He gave His life and shed His blood that "whosoever will" can be saved and delivered from death and judgment—*God's Word declares it:*

"There is therefore now *NO condemnation* to them which are in Christ Jesus . . ." (Rom. 8:1), and He Himself said, "He that heareth my Word, and believeth on Him that sent me, *hath everlasting life, and SHALL NOT come into CONDEMNATION* (judgment); *but IS* (already) *PASSED from death unto life*" (John 5:24).

Just as surely as men die, and just as surely as Jesus died on the cross, He is coming again: *"Unto them that look for Him shall He appear the second time without sin unto salvation"* (Heb. 9:28b).

In this Scripture we have, indirectly, a reference to the high priest of the Old Testament era. On the Day of Atonement, when the priest went into the holy of holies to make atonement for his own sins, he then came out in his robes of glory and beauty to bless the people. Jesus came as the Lamb of God and offered *Himself.* He died on the cross for our sins, but He is alive forevermore. He is coming a second time—not as a babe in a manger, but as King of kings and Lord of lords. Yes, *this same Jesus* will surely come exactly as He went away.

He assured His disciples, "Let not your heart be troubled: ye believe in God, believe also in me. In my Father's house are many mansions: if it were not so, I would have told you. *I go to prepare a place for YOU. And if I go and prepare a place for you, I WILL COME AGAIN, AND RECEIVE YOU UNTO MYSELF; THAT WHERE I AM, THERE YE MAY BE ALSO"* (John 14:1–3).

As the resurrected Lord spoke with His disciples only moments before His ascension, He promised them that they would receive power after the Holy Ghost came upon them, and instructed them that they were then to be His witnesses "in Jerusalem, and in all

Judaea, and in Samaria, and unto the uttermost part of the earth. And when He had spoken these things, while they beheld, *He was taken up; and a cloud received Him out of their sight.* And while they looked stedfastly toward heaven as He went up, behold, two men stood by them in white apparel; which also said, *Ye men of Galilee, why stand ye gazing up into heaven? THIS SAME JESUS, which is taken up from you into heaven, shall so COME IN LIKE MANNER AS YE HAVE SEEN HIM GO INTO HEAVEN"* (Acts 1:8—11).

Christ's *first* coming (to take away the sin of the world) and His *future* coming (to call His Church to meet Him in the clouds in the air) are very closely and intimately connected. They are the foundation and the capstone of the Gospel, the alpha and omega of truth, the beginning and the ending of revelation. They are the cause and the effect of love's provision, the guarantee that *full payment of the sin-debt has been made* and eternal life is assured for the believer. Christ's first and second comings are the grounds and the outcome of saving grace.

Christ's Atonement Brings a Fourfold Blessing

"But of Him are ye in Christ Jesus, who of God is made unto us *wisdom,* and *righteousness,* and *sanctification,* and *redemption"* (I Cor. 1:30).

Salvation is of the Lord (Psalm 3:8; Jonah 2:9). In the wisdom and love of God's grace He has provided all that Divinity demands to settle the sin-debt and provide eternal life for all who will believe; but "the fear of the Lord is the beginning of knowledge" (Prov. 1:7), and man will never repent in verity and truth *until* the fear of God grips his heart!

The only possible way anyone can know that "the wages of sin is death but the gift of God is eternal life" is to discover this truth in the Word of God. Even the knowledge, wisdom, and understanding that make it possible for sinners to exercise faith in the shed blood of Jesus are imparted through God's infallible Word—*and the Word IS God* (John 1:1,2).

Christ is made unto us WISDOM:

Jesus was the Word, He was in the beginning with the Father, but in the fulness of time *"the Word was made flesh,* and dwelt among us, (and we beheld His glory, the glory as of the only begotten of the Father,) *full of GRACE and TRUTH"* (John 1:14). Grace *saves* us, and *truth* tells us that *grace has been provided* for the salvation of the sinner. In John 8:32 Jesus said, *"Ye shall know the TRUTH, and the truth shall make you FREE."* To Thomas He said, *"I AM TRUTH"* (John 14:6). In John 17:17 He prayed to the heavenly Father, "Sanctify them through thy truth: *thy WORD is truth."*

Christ is made unto us RIGHTEOUSNESS:

Only in the Word of God do we learn that sin and death passed upon the whole human race because of the disobedience of the first Adam; and only in the Word do we learn that through one *righteous* act of the *last Adam* (the Lord Jesus Christ) all claims of God's holiness, righteousness, and law were fully met: "Therefore as by the *offence* of one *judgment came upon ALL men to condemnation;* even so by *the righteousness of One* the free gift came upon all men unto justification of life. For as by one man's *disobedience* many were made *sinners,* so by the *obedience of One* shall many be made *righteous"* (Rom. 5:18,19).

Therefore, through the one righteous act of the last Adam, all who believe in His shed blood and finished work are reckoned righteous:

"For what saith the Scripture? *Abraham believed*

God, and it was counted unto him for righteousness.
Now to him that worketh is the reward not reckoned
of grace, but of debt. But *to him that worketh not,
but believeth on Him that justifieth the ungodly,
his faith is counted for righteousness.* Even as David
also describeth the blessedness of the man, unto whom
God imputeth righteousness without works, saying,
Blessed are they whose iniquities are forgiven, and
whose sins are covered. Blessed is the man to whom
the Lord will not impute sin.

"Cometh this blessedness then upon the circumcision only, or upon the uncircumcision also? for we
say that faith was reckoned to Abraham for righteousness. How was it then reckoned? when he was
in circumcision, or in uncircumcision? Not in circumcision, but in uncircumcision. . . .

*"Now it was not written for his sake alone, that
it was imputed to him; but FOR US ALSO, to whom
it shall be imputed, IF WE BELIEVE ON HIM
THAT RAISED UP JESUS OUR LORD FROM THE
DEAD"* (Rom. 4:3–10, 23, 24).

Christ IS the righteousness of God. Christ *in
the Christian* is "the hope of glory" (Col. 1:27), and
apart from Christ there *is* no hope. Only the *righteous* will enter heaven, and we become righteous *by
imputation* when the righteousness of *Christ* is imputed
to us.

The Lord Jesus Christ knew no sin, but He was
made *"to be sin for us . . .* that we might be made
the righteousness of God IN HIM" (II Cor. 5:21).
Please notice—the Scripture says, *"that we might
be MADE* the righteousness of God." It does not
say, "that we might *gradually become* righteous,"
or that we "might *attain* righteousness *through faithful living." We are MADE righteous by imputation*
when we exercise faith in the finished work of the
Lord Jesus Christ who is "the righteousness of God."

Christ is made unto us SANCTIFICATION:

The Greek word here translated *"sanctification"* is rendered "holiness" in Romans 6:22: "But now being made free from sin, and become servants to God, *ye have your fruit unto HOLINESS*, and the end everlasting life." In the spiritual sense, holiness means that which is set apart for sacred use. Believers are "sanctified in Christ Jesus" (I Cor. 1:2), set apart unto God in their identification with Him by being *born* of God (John 1:12,13).

Sanctification is conformity to God's nature. *God is holy*, and without holiness "no man shall see the Lord" (Heb. 12:14). In I Peter 1:16 God commands, *"Be ye holy; for I AM HOLY,"* and the only way man can *be* holy is to possess divine nature. When we are saved we are made *"partakers of the divine nature"* (II Pet. 1:4) and we are *"hid with Christ in God"* (Col. 3:3).

During the Old Testament economy the words *"holiness to the Lord"* were written on the mitre of God's anointed high priest in order that the children of Israel might always be assured of being accepted before Jehovah (Ex. 28:36−38). In like manner, the Man Christ Jesus ever lives at the right hand of God to represent the believer: "Wherefore He is able also to save them to the uttermost that come unto God by Him, seeing He ever liveth to make intercession for them" (Heb. 7:25).

Christ is made unto us REDEMPTION:

Redemption is threefold:
(1) When we exercise faith in the finished work of Jesus, redemption from the curse and condemnation of sin becomes ours (Eph. 1:7).
(2) Day by day as we walk with Christ and fellowship with Him in the power of the Spirit we are re-

deemed from self-will and from sins that would rob us
of the joy of our salvation (Tit. 2:14; I John 2:1,2).

(3) Then one day—no man knows the day or the
hour—we will be redeemed from the very *presence* of
sin. We will be caught up out of this sinful world to
meet Jesus in the clouds in the air (I Thess. 4:17).

Christ is the author and the finisher of our faith,
the alpha and omega of our salvation, and through
His atonement He *secures our redemption*—that is,
our redemption from the penalty of sin is just as secure
as *Jesus* is secure, because we are *IN Christ, in God.*
But there is more:

Believers, saved by God's grace, *are "waiting for
the adoption, to wit, the redemption of our body"*
(Rom. 8:23). Thus does God's Word assure us that our
bodies will be redeemed. Just as surely as *Christ* rose
again—incorruptible—and sits at the right hand of
God the Father in a glorified body, we who believe
on Him and receive His finished work will one day
receive a glorified body and will sit with Jesus to
reign with Him: "When Christ, who is our life, shall
appear, *then shall (we) also appear WITH HIM in
glory*" (Col. 3:4).

Christ's atonement answers for the past, provides
for the present, and secures the future. Therefore in
the words of Peter, *we "rejoice with JOY UNSPEAK-
ABLE AND FULL OF GLORY"* (I Pet. 1:8).

Christ's Atonement Gives Comfort
in a World of Unrest

"Wherefore comfort one another with these words"
(I Thess. 4:18).

The believers in the church at Thessalonica were
disturbed about their loved ones who had departed
this life and whose bodies had been laid in the tomb.
Would these departed loved ones be left behind when

Jesus came to set up His kingdom and glory? Through the inspired pen of the Apostle Paul, God assured the Thessalonian believers (and us) that death does not change the believer's oneness with Christ:

"But *I would not have you to be ignorant, brethren, concerning them which are asleep, that ye sorrow not, even as others which have no hope. For if we believe that Jesus died and rose again, even so them also which sleep in Jesus will God bring with Him.*

"For this we say unto you by the word of the Lord, that we which are alive and remain unto the coming of the Lord *shall not prevent them which are asleep.* For the Lord Himself shall descend from heaven with a shout, with the voice of the archangel, and with the trump of God: *AND THE DEAD IN CHRIST SHALL RISE FIRST:* Then we which are alive and remain *shall be caught up together with them in the clouds, to meet the Lord in the air: and so shall we ever be with the Lord. WHEREFORE comfort one another with these words*" (I Thess. 4:13–18).

In verse 14 of this passage the Holy Spirit emphasizes the fact that *Jesus died AND ROSE AGAIN.* He conquered death, hell, and the grave. *Believers are IN Christ,* therefore death and the grave cannot separate the believer *from* Christ. The divine fact that He died on the cross and rose again assures the believer a place *with Christ* in glory. His resurrection from the dead assures us that the grave cannot hold our departed loved ones who died in Him. Their spirits are with the Lord now, and their bodies will be raised in the first resurrection. When Jesus comes in the Rapture our departed loved ones will come with Him in the air, their bodies having been raised incorruptible. Living believers will be changed "in a moment, in the twinkling of an eye," and together all believers will be caught up to meet the Lord, to be with Him forever.

Matthew 17:1—8 presents a *picture* of the coming of Christ in glory. Jesus took Peter, James, and John "and bringeth them up into an high mountain apart, and was *transfigured* before them: and *His face did shine as the sun, and His raiment was white as the light.* And, behold, there appeared unto them *Moses and Elias* talking with Him." Later, in writing of this experience, Peter declared, "We have not followed cunningly devised fables, when we made known unto you the power and coming of our Lord Jesus Christ, but were eyewitnesses of His majesty. For He received from God the Father honour and glory, when there came such a voice to Him from the excellent glory, This is my beloved Son, in whom I am well pleased. And this voice which came from heaven we heard, when we were with Him in the holy mount" (II Pet. 1:16—18).

Moses, to whom God gave the law, was a type of Christians who will be raised from the dead. He is the only person whose funeral God personally supervised. Moses died in the land of Moab, and *God "buried him* in a valley in the land of Moab, over against Beth-peor: *BUT NO MAN KNOWETH OF HIS SEPULCHRE UNTO THIS DAY"* (Deut. 34:6). But *GOD knows* where the body of Moses lies, just as He knows where *every believer* is buried. Whether it be on the bottom of the sea, in the deepest valley, or on the highest mountain, He knows exactly where the body of each of His children rests, and in due time He will raise them all!

Elijah—the other man who appeared with Jesus on the Mount of Transfiguration—*did not die:* God took him to heaven in a chariot of fire (II Kings 2:11). Elijah is a type of the saints who will be living when Jesus comes in the Rapture, saints who will be changed "in a moment, in the twinkling of an eye," translated without seeing death.

But Matthew does not give the complete account of what happened on the Mount of Transfiguration. (That is why there are *four* Gospels. Each writer reveals some part of the life, ministry, death, and resurrection of Jesus which the other three writers *do not* reveal.) In this particular instance *Luke* tells us what Jesus, Moses, and Elijah discussed in their meeting:

"And behold, there talked with Him two men, which were Moses and Elias: who appeared in glory, *and SPAKE OF HIS DECEASE WHICH HE SHOULD ACCOMPLISH AT JERUSALEM"* (Luke 9:30,31). His "decease" was, of course, His death on the cross, and it is especially significant that His glory should be identified with His death because the death of Jesus on the cross opened the door for believers to *enter into* His glory—and *ONLY through His death* can this be accomplished!

Through Christ's atonement, believers are "appointed" to the glory of His fellowship with the Father:

"For God *hath not appointed us to WRATH*, but to obtain salvation by our Lord Jesus Christ, who died for us, that, whether we wake or sleep, *we should live together with HIM"* (I Thess. 5:9,10).

The Greek word here translated *"appointed"* means "to set *in a place,* as we would set a candle under a bushel." The same word is thus used in Matthew 5:15, and in Mark 6:29 it is used in speaking of a body *"laid"* in the tomb. In John 2:10 the same word speaks of wine *"set forth,"* and in John 15:16 it is used in speaking of one *"ordained."* In I Corinthians 12:18 the word is used in speaking of God having *"set" the members* in the body, and in verse 28 of the same chapter it speaks of one *"set" in an office.*

Therefore we are assured that God's wrath is *not appointed for believers.* We are appointed unto salvation, and just as surely as God lives we will enjoy eternal life and share God's glory in the place Jesus has gone to prepare for us!

In Christ's atonement we are assured of a home in heaven: "Therefore we are always confident, knowing that, whilst we are at home in the body, we are absent from the Lord . . . We are confident, I say, and willing rather to be absent from the body, and to be present with the Lord. Wherefore we labour, that, whether present or absent, we may be accepted of Him" (II Cor. 5:6, 8, 9). In these verses, the same Greek word is translated "at home" and "be present." The true meaning of the word is "to be at home." Therefore, as long as we are "at home" in this tabernacle of flesh we are absent from the Lord; but the second we depart this mortal body we will "be at home" *with the Lord.*

In the beginning Jesus the Son was at home with the Father (John 1:1, 14, 18); but it was agreed between the members of the Holy Trinity that He would take a body of flesh, leave the Father's bosom, and come into the world "to put away sin by the sacrifice of Himself" (Heb. 9:26). He left the glory of the Father's house and the Father's presence in order that He might *bring INTO* that glory all who will believe in His shed blood.

Jesus did many things during His earthly ministry— He healed the sick, fed the hungry, comforted the sorrowing, raised the dead—but those things were side lines with Him. His primary purpose in coming into this world was to lay down His life that *we* might *have* life, and that we might share His glory with the Father throughout eternity. He made this very plain in His intercessory prayer recorded in John's Gospel, chapter 17. There are seven places in that prayer where He spoke of a sevenfold glory:

1. "These words spake Jesus, and lifted up His eyes
   to heaven, and said, Father, the hour is come;
   GLORIFY THY SON, that thy Son also may glorify

thee" (John 17:1). Christ's life on earth was lived to glorify His heavenly Father and to finish the work the Father had given Him to do.

2. *"I have GLORIFIED THEE on the earth:* I have finished the work which thou gavest me to do" (John 17:4). The cross of Jesus expresses glory. It was the work to which He consecrated His every thought, word, and deed. From the time He entered this world until He said, "It is finished," He was dedicated to the work of redemption for sinners. To human eyes, the cross is ugly and degrading; but the light of Calvary is the Light of the world, and the only way to become *children of light* is through the blood Jesus shed on Calvary's cross.

3. "And now, O Father, *GLORIFY THOU ME WITH THINE OWN SELF with the glory which I had with thee BEFORE THE WORLD WAS"* (John 17:5). The Prophet Isaiah gives us some idea of Christ's preincarnation glory in his testimony concerning his vision of the Lord *in* glory:

"In the year that King Uzziah died I saw also the Lord sitting upon a throne, high and lifted up, and His train filled the temple. Above it stood the seraphims: each one had six wings; with twain he covered his face, and with twain he covered his feet, and with twain he did fly. And one cried unto another, and said, Holy, holy, holy, is the Lord of hosts: the whole earth is full of His glory. And the posts of the door moved at the voice of him that cried, and the house was filled with smoke.

"Then said I, Woe is me! for I am undone; because I am a man of unclean lips, and I dwell in the midst of a people of unclean lips: for mine eyes have seen the King, the Lord of hosts" (Isa. 6:1—5).

4. "And all mine are thine, and thine are mine; *and I am GLORIFIED IN THEM"* (John 17:10). Believers bring glory to the Lord Jesus Christ. Paul

commanded the Corinthian believers, "Whether therefore ye eat, or drink, or whatsoever ye do, *do all to
the glory of God*" (I Cor. 10:31). Believers should be
careful always to do those things that bring *glory and
honor* to the name of Jesus, refusing to partake of
anything that would bring *dishonor* to His precious
name.

5. "And *THE GLORY WHICH THOU GAVEST ME
   I have given them;* that they may be one, even as
we are one" (John 17:22). Jesus is the head of the
New Testament Church, His body, which is made up
of born again believers—"we are members of His body,
of His flesh, and of His bones" (Eph. 5:30). Therefore
Christ is glorified by the members of His body. (Please
read I Corinthians 12:12—31 and Ephesians 5:25—30.)

6. "Father, I will that they also, whom thou hast
   given me, be with me where I am; *that they may
behold MY GLORY, which thou hast given me; for
thou lovedst me before the foundation of the world*"
(John 17:24). The Lord Jesus has a *personal glory*
which is distinct from the glory acquired by Him because of His finished work on earth. He possesses
glory which He had in the beginning because of His
personal worth. He is the Pearl of great price, the
Jewel of all jewels. He is the bright and morning
Star.

7. "And *the glory which thou gavest me I HAVE
   GIVEN THEM . . .*" (John 17:22). Born again believers possess glory with Christ. To illustrate: When
a young man from a royal family marries a commoner,
the girl takes the title of royalty and is exalted in
position from poverty to wealth and splendor. *All
unbelievers are poor, wretched, hopeless*—children of
the devil (John 8:44; Eph. 2:1—3). But no matter how
wretched and sinful a person may be, when that person believes on the Lord Jesus Christ he is exalted
from poverty to the manifold riches of God's grace,

he is raised from disgrace to glory! Believers share the glory of Christ, the Son of God, in all that He is and all that He possesses:

"The Spirit Himself beareth witness with our spirit, that we are the children of God: and if children, then HEIRS; heirs of GOD, and JOINT-HEIRS WITH CHRIST; if so be that we suffer with Him, that we may be also GLORIFIED TOGETHER" (Rom. 8: 16,17).

Believers have a place of glory with Jesus. When we depart this tabernacle of flesh, we will be at home in the glory of His presence and we will share His glory throughout eternity. However, we know that something must happen to these mortal bodies if we are to share Christ's glory—and something *will* happen when we see Him:

"Beloved, *NOW ARE WE THE SONS OF GOD*, and it doth not yet appear what we *shall be:* but we know that, *when He shall appear, WE SHALL BE LIKE HIM; for we shall see Him as He IS"* (I John 3:2).

"For whom He did foreknow, He also did PRE-DESTINATE to be conformed TO THE IMAGE OF HIS SON, that He might be the firstborn among many brethren" (Rom. 8:29).

"For our conversation (citizenship) is in heaven; from whence also we look for the Saviour, the Lord Jesus Christ: who shall *change our vile body*, that it may be fashioned *like unto HIS GLORIOUS BODY*, according to the working whereby He is able even to subdue all things unto Himself" (Phil. 3:20,21).

Revelation 22:4 tells us that in that city where shall be no night, we shall eternally behold the face of the Lamb, and His name shall be in our foreheads. When Jesus looks at us He will see Himself, for we will be *like Him*.

Believers will not *begin* to have eternal life when

we stand face to face with Jesus in heaven. We have
eternal life NOW, from the very moment we believed
in His finished work on our behalf. But that life in
its completeness and fulness will have its consummation in the glory that shall be revealed in us when we
stand in His presence in the Father's glory: *"When
Christ, who is our life, shall appear, then shall ye
also appear with Him in glory"* (Col. 3:4).

The Gospel is threefold in its message:

1. The Gospel message reveals the grace of God.
It is therefore *the Gospel of GRACE*, making known
the truth of John 3:16—God so loved the world that
He gave Jesus to die for us—yes, *even while we were
yet sinners* (Rom. 5:8). Jesus was the Word Incarnate,
the only begotten of the Father, *"full of GRACE and
truth"* (John 1:14).

2. The Gospel message reveals the power of God.
It is therefore *the Gospel of POWER.* "As many as
received Him, *to them gave He POWER to become
the sons of God* . . . which were born . . . of God"
(John 1:12,13). The Apostle Paul testified, "I am not
ashamed of the Gospel of Christ: *for it is the POWER
OF GOD unto salvation to every one that believeth;*
to the Jew first, and also to the Greek" (Rom. 1:16).

Jesus told His disciples, "Behold, I send the promise of my Father upon you: but tarry ye in the city
of Jerusalem, *until ye be endued with POWER from
on high"* (Luke 24:49). In Acts 1:8 He promised, *"Ye
shall receive POWER, after that the Holy Ghost is
come upon you: and ye shall be witnesses unto me*
both in Jerusalem, and in all Judaea, and in Samaria,
and unto the uttermost part of the earth."

3. The Gospel message reveals the fact that we
will share the glory of Christ in the presence of the
glory of God. It is therefore *the Gospel of GLORY.*
"If our Gospel be hid, it is hid to them that are lost:
in whom the god of this world hath blinded the minds

of them which believe not, *lest the light of THE GLO-RIOUS GOSPEL OF CHRIST, who is the image of God, should shine unto them*" (II Cor. 4:3,4).

Paul defined the Gospel in his letter to the Corinthian believers: "For I delivered unto you first of all that which I also received, how that *CHRIST DIED for our sins* according to the Scriptures; and that *HE WAS BURIED*, and that *HE ROSE AGAIN the third day* according to the Scriptures . . .

"For as in Adam all die, even so in Christ shall all be made alive. But every man in his own order: Christ the firstfruits; afterward they that are Christ's at His coming. Then cometh the end, when He shall have delivered up the kingdom to God, even the Father; when He shall have put down all rule and all authority and power. For He must reign, till He hath put all enemies under His feet. The last enemy that shall be destroyed is death. . . .

"So when this corruptible shall have put on incorruption, and this mortal shall have put on immortality, then shall be brought to pass the saying that is written, Death is swallowed up in victory. O death, where is thy sting? O grave, where is thy victory? The sting of death is sin; and the strength of sin is the law. BUT THANKS BE TO GOD, WHICH GIVETH US THE VICTORY THROUGH OUR LORD JESUS CHRIST. Therefore, my beloved brethren, be ye stedfast, unmoveable, always abounding in the work of the Lord, forasmuch as ye know that your labour is not in vain in the Lord" (I Cor. 15:3,4,22−26, 54−58).

The Gospel message reveals the saving *grace* of God, the transforming *power* of God, and the *glory* of God. Through Christ's atonement *believers possess* grace, power, and glory—and when this mortal puts on immortality we shall know and share *the fulness* of God's glory.

Adam was *innocent,* but he did not possess immortality. If he *had* been immortal he could not have sinned because immortality proclaims a state of incorruptible bliss and holiness *in a body* that is incorruptible (I Cor. 15:54). But *Christ,* the last Adam, *WAS immortal* (I Tim. 6:14—16). Life and immortality have been brought to light through the glorious Gospel of God's saving grace, His transforming power, and His eternal glory (II Tim. 1:10). Believers will know these things experimentally when Jesus comes and we are caught up to meet Him in the clouds in the air. This mortal will then put on immortality, this corruptible will put on incorruption, and we will be *like Jesus* when we share His glory in the glory of God's eternal kingdom.

Believers Are Sealed for Glory

In Ephesians 1:13,14 Paul wrote, under inspiration, that after we believe we are *"sealed with that Holy Spirit of promise, which is the EARNEST of our inheritance* until the redemption of the purchased possession, unto the praise of His glory."

Then in Ephesians 4:30 Paul says, "Grieve not the Holy Spirit of God, *whereby ye are SEALED unto the day of redemption."*

"Earnest" means "guarantee or security." The *"day of redemption"* here speaks of the redemption of *the body,* the time when this mortal puts on immortality, not the redemption of the soul when one believes on the Lord Jesus. We are sealed until the redemption of the *"purchased possession."* Calvary provided the purchase price of our salvation. The blood of Jesus redeems us from the *penalty* of sin, and we are *"kept* by the power of God through faith unto salvation ready to be revealed in the last time" (I Pet. 1:5).

The "salvation" of which Peter spoke here is not

salvation of the soul, but the glorious body we will receive when we see Jesus and enter into God's glory: *"For we know that if our earthly house of this tabernacle were dissolved, we have a building of God, an house not made with hands, eternal in the heavens"* (II Cor. 5:1). We are saved from sin the moment we believe on Jesus, but we will be saved from the very *presence* of sin when we are caught up to meet Jesus in the clouds in the air and enter into the glory of God's eternal kingdom.

In Revelation 22:14 we read, "Blessed are they that do His commandments, that they may have RIGHT to the tree of life, and may enter in through the gates into the city."

(In this verse, "commandments" does not speak of the law of Moses but of *the commandments of Jesus*—"Believe, trust, and obey.") The New Testament command that brings salvation is to hear the words of Jesus, believe on Him who sent Jesus, and we who obey this commandment will not come into condemnation: "Verily, verily, I say unto you, *He that heareth my WORD, and believeth on Him that sent me, hath everlasting life, and SHALL NOT come into condemnation; but IS PASSED from death unto life"* (John 5:24).

"And the Spirit and the bride say, Come. And let him that heareth say, Come. And let him that is athirst come. And *WHOSOEVER WILL, let him take the water of life FREELY"* (Rev. 22:17).

God's New Paradise and the River of Life

"And he shewed me a pure river of water of life, clear as crystal, proceeding out of the throne of God and of the Lamb. In the midst of the street of it, and on either side of the river, was there the tree of life, which bare twelve manner of fruits, and yielded her fruit every month: and the leaves of the tree were for the healing of the nations.

"And there shall be no more curse: but the throne of God and of the Lamb shall be in it; and His servants shall serve Him: And they shall see His face; and His name shall be in their foreheads. And there shall be no night there; and they need no candle, neither light of the sun; for the Lord God giveth them light: and they shall reign for ever and ever. And He said unto me, These sayings are faithful and true: and the Lord God of the holy prophets sent His angel to shew unto His servants the things which must shortly be done. Behold, I come quickly: blessed is he that keepeth the sayings of the prophecy of this book" (Rev. 22:1–7).

As I bring this message to a close, I ask: *Are YOU saved by God's grace?* Are your sins covered by the blood of the Lamb? Are you trusting in Christ's finished work through which we have the atonement? If you are not, then regardless of how "religious" you may be or how much good you may do, *you are hopelessly lost!* There is only one way to become a child of God, and that is *GOD'S way*—through Christ's atonement. The blood of Jesus Christ cleanses from all sin, and *only* through His blood can anyone *be cleansed* from sin.

God's Word plainly declares that "there shall in no wise enter into (heaven) any thing that defileth, neither whatsoever worketh abomination, or maketh a lie: but they which are written in the Lamb's book of life" (Rev. 21:27). Therefore if you hope to enter heaven's glory you must trust in the shed blood of the Lamb of God.

If you have not trusted Him, *trust Him NOW* as your personal Saviour. He will save you and give you assurance that He lives in your heart:

"If thou shalt confess with thy mouth the Lord

Jesus, and shalt believe in thine heart that God hath raised Him from the dead, thou shalt be saved. For with the heart man believeth unto righteousness; and with the mouth confession is made unto salvation" (Rom. 10:9,10).

"For when we were yet without strength, in due time Christ died for the ungodly. . . . But God commendeth His love toward us, in that, while we were yet sinners, Christ died for us. . . . For if, when we were enemies, we were reconciled to God by the death of His Son, much more, being reconciled, we shall be saved by His life. And not only so, but we also joy in God through our Lord Jesus Christ, by whom we have now received the atonement" (Rom. 5:6, 8, 10, 11).

"For by grace are ye saved through faith; and that not of yourselves: it is the gift of God: not of works, lest any man should boast" (Eph. 2:8,9).

"In whom we have redemption through His blood, the forgiveness of sins, according to the riches of His grace" (Eph. 1:7).

"Be ye kind one to another, tenderhearted, forgiving one another, *even as God FOR CHRIST'S SAKE hath forgiven you*" (Eph. 4:32).

"According to the riches of God's grace" is the measure of God's forgiveness when we exercise faith in the finished work of Jesus. God forgives us "for Christ's sake"!

"But God, who is rich in mercy, for His great love wherewith He loved us, even when we were dead in sins, hath quickened us together with Christ, (by grace ye are saved;) and hath raised us up together, and made us sit together in heavenly places in Christ Jesus: That in the ages to come He might shew the exceeding riches of His grace in His kindness toward us through Christ Jesus" (Eph. 2:4—7).